CHICKASAW BY BLOOD ENROLLMENT CARDS 1898-1914

VOLUME III

TRANSCRIBED BY

JEFF BOWEN

NATIVE STUDY
Gallipolis, Ohio
USA

Originally published:
Baltimore, Maryland
2010

Reprinted by:

Native Study LLC
Gallipolis, OH
www.nativestudy.com

Library of Congress Control Number: 2020915583

ISBN: 978-1-64968-041-9

Made in the United States of America.

Other Books and Series by Jeff Bowen

1901-1907 Native American Census Seneca, Eastern Shawnee, Miami, Modoc, Ottawa, Peoria, Quapaw, and Wyandotte Indians (Under Seneca School, Indian Territory)

1932 Census of The Standing Rock Sioux Reservation with Births And Deaths 1924-1932

Census of The Blackfeet, Montana, 1897- 1901 Expanded Edition

Eastern Cherokee by Blood, 1906-1910, Volumes I thru XIII

Choctaw of Mississippi Indian Census 1929-1932 with Births and Deaths 1924-1931   Volume I

Choctaw of Mississippi Indian Census 1933, 1934 & 1937, Supplemental Rolls to 1934 & 1935 with Births and Deaths 1932-1938, and Marriages 1936-1938 Volume II

Eastern Cherokee Census Cherokee, North Carolina 1930-1939 Census 1930-1931 with Births And Deaths 1924-1931 Taken By Agent L. W. Page Volume I

Eastern Cherokee Census Cherokee, North Carolina 1930-1939 Census 1932-1933 with Births And Deaths 1930-1932 Taken By Agent R. L. Spalsbury   Volume II

Eastern Cherokee Census Cherokee, North Carolina 1930-1939 Census 1934-1937 with Births and Deaths 1925-1938 and Marriages 1936 & 1938 Taken by Agents R. L. Spalsbury And Harold W. Foght Volume III

Seminole of Florida Indian Census, 1930-1940 with Birth and Death Records, 1930-1938

Texas Cherokees 1820-1839 A Document For Litigation 1921

Choctaw By Blood Enrollment Cards 1898-1914 Volumes I thru XVII

Starr Roll 1894   (Cherokee Payment Rolls) Districts: Canadian, Cooweescoowee, and Delaware Volume One

Starr Roll 1894 (Cherokee Payment Rolls) Districts: Flint, Going Snake, and Illinois   Volume Two

Starr Roll 1894 (Cherokee Payment Rolls) Districts: Saline, Sequoyah, and Tahlequah; Including Orphan Roll Volume Three

Other Books and Series by Jeff Bowen

Cherokee Intruder Cases Dockets of Hearings 1901-1909 Volumes I & II

Indian Wills, 1911-1921 Records of the Bureau of Indian Affairs
Books One thru Seven;

Native American Wills & Probate Records 1911-1921

Turtle Mountain Reservation Chippewa Indians 1932 Census with Births & Deaths, 1924-1932

Chickasaw By Blood Enrollment Cards 1898-1914 Volume I & II

Visit our website at **www.nativestudy.com** to learn more about these
and other books and series by Jeff Bowen

This whole series is dedicated to my wife and best friend, Kathy.

ENROLLMENT CARDS FOR THE
FIVE CIVILIZED TRIBES
1898-1914

On 93 rolls of this microfilm publication are reproduced the enrollment cards that were prepared by the staff of the Commission to the Five Civilized Tribes between 1898 and 1914. These records are part of Records of the Bureau of Indian Affairs, Record Group (RG) 75, and are housed in the Archives Branch of the Federal Archives and Records Center, Fort Worth, Tex. An act of Congress approved March 3, 1893 (27 Stat. 645), authorized the establishment of the Commission to negotiate agreements with the Cherokee, Choctaw, Chickasaw, Creek, and Seminole tribes providing for the dissolution of the tribal governments and the allotment of land to each tribal member. Senator Henry L. Dawes of Massachusetts was appointed Chairman of this Commission on November 1, 1893, after which it has commonly been referred to as the Dawes Commission. The Commission was authorized by an act of Congress approved June 28, 1898 (30 Stat. 495), to prepare citizenship (tribal membership) rolls for each tribe. These final rolls were the basis for allotment. Under this act, subsequent acts, and resulting agreements negotiated with each tribe, the Commission received applications for membership covering more than 250,000 people and enrolled more than 101,000. The tribal membership rolls were closed on March 4, 1907, by an act of Congress approved on April 26, 1906 (34 Stat. 370), although an additional 312 persons were enrolled under an act approved August 1, 1914. The Commission enrolled individuals as "citizens" of a tribe under the following categories: Citizens By Blood, Citizens by Marriage, New Born Citizens By Blood (enrolled under an act of Congress approved March 3, 1905), Minor Citizens By Blood (enrolled under an act of Congress approved April 26, 1906), Freedmen (former black slaves of Indians, later freed and admitted to tribal citizenship), New Born Freedmen, and Minor Freedmen. Delaware Indians adopted by the Cherokee tribe were enrolled as a separate group within the Cherokee. Within each enrollment category, the Commission generally maintained three types of cards: "Straight" cards for persons whose applications were approved, "D" cards for persons whose applications were considered doubtful and subject to question, and "R" cards for persons whose applications were rejected. Persons listed on "D" cards were subsequently transferred to either "Straight" or "R" cards depending on the Commission's decisions. All decisions of the Commission were sent to the Secretary of the Interior for final approval.

An enrollment card, sometimes referred to by the Commission as a "census card," records the information provided by individual applications submitted by members of the same family group or household and includes notation of the actions taken. The information given for each applicant includes name, roll number (individual's number if enrolled), age, sex, degree of Indian blood, relationship to the head of the family group, parents' names, and references to enrollment on earlier rolls used by the Commission for verification of eligibility. The card often includes references to kin-related enrollment cards and notations about births, deaths, changes in marital status, and actions taken by the Commission and the Secretary of the Interior. Within each enrollment category, the cards are arranged numerically by a "field" or "census card" number, which is separate from the roll number. The index to the final rolls, which is reproduced on roll 1 of this publication, provides the roll number for each person while the final rolls themselves provide the census card numbers for each enrollee. No indexes have been located for the majority of the "D" and "R" cards. There are a few Mississippi Choctaw "Identified" and "Field Cards" as well as some Chickasaw "Cancelled" that refer to person never finally enrolled.

National Archives and Records Administration
American Indians Catalogue, p. 41

INTRODUCTION

The following Introduction describes the considerations employed in transcribing the Chickasaw enrollment cards that comprise the basis for this series. The Chickasaw by Blood enrollment cards, sometimes called "census cards" by the Dawes Commission, were pre-printed cards or loose sheets of paper labeled **Chickasaw Nation. Chickasaw Roll (Not Including Freedmen) with Residence County**. The heading **Post Office** appeared on the left side of each card, and **Card No., Field No.** on the right. The cards were further broken down into the categories *Dawes No., Name, Relationship to Person First Named, Age, Sex, Blood, Tribal Enrollment (Year, Town, Page), Name of Father, Year, Town, Name of Mother, Year, Town*, as well as *Tribal Enrollments of Parents*. For whatever reason, no card numbers were recorded in the corresponding field on any of the cards.

This and subsequent volumes have been transcribed from National Archives microfilm series M-1186: Roll 67, 1-662 and Roll 68, 663-1424. The page format of this transcription does not follow the microfilm exactly, owing to the space restrictions of the book format, but I have endeavored to include all categories of information supplied in the original. Also, the Dawes Roll No. has been relegated to the Notes area of each transcribed page. The notes section also contains information such as, Other name listings, Transfers to different cards, Birth dates, Death dates, listings on various payrolls with years, even sometimes a mention of a spouse in the doubtful category with card number, spouse possibly from another tribe, or a marriage license and certificate that was on file along with location. Sometimes the notes contain revealing information such as the following, "5/31/99. It is reported that Wm. Washington has this woman on his place and had parties to marry and they have never lived together—Investigate." Interestingly, this tidbit was found not under the representation of Wm. Washington but under that of Head of Household "Frank Osavior." Finally, the category "County" indicates the status of Non-Citizen, ethnicity, or Creek Roll, Cherokee Roll, Chocktaw Roll, etc.

Jeff Bowen
Gallipolis, OH
NativeStudy.com

Chickasaw Enrollment Cards 1898-1914
Chickasaw by Blood   Volume III

RESIDENCE: Choctaw Nation ~~COUNTY~~   **CARD NO.**

POST OFFICE: South McAlester, Ind. Ter.   **FIELD NO.**

	NAME	RELATION-SHIP TO PERSON FIRST NAMED	AGE	SEX	BLOOD	TRIBAL ENROLLMENT		
						YEAR	COUNTY	PAGE
1	Sittel, Fritz	NAMED	36	M	I.W.			
2	" Malvina	Wife	30	F	1/4			
3	" Edward	Son	14	M	1/8			
4	" William B	"	11	"	1/8			
5	" Myrtle	Dau	9	F	1/8			
6	" Lottie	"	7	"	1/8			
7	" Josie	"	5	"	1/8			
8	" Fritz, Jr	Son	3	M	1/8			
9	" Farris G	"	7mo	"	1/8			
10	" Melven Cornish	Son	9mo	M	1/8			

TRIBAL ENROLLMENT OF PARENTS

	NAME OF FATHER	YEAR	COUNTY	NAME OF MOTHER	YEAR	COUNTY
1	Edward Sittel		Non citizen	Lena Sittel		Non Citizen
2	Wm B. Pitchlynn	Dead	Choctaw roll	Elsie Pitchlynn	Dead	Chick residing in Choctaw N. 1st Dist.
3	No. 1			No. 2		
4	No. 1			No. 2		
5	No. 1			No. 2		
6	No. 1			No. 2		
7	No. 1			No. 2		
8	No. 1			No. 2		
9	No. 1			No. 2		
10	No. 1			No. 2		

(NOTES)

No. 1 on Choctaw Roll Tobucksy Co. No. 15031 transferred to Chickasaw roll
No. 2 "   "   "   "   "   " 11257
No. 3 "   "   "   "   "   " 11258
No. 4 "   "   "   "   "   " 11259
No. 5 "   "   "   "   "   " 11260
No. 6 "   "   "   "   "   " 11261
No. 7 "   "   "   "   "   " 11262
No. 8 "   "   "   "   "   " 11263
No. 9 Enrolled Nov. 4/99
No. 10 Born Dec. 28, 1901. enrolled Sept. 24, 1902.

Mar. 20/99.

CANCELLED Stamped across card

1

Chickasaw Enrollment Cards 1898-1914
Chickasaw by Blood   Volume III

RESIDENCE: Choctaw Nation   ~~COUNTY~~   CARD NO.

POST OFFICE: South Canadian, Ind. Ter.   FIELD NO.

NAME	RELATION-SHIP TO PERSON	AGE	SEX	BLOOD	TRIBAL ENROLLMENT		
					YEAR	COUNTY	PAGE
1 Priddy, Melvin	FIRST NAMED	20	M	1/16	1897	Chick residing in Choctaw N. 1st Dist.	67
2 " Cecile Lewis	Son	2m	M	1/32			
3 " Siddie	Wife	20	F	I.W.			

TRIBAL ENROLLMENT OF PARENTS

	NAME OF FATHER	YEAR	COUNTY	NAME OF MOTHER	YEAR	COUNTY
1	Louis Priddy	Dead	Chick residing in Choctaw N. 1st Dist.	Caroline Priddy	Dead	Non Citizen
2	No. 1			Siddie Priddy		
3	Jno Bowman		non citz	Alice Bowman		non citz.

(NOTES)

No. 1 is the husband of Siddie Priddy on Chickasaw Card #D.284.

Evidence of marriage filed Jany. 30, 1901.

No. 2 Enrolled January 30, 1901.

No. 3 transferred from Chickasaw card #D284 April 1, 1903. See

decision of March 10, 1903.   *(No. 3 Dawes' Roll No. 64)*

Mar. 20/99.

RESIDENCE: Choctaw Nation   COUNTY   CARD NO.

POST OFFICE: Krebs, Ind. Ter.   FIELD NO.

NAME	RELATION-SHIP TO PERSON	AGE	SEX	BLOOD	TRIBAL ENROLLMENT		
					YEAR	COUNTY	PAGE
1 Jefferson, Simeon	FIRST NAMED	21	M	1/2	1896	Chick residing in Choc Nation	69

TRIBAL ENROLLMENT OF PARENTS

	NAME OF FATHER	YEAR	COUNTY	NAME OF MOTHER	YEAR	COUNTY
1	Isham Jefferson	Dead	Tobucksy	Latoe Jefferson	Dead	Chick residing in Choctaw N. 1st Dist.

(NOTES)

No. 1 See decision of June 13, 04.

On 1893 Tobucksy Co., Pay Roll, Page 51, No. 454.

No. 1 is the husband of Mary Jefferson on Choctaw Card No. 5361

No. 1 elects to be enrolled as a Chick. Feb. 26, 1904.

P.O. Calvin, I.T. 12/23/02

Mar. 22/99.

RESIDENCE: COUNTY					CARD NO.			
POST OFFICE: Buckhorn, Ind. Ter.					FIELD NO.			
NAME	RELATION-SHIP TO PERSON FIRST NAMED	AGE	SEX	BLOOD	TRIBAL ENROLLMENT			
					YEAR	COUNTY	PAGE	
1 Lowrance, Robert H.	NAMED	20	M	1/16	1897	Tishomingo	28	
2 " Sophia Elizabeth	Wife	16	F	I.W.				
3 " Dora Isabella	Dau	2mo	F	1/32				
4 " Bernice Sloan	Son	2mo	M	1/32				

TRIBAL ENROLLMENT OF PARENTS

	NAME OF FATHER	YEAR	COUNTY	NAME OF MOTHER	YEAR	COUNTY
1	Willis B. Lowrance I.W.	1897	Tishomingo	Mary Easter Lowrance	1897	Tishomingo
2	(Illegible) Hodges	Dead	Non Citizen	Kale Hodges	Dead	Non Citizen
3	No. 1			No. 2		
4	No. 1			No. 2		

(NOTES)

No. 1 transferred from Chickasaw Card #618.
No. 2 Enrolled Mar. 20/99.   *(No. 2 Dawes' Roll No. 172)*
No. 3 Enrolled May 24, 1900.
No. 4 Born Jany. 6, 1902; enrolled March 1, 1902.

RESIDENCE: COUNTY					CARD NO.			
POST OFFICE: Johnson, Ind. Ter.					FIELD NO.			
NAME	RELATION-SHIP TO PERSON FIRST NAMED	AGE	SEX	BLOOD	TRIBAL ENROLLMENT			
					YEAR	COUNTY	PAGE	
1 Williams, Chas. L.	NAMED	25	M	I.W.				
2 " Emely	Wife	15	F	1/16	1897	Pontotoc	61	
3 " Katie M.	Dau	3mo	F	1/32				

TRIBAL ENROLLMENT OF PARENTS

	NAME OF FATHER	YEAR	COUNTY	NAME OF MOTHER	YEAR	COUNTY
1	D.M. Williams		Non Citizen	Arminta Williams		Non Citizen
2	Joseph E. Johnston	1897	Pontotoc	Mary C. Johnston I.W.	1897	Pontotoc
3	No. 1			No. 2		

(NOTES)

No. 2 on Chickasaw roll as Emely Johnston   *(No. 1 Dawes' Roll No. 171)*
No. 3 Born April 13, 1902; Enrolled July 3, 1902.

Mar. 20/99.

Chickasaw Enrollment Cards 1898-1914
Chickasaw by Blood   Volume III

RESIDENCE:	COUNTY					CARD NO.			
POST OFFICE:	Stonewall, Ind. Ter.					FIELD NO.			

NAME	RELATIONSHIP TO PERSON FIRST NAMED	AGE	SEX	BLOOD	TRIBAL ENROLLMENT		
					YEAR	COUNTY	PAGE
1 Byrd, James M.	NAMED	28	M	I.W.			

TRIBAL ENROLLMENT OF PARENTS

	NAME OF FATHER	YEAR	COUNTY	NAME OF MOTHER	YEAR	COUNTY
1	M. Byrd		Non Citizen	D.A. Byrd		Non Citizen

(NOTES)

(All notations illegible)   *(No. I Dawes' Roll No. 170)*

P.O. Roff, I.T. 11/15/02.

RESIDENCE:	Pontotoc COUNTY					CARD NO.			
POST OFFICE:	Purcell, Ind. Ter.					FIELD NO.			

NAME	RELATIONSHIP TO PERSON FIRST NAMED	AGE	SEX	BLOOD	TRIBAL ENROLLMENT		
					YEAR	COUNTY	PAGE
1 Fox, Franklin Marion	NAMED	52	M	I.W.	1897	Pontotoc	81
2 " Sallie J.	Wife	43	F	1/8	1897	"	63
3 " Frank F.	Son	18	M	1/16	1897	"	64
4 " Jay J.	"	16	"	1/16	1897	"	64
5 " Wallace W.	"	3 1/2	"	1/16	1897	"	64

TRIBAL ENROLLMENT OF PARENTS

	NAME OF FATHER	YEAR	COUNTY	NAME OF MOTHER	YEAR	COUNTY
1	John Fox	Dead	Non Citizen	Elizabeth Fox	Dead	Non Citizen
2	James P. Pridley[sic]	"	" "	Elizabeth Priddy	"	Pontotoc
3	No. I			No. 2		
4	No. I			No. 2		
5	No. I			No. 2		

(NOTES)

No. I on Chickasaw roll as F.M. Fox   *(No. I Dawes' Roll No. 487)*
No. 2 "   "   "   " Sallie " Grand daughter of Mary of Polly Johnson
No. 3 "   "   "   " F.F.   "
No. 4 "   "   "   " J.J.   "
     All admitted by Dawes Com. Case No. 48, and no appeal taken.
     All except No. 1, descendants of John McLish
No. 2 Died June 2, 1899; Proof of death filed Nov. 1, 1902.
See letter of J.M. Folsom of Jany. 15, 1902, filed 1/17/01.

                                        Transferred Nov. 30/98.
P.O. address is now at Ardmore, I.T.   From white card No. D.158.

Chickasaw Enrollment Cards 1898-1914
Chickasaw by Blood   Volume III

RESIDENCE: Pontotoc COUNTY					CARD NO.			
POST OFFICE: Purcell, Ind. Ter.					FIELD NO.			

NAME	RELATION-SHIP TO PERSON FIRST NAMED	AGE	SEX	BLOOD	TRIBAL ENROLLMENT		
					YEAR	COUNTY	PAGE
1 Costello, Charles E.	NAMED	28	M	I.W.	1897	Pontotoc	80
2 " Charles Leavitt `	Son	1	"	1/32	1897	"	89

TRIBAL ENROLLMENT OF PARENTS

	NAME OF FATHER	YEAR	COUNTY	NAME OF MOTHER	YEAR	COUNTY
1	John Costello		Non citizen	Anna Costello		Non citizen
2	No. 1			Cleo Inez "	Dead	Pontotoc

(NOTES)

No. 1 and his Wife, Cleo Inez Costello, admitted by Dawes Com, Case No. 33 and no appeal taken.

No. 2 On Chickasaw roll as Charles Levett Costello; registered under Act of Legislature, July 31, 1897 (Chickasaw roll, Page 89.)

No. 2 descendant of John McLish.

No. 2 Affidavits as to birth received and filed Oct. 20, 1902.

Transferred Nov. 30/98.

P.O. Lindsay, I.T. 10/3/02.

From white card No. D.5.

RESIDENCE: Pickens COUNTY					CARD NO.			
POST OFFICE: Ardmore, Ind. Ter.					FIELD NO.			

NAME	RELATION-SHIP TO PERSON FIRST NAMED	AGE	SEX	BLOOD	TRIBAL ENROLLMENT		
					YEAR	COUNTY	PAGE
1 Drew, Mary V.	NAMED	39	F	1/32	1893	Pickens	P.R. #2 223
2 Wallace, Harold M.	Son	15	M	1/64	"	"	"
3 Drew, Byron	Husband	47	"	I.W.			

TRIBAL ENROLLMENT OF PARENTS

	NAME OF FATHER	YEAR	COUNTY	NAME OF MOTHER	YEAR	COUNTY
1	John G. Moore	Dead	Chick Indian	Susan Moore		non-citizen
2	Saml W. Wallace	"	non citizen	No. 1		
3	Monroe Drew	"	" "	Mary Drew		non cit.

(NOTES)

No. 1 on Chickasaw roll as Mary V. Wallace   (No. 1 Dawes' Roll No. 4925)

No. 1 is the Wife of Byron Drew on Chickasaw card #D.279.   (No. 2 Dawes' Roll No. 4926)

No. 1 admitted by Chickasaw Citizenship Committee on November 10, 1889.   (No. 3 Dawes' Roll No. 62)

No. 3 originally listed for enrollment on Chickasaw card #D.279. 9/4/99; transferred to this card July 6, 1905. See decision of June 6, 1905.

Sept. 8, 1904: Decision un*(illegible)*by Commission admitting Nos. 1 and 2 as citizens by blood of Chickasaw Nation.

Chickasaw Enrollment Cards 1898-1914
Chickasaw by Blood   Volume III

Sept. 20, 1904: Protest filed by attorneys for Choctaw and Chickasaw Nations.
Sept. 20, 1904: Record forwarded the Secty of Interior
Nov. 29, 1904: Decision of Commission of Sept. 8, 1904, enrolling Nos. 1 and 2 affirmed by
         Secretary of Interior (I.T.D. 10736 1904) *(remainder illegible)*

Nov. 26/98.

	NAME	RELATION-SHIP TO PERSON FIRST NAMED	AGE	SEX	BLOOD	TRIBAL ENROLLMENT		
						YEAR	COUNTY	PAGE
1	Roberts, Mollie	NAMED	21	F	1/2			

RESIDENCE: Choctaw Nation ~~COUNTY~~   CARD NO.
POST OFFICE: Goodland, Ind. Ter.   FIELD NO.

TRIBAL ENROLLMENT OF PARENTS

	NAME OF FATHER	YEAR	COUNTY	NAME OF MOTHER	YEAR	COUNTY
1	Washington Burney	Dead	Choctaw roll	Rhoda Wachubbe		Chick residing in Choctaw N. 3rd Dist.

(NOTES)
    On Choctaw Census Record, No. 2, Page 411; transferred to Chickasaw roll by Dawes Com.
    On Choctaw, 1896, Kiamitia County, No. 10852.
No. 1 Died March 10, 1902. Proof of death filed Oct. 11, 1902.

Nov. 26/98.

CANCELLED Stamped across card
Died prior to Sept. 25, 1902

RESIDENCE: Pickens   COUNTY   CARD NO.
POST OFFICE: Bradley, Ind. Ter.   FIELD NO.

	NAME	RELATION-SHIP TO PERSON FIRST NAMED	AGE	SEX	BLOOD	TRIBAL ENROLLMENT		
						YEAR	COUNTY	PAGE
1	Gaddis, George L.	NAMED	27	M	1/8	1897	Pickens	19
2	" Lee Jefferson	Son	1	M	1/16			

TRIBAL ENROLLMENT OF PARENTS

	NAME OF FATHER	YEAR	COUNTY	NAME OF MOTHER	YEAR	COUNTY
1	Wm. Gaddis	Dead	Chickasaw roll	Susan Gaddis	Dead	non citizen
2	No. 1			Martha Gaddos		" "

(NOTES)
    On Chickasaw roll as G.L. Gaddis.
No. 1 is now the husband of Martha Gaddis, a non-citizen. Evidence of marriage filed May 3, 1902.
No. 2 Born April 14, 1901. enrolled May 3, 1902.

P.O. Commanche, I.T. 4/22/02.

Nov. 26/98.

Chickasaw Enrollment Cards 1898-1914
Chickasaw by Blood   Volume III

RESIDENCE: Pontotoc   COUNTY   CARD NO.
POST OFFICE: Stonewall, Ind. Ter.   FIELD NO.

NAME	RELATION-SHIP TO PERSON FIRST NAMED	AGE	SEX	BLOOD	TRIBAL ENROLLMENT		
					YEAR	COUNTY	PAGE
1 McKeel, John Francis	NAMED	32	M	I.W.			
2 " Cora Chisholm	Wife	25	F	1/8	1897	Pontotoc	47
3 " John C.	Son	5mo	M	1/16			
4 " William Bynum	Son	3wks	M	1/16			

TRIBAL ENROLLMENT OF PARENTS

	NAME OF FATHER	YEAR	COUNTY	NAME OF MOTHER	YEAR	COUNTY
1	J.N. McKeel		non citizen	Caroline McKeel		non citizen
2	Wm Chisholm	Dead	Creek Citz	Julia McLish	Dead	Chickasaaw roll
3	No. 1			No. 2		
4	No. 1			No. 2		

(NOTES)

No. 2 on Chickasaw roll as Cora Chisolm
No. 3 enrolled Nov. 4/99.
No. 4 enrolled January 3, 1901.
    Copy of divorce proceedings between John F. McKeel and Helen McKeel filed Nov. 15, 1902.

Nov. 25/98.

P.O. Ada, I.T. 11/12/02.   No. 2 transferred from Card #447 Nov. 25/98.

RESIDENCE: Pickens   COUNTY   CARD NO.
POST OFFICE: Ardmore, Ind. Ter.   FIELD NO.

NAME	RELATION-SHIP TO PERSON FIRST NAMED	AGE	SEX	BLOOD	TRIBAL ENROLLMENT		
					YEAR	COUNTY	PAGE
1 Yates, Alonzo Pleasant	NAMED	40	M	I.W.			
2 " Rachael	Wife	41	F	1/2	1897	Pickens	15
3 ~~Parris, Will~~	~~StepSon~~	~~19~~	~~M~~	~~1/4~~	~~1897~~	"	~~15~~

TRIBAL ENROLLMENT OF PARENTS

	NAME OF FATHER	YEAR	COUNTY	NAME OF MOTHER	YEAR	COUNTY
1	G.F. Yates	Dead	Non Citizen	Tenney Yates	Dead	Non citizen
2	Joe Wolf	"	Chickasaw roll	Jennie Wolfe	"	" "
3	~~Henry Parris~~	"	~~non-citizen~~	~~No. 2~~		

(NOTES)

No. 3 Died Oct. 1901. Enrollment cancelled by Dept. July , 1904.
No. 2 on Chickasaw roll as Rachael Owens
No. 2 said to be on Cherokee rolls; not on *(illegible)*
No. 3 Died Oct. 1901. Proof of death filed Nov. 3, 1902.

On this card   Nov. 25/98.
from white card No. D.III.

RESIDENCE: Tishomingo   COUNTY   CARD NO.

POST OFFICE: Dougherty, Ind. Ter.   FIELD NO.

	NAME	RELATION-SHIP TO PERSON FIRST NAMED	AGE	SEX	BLOOD	TRIBAL ENROLLMENT		
						YEAR	COUNTY	PAGE
1	Johnson, James M.	NAMED	33	M	1/16	1897	Tishomingo	34
2	" Lenorah	Dau	4	F	1/32	1897	"	34
3	" Maggie	Wife	26	F	I.W.			

TRIBAL ENROLLMENT OF PARENTS

	NAME OF FATHER	YEAR	COUNTY	NAME OF MOTHER	YEAR	COUNTY
1	Wyatt M. Johnson	Dead	Chickasaw roll	Malissa Johnson	Dead	non-citizen
2	No. 1			Maggie Johnson	"	"
3	John W. Moore		non citizen	Amanda L. Moore	Dead	" "

(NOTES)

No. 1 on Chickasaw roll as J.M. Johnson.

Descendants of John McLish.

See marriage license filed herein where the name of No. 1 appears as James McJohnson

No. 3 placed on this card September 28th 1905 in accordance with order of the Commissioner to the Five Civilized Tribes of that date holding application was made within the time prescribed by Act of Congress, approved July 1, 1902 (32 Stat 641)

Nov. 25/98.

RESIDENCE: Tishomingo   COUNTY   CARD NO.

POST OFFICE: Dougherty, Ind. Ter.   FIELD NO.

	NAME	RELATION-SHIP TO PERSON FIRST NAMED	AGE	SEX	BLOOD	TRIBAL ENROLLMENT		
						YEAR	COUNTY	PAGE
1	Turner, Edward B.	NAMED	26	M	1/16	1897	Tishomingo	27
2	" Clifford	Son	3	"	1/32	1897	"	27
3	" Laura E.	Dau	1	F	1/32	1897	"	88
4	" Ethel	Dau	11/2	F	1/32			

TRIBAL ENROLLMENT OF PARENTS

	NAME OF FATHER	YEAR	COUNTY	NAME OF MOTHER	YEAR	COUNTY
1	Mazeppa Turner		white man	Laura Turner	Dead	Chickasaw roll
2	No. 1			Ada B. Turner		non-citizen
3	No. 1			" " "		" "
4	No. 1			" " "		" "

(NOTES)

Descendants of John McLish.

No. 3 Proof of birth received and filed Oct. 14, 1902.

No. 4 Enrolled April 10, 1901.

(No. 3 Dawes' Roll No. 4213)

Nov. 25/98.

RESIDENCE: Tishomingo **COUNTY**   **CARD NO.**

POST OFFICE: Dougherty, Ind. Ter.   **FIELD NO.**

	NAME	RELATION-SHIP TO PERSON FIRST NAMED	AGE	SEX	BLOOD	TRIBAL ENROLLMENT		
						YEAR	COUNTY	PAGE
1	Harrison, Pollie	NAMED	21	F	1/16	1897	Tishomingo	32
2	" Laura J.	Dau	5	"	1/32	1897	"	32
3	" John Thomas	Son	3	M	1/32	1897	"	32

TRIBAL ENROLLMENT OF PARENTS

	NAME OF FATHER	YEAR	COUNTY	NAME OF MOTHER	YEAR	COUNTY
1	Mazeppa Turner		white man	Laura Turner	Dead	Chickasaw roll
2	W.S. Harrison		Non Citizen	No. 1		
3	" " "		" "	No. 1		

(NOTES)

Descendants of John McLish

No. 2 on Chickasaw roll as Joel Harrison

No. 3 "   "   "   " Thomas "

Nov. 25/98.

RESIDENCE: Tishomingo **COUNTY**   **CARD NO.**

POST OFFICE: Dougherty, Ind. Ter.   **FIELD NO.**

	NAME	RELATION-SHIP TO PERSON FIRST NAMED	AGE	SEX	BLOOD	TRIBAL ENROLLMENT		
						YEAR	COUNTY	PAGE
1	Johnson, Willie	NAMED	22	M	1/16	1897	Tishomingo	30

TRIBAL ENROLLMENT OF PARENTS

	NAME OF FATHER	YEAR	COUNTY	NAME OF MOTHER	YEAR	COUNTY
1	Thos. W. Johnson	Dead	Chickasaw roll	Rosa B. Johnson		white woman

(NOTES)

Descendant of John McLish.

For evidence of marriage of parents see card of Rosa B. Johnson, No. D.214.

Nov. 25/98.

RESIDENCE: Tishomingo COUNTY					CARD NO.		
POST OFFICE: Dougherty, Ind. Ter.					FIELD NO.		

	NAME	RELATION-SHIP TO PERSON FIRST NAMED	AGE	SEX	BLOOD	TRIBAL ENROLLMENT		
						YEAR	COUNTY	PAGE
1	Cooper, William W.	NAMED	49	M	I.W.	1897	Pontotoc	81
2	" Demis Mattie	Wife	33	F	1/32	1897	Pontotoc	66
3	" Lysal F.	Son	15	M	1/64	1897	"	66
4	" Charles Christopher	"	12	"	1/64	1897	"	66
5	" Frances M.	Dau	7	F	1/64	1897	"	66
6	" Pattie Ross	"	5	"	1/64	1897	"	66
7	" Happy	"	8mo	"	1/64			
8	Wells, John Franklin	Bro in law	25	M	1/32	1893	Pontotoc	PR #2 229
~~9~~	~~Cooper, William M~~	~~Son~~	~~5mo~~	~~M~~	~~1/64~~			
~~10~~	~~" Minnie Maria~~	~~Dau~~	~~5mo~~	~~F~~	~~1/64~~			

			TRIBAL ENROLLMENT OF PARENTS				
	NAME OF FATHER	YEAR	COUNTY	NAME OF MOTHER	YEAR	COUNTY	
1	L.B. Cooper	Dead	Non Citizen	Frances M. Cooper		Non Citizen	
2	Frank P. Wells	Dead	Non Citizen	Malissa A. Wells	Dead	Chickasaw roll	
3	Wm. W. Cooper	1897	Pontotoc	No. 2			
4	" " "	1897	"	No. 2			
5	" " "	1897	"	No. 2			
6	" " "	1897	"	No. 2			
7	" " "	1897	"	No. 2			
8	Frank P. Wells	Dead	Non Citizen	Malissa A. Wells	Dead	Chickasaw roll	
9	~~No.1~~			~~No. 2~~			
~~10~~	~~No.1~~			~~No. 2~~			

(NOTES)

No. 1 on Chickasaw roll as W.W. Cooper   *(No. 1 Dawes' Roll No. 63)*
No. 2 "   "   "   Mattie "
No. 3 "   "   "   L.F. Cooper
No. 4 "   "   "   Cecil "
No. 5 "   "   "   Francis W. "
No. 6 "   "   "   P.R. "
No. 8 "   "   "   J.F. Wells, Sr.
Nos. 9 and 10 Enrolled May 24, 1900.
No. 9 Died June 20, 1900; Proof of death filed Nov. 12, 1902.
No. 10 Died June 4, 1900; Proof of death filed Nov. 12, 1902.
No. 9 Died June 20, 1900. Enrollment cancelled by Dept. July 2, 1904
No. 10 Died June 21[sic], 1900. Enrollment cancelled by Dept. July 2, 1904.

All except No. 1 descendants of John McLish.

P.O. Hickory, I.T. 11/5/02.   Nov. 25/98.

	NAME	RELATION-SHIP TO PERSON FIRST NAMED	AGE	SEX	BLOOD	TRIBAL ENROLLMENT		
						YEAR	COUNTY	PAGE
1	Wright, Isaac S.	NAMED	46	M	I.W.	1897	Pickens	79
2	" Lizzie B.	Wife	33	F	1/16	1897	"	28
3	" Willie Mazeppa	Son	9	M	1/32	1897	"	31
4	" Pearl	Dau	5	F	1/32	1897	"	32

RESIDENCE: Tishomingo COUNTY   CARD NO.
POST OFFICE: Dougherty, Ind. Ter.   FIELD NO.

TRIBAL ENROLLMENT OF PARENTS

	NAME OF FATHER	YEAR	COUNTY	NAME OF MOTHER	YEAR	COUNTY
1	David W. Wright	Dead	non citizen	Eliza Wright		non citizen
2	Mayzeppa Turner		white man	Laura Turner	Dead	Chickasaw roll
3	No. 1			No. 2		
4	No. 1			No. 2		

(NOTES)

No. 2 Died Dec. 31, 1901. Enrollment cancelled by Dept, July 2, 1904.
No. 1 on Chickasaw roll as Isaac Wright.   *(No. 1 Dawes' Roll No. 62)*
No. 2 "   "   "   " Lizzie   "
No. 3 "   "   "   " Willie   "
No. 2 Died Dec. 31, 1901; Proof of death filed Nov. 6, 1902.
All except No. 1 descendants of John McLish.

11/6/02 P.O. Sulphur, I.T.   Nov. 25/98.

	NAME	RELATION-SHIP TO PERSON FIRST NAMED	AGE	SEX	BLOOD	TRIBAL ENROLLMENT		
						YEAR	COUNTY	PAGE
1	Johnson, James T.	NAMED	25	M	1/16	1897	Tishomingo	32
2	" Thomas Wreen	Son	4	"	1/32	1897	"	32
3	" Dewey Reeves	"	4mo	"	1/32			

RESIDENCE: Tishomingo COUNTY   CARD NO.
POST OFFICE: Dougherty, Ind. Ter.   FIELD NO.

TRIBAL ENROLLMENT OF PARENTS

	NAME OF FATHER	YEAR	COUNTY	NAME OF MOTHER	YEAR	COUNTY
1	Thos. W. Johnson	Dead	Chickasaw roll	Rosa B. Johnson		white woman

11

Chickasaw Enrollment Cards 1898-1914
Chickasaw by Blood   Volume III

2	No. 1			Hattie Johnson		non citizen
3	No. 1			" "		" "

(NOTES)

No. 1 As to evidence of marriage of parents, see card of Rosa B. Johnson, No. D.214.

No. 2 on Chickasaw roll as Ream Johnson.

Descendants of John McLish.

Nov. 25/98.

RESIDENCE: Tishomingo   COUNTY   CARD NO.

POST OFFICE: Dougherty, Ind. Ter.   FIELD NO.

	NAME	RELATIONSHIP TO PERSON FIRST NAMED	AGE	SEX	BLOOD	TRIBAL ENROLLMENT		
						YEAR	COUNTY	PAGE
1	Jack, Mary	NAMED	20	F	1/16	1897	Tishomingo	30
2	" Walter	Son	4	M	1/32	1897	"	30
3	" Hazel Gladys	Dau	1 1/2	F	1/32			

TRIBAL ENROLLMENT OF PARENTS

	NAME OF FATHER	YEAR	COUNTY	NAME OF MOTHER	YEAR	COUNTY
1	Thos. W. Johnson	Dead	Chickasaw roll	Rosa B. Johnson		White Woman
2	Thomas Jack		non citizen	No. 1		
3	" "		" "	No. 1		

(NOTES)

Descendants of John McLish.

No. 1 Evidence of marriage of parents attached to card of mother, No. D.214. Jan. 4, 1900.

No. 3 Proof of birth received and filed Oct. 29, 1902.   (No. 3 Dawes' Roll No. 4242)

Nov. 25/98.

RESIDENCE: Tishomingo   COUNTY   CARD NO.

POST OFFICE: Dougherty, Ind. Ter.   FIELD NO.

	NAME	RELATIONSHIP TO PERSON FIRST NAMED	AGE	SEX	BLOOD	TRIBAL ENROLLMENT		
						YEAR	COUNTY	PAGE
1	Short, William Walter	NAMED	10	M	1/32	1897	Tishomingo	30
2	" Robert P, Jr.	Bro	8	"	1/32	1897	"	30
3	" Thomas Clyde	"	5	"	1/32	1897	"	30

TRIBAL ENROLLMENT OF PARENTS

	NAME OF FATHER	YEAR	COUNTY	NAME OF MOTHER	YEAR	COUNTY
1	R.P. Short		Non citizen	Hattie J. Deel	1897	Tishomingo
2	" " "		" "	" " "	1897	"
3	" " "		" "	" " "	1897	"

12

(NOTES)

No. 1 on Chickasaw roll as Willie Short
No. 2 "   "   "   " Robert "   Jr.
No. 3 "   "   "   " Clyde "
    Descendants of John McLish.

Nov. 25/98.

Hattie Johnson Deel, Chick card #1358, protests against allowing R.P. Short, father of Wm. Walter Short, et al, to make selection for said children. See Chickasaw jacket #3841.

RESIDENCE: Pickens   **COUNTY**   **CARD NO.**

POST OFFICE: Dougherty, Ind. Ter.   **FIELD NO.**

	NAME	RELATION-SHIP TO PERSON FIRST NAMED	AGE	SEX	BLOOD	TRIBAL ENROLLMENT		
						YEAR	COUNTY	PAGE
1	Deel, Hattie Johnson	NAMED	31	F	1/16	1897	Tishomingo	30
2	" Bonnie Owenby	Dau	9mos	"	1/32			
3	" Homer	Son	4mo	M	1/32			
4	" Bennett B.	Husb	43	M	I.W.			

TRIBAL ENROLLMENT OF PARENTS

	NAME OF FATHER	YEAR	COUNTY	NAME OF MOTHER	YEAR	COUNTY
1	Thos. W. Johnson	Dead	Chickasaw roll	Rosa B. Johnson I.W.		White woman
2	Bennett B. Deel		White man	No. 1		
3	" " "		" "	No. 1		
4	R.C. Deel		non citizen	Nancy Deel	Dead	non citizen

(NOTES)

No. 1 on Chickasaw roll as Hattie Johnson Short
    Bennett B. Deel, husband of No. 1 on Chickasaw D.216.
    Descendants of John McLish.
No. 3 Affidavit received but irregulat and returned for correction Dec. 14/99, Filed Dec. 19/99.
    For evidence of marriage of parents of No. 1, see card of Rosa B. Johnson, Card No. D.214.
No. 4 transferred from Chickasaw card #D.216.
    See decision of March 5, 1904. Mar. 23, 1904,   *(No. 4 Dawes' Roll No. 293)*

Nov. 25/98,

RESIDENCE: Tishomingo   **COUNTY**   **CARD NO.**

POST OFFICE: Dougherty, Ind. Ter.   **FIELD NO.**

	NAME	RELATION-SHIP TO PERSON FIRST NAMED	AGE	SEX	BLOOD	TRIBAL ENROLLMENT		
						YEAR	COUNTY	PAGE
1	Green, Fred C.	NAMED	35	M	I.W.			
2	" Minnie	Wife	27	F	1/16	1897	Tishomingo	32

13

Chickasaw Enrollment Cards 1898-1914
Chickasaw by Blood   Volume III

3	" Roy C.		Son	9	M	1/32	1897		"		32

TRIBAL ENROLLMENT OF PARENTS

	NAME OF FATHER	YEAR	COUNTY	NAME OF MOTHER	YEAR	COUNTY
1	Charles H. Green	Dead	Non Citz	Rena Green		Non Citz
2	Thos. W. Johnson	Dead	Chickasaw roll	Rosa B. Johnson		White woman
3	Fred C. Green		white man	No. 2		

(NOTES)

No. 1 married to Minnie Johnson Dec. 22, 1888 Under U.S. law. remarried to Minnie Johnson
    July 11, 1893 Under Chickasaw law.   *(No. 1 Dawes' Roll No. 486)*
No. 1 transferred from Chickasaw *(remainder illegible)*
No. 2 as to evidence of marriage of parents, see Card of Rosa B. Johnson No. D.214.
Nos. 2 and 3 descendants of John McLish
No. 3 on Chickasaw roll as Roy Green.
    Fred C. Green husband of No. 2 on Chickasaw D.215.

         Nov. 25/98.

RESIDENCE: Tishomingo **COUNTY**						*CARD NO.*		
POST OFFICE: Dougherty, Ind. Ter.						*FIELD NO.*		

NAME	RELATION-SHIP TO PERSON FIRST NAMED	AGE	SEX	BLOOD	TRIBAL ENROLLMENT		
					YEAR	COUNTY	PAGE
1 Johnson, Claudie		13	M	1/16	1897	Tishomingo	32

TRIBAL ENROLLMENT OF PARENTS

	NAME OF FATHER	YEAR	COUNTY	NAME OF MOTHER	YEAR	COUNTY
1	Thos. W. Johnson	Dead	Chickasaw roll	Rosa B. Johnson		white woman

(NOTES)

Descendants of John McLish.
Jany. 4, 1900: Evidence of marriage of parents attached to Card No. D.214.

         Nov. 25/98.

RESIDENCE: Tishomingo **COUNTY**						*CARD NO.*		
POST OFFICE: Palmer, Ind. Ter.						*FIELD NO.*		

	NAME	RELATION-SHIP TO PERSON FIRST NAMED	AGE	SEX	BLOOD	TRIBAL ENROLLMENT		
						YEAR	COUNTY	PAGE
1	Jordan, Ethel	NAMED	24	F	1/16	1897	Tishomingo	30
2	" Benj. Gaston	Son	6	M	1/32	1897	"	30
3	" Ola May	Dau	4	F	1/32	1897	"	28
4	" James Earl	Son	2	M	1/32	1897	"	88
5	" Gracie	Dau	4mo	F	1/32			

6	"	Earnest Cecil	Son	2mo	M	1/32			
7	"	William Gaston	Hus	32	M	I.W.			

TRIBAL ENROLLMENT OF PARENTS

	NAME OF FATHER	YEAR	COUNTY	NAME OF MOTHER	YEAR	COUNTY
1	Charles Patterson I.W.	1897	Tishomingo	Louisa Patterson	1897	Tishomingo
2	Wm Gaston Jordan		white man	No. 1		
3	" " "		" "	No. 1		
4	" " "		" "	No. 1		
5	" " "		" "	No. 1		
6	" " "		" "	No. 1		
7	John Jordan		non citizen	Frances J. Jordan		non citizen

(NOTES)

No. 1 admitted by Dawes Com. Case No. 113, and no appeal taken.
No. 1 on Chickasaw roll as Ethel Jurdan
No. 2 "   "   "   " Ben H.   "
No. 3 "   "   "   " Olan   "
No. 5 Enrolled May 24, 1900.
No. 5 Died Aug. 1901; proof of death filed Nov. 4, 1902.
No. 6 Born May 27, 1902; Enrolled July 22, 1902.
    Descendants of John McLish.
    William Gaston Jordan husband of No. 1 on Chickasaw D. 213.
No. 7 transferred from Chickasaw card D.213, April 7, 1904.
    See decision of March 15, 1904.   *(No. 7 Dawes' Roll No. 344)*
           Nov. 25/98.

RESIDENCE: Tishomingo   **COUNTY**   **CARD NO.**
POST OFFICE: Davis, Ind. Ter.   **FIELD NO.**

	NAME	RELATION-SHIP TO PERSON FIRST NAMED	AGE	SEX	BLOOD	TRIBAL ENROLLMENT		
						YEAR	COUNTY	PAGE
1	Patterson, James E.	NAMED	22	M	1/16	1897	Tishomingo	29
2	" Mollie J.	Wife	25	F	I.W.			
3	" Docia M.	Dau	2	F	1/32	1897	Tishomingo	88
4	" Charles Olander	Son	2mos	M	1/32			
5	" Leona	Dau	2mo	F	1/32			
6	" James Earl	Son	5wks	M	1/32			

TRIBAL ENROLLMENT OF PARENTS

	NAME OF FATHER	YEAR	COUNTY	NAME OF MOTHER	YEAR	COUNTY
1	Charles Patterson I.W.	1897	Tishomingo	Louisa Patterson	1897	Tishomingo
2	O.M. Ware		non citizen	Lizzie Ward		non-citizen
3	No. 1			Mollie Patterson		white woman

15

4	No. 1			"	"		"	"
5	No. 1			"	"		"	"
6	No. 1			"	"		"	"

(NOTES)

No. 1 on Chickasaw roll as James A. Patterson   *(No. 2 Dawes' Roll No. 343)*

No. 4 affidavit of attending physician to be supplied. Received Dec. 13/98.

Nos. 1, 3 and 4 descendants of John McLish.

No. 1 admitted by Dawes Commission in 1896 in Chickasaw case #113; No appeal.
    Wife of No. 1 is enrolled Chickasaw card #D.212.

No. 5 was born March 18, 1900, was Enrolled on Chickasaw card #D.212 May 24, 1900 and
    transferred to this card Feby. 20, 1901.

No. 6 born Dec. 3, 1901; enrolled Jan. 9, 1902.

No. 2 transferred from Chickasaw card D.212, April 7, 1904.
    See decision of March 15, 1904.

Nov. 25/98.

RESIDENCE: Tishomingo   COUNTY   CARD NO.

POST OFFICE: Davis, Ind. Ter.   FIELD NO.

NAME	RELATION- SHIP TO PERSON FIRST NAMED	AGE	SEX	BLOOD	TRIBAL ENROLLMENT		
					YEAR	COUNTY	PAGE
1 Patterson, Charles	NAMED	61	M	I.W.	1897	Tishomingo	97
2 " ~~Louisa~~	~~Wife~~	~~59~~	F	~~1/8~~	~~1897~~	"	~~29~~

TRIBAL ENROLLMENT OF PARENTS

	NAME OF FATHER	YEAR	COUNTY	NAME OF MOTHER	YEAR	COUNTY
1	Chesley Patterson	Dead	Non citizen	Nancy Patterson	Dead	non-citizen
2	~~Richard Humphreys~~	"	" "	~~Sarah Humphreys~~	"	~~Chickasaw roll~~

(NOTES)

No. 2 Died Feb. 24, 1902. Enrollment cancelled by Dept. July 2, 1904.

No. 1 Admitted as an intermattied citizen and No. 2 as a citizen by blood: by Dawes Commission in 1896.
    Chickasaw case #113; no appeal.

No. 1 Died Oct. 23, 1898; Proof of death filed Nov. 3, 1902.

No. 2 Descendant of John McLish.

No. 2 Died Feb. 24, 1902; Proof of death filed Nov. 3, 1902.

Nov. 25/98.

Chickasaw Enrollment Cards 1898-1914
Chickasaw by Blood   Volume III

RESIDENCE: Pickens   COUNTY   CARD NO.

POST OFFICE: Pauls Valley, Ind. Ter.   FIELD NO.

	NAME	RELATION-SHIP TO PERSON FIRST NAMED	AGE	SEX	BLOOD	TRIBAL ENROLLMENT		
						YEAR	COUNTY	PAGE
1	Allender, Udolph S.	NAMED	30	M	I.W.	1897	Pickens	78
2	" Annie E.	Wife	24	F	1/16	1897	"	15
3	" Dorella	Dau	11/2	"	1/32	~~1897~~	"	~~86~~
4	" Marian B.	"	1mo	"	1/32			

TRIBAL ENROLLMENT OF PARENTS

	NAME OF FATHER	YEAR	COUNTY	NAME OF MOTHER	YEAR	COUNTY
1	Saml. S. Allender	Dead	non citizen	Hattie B. Allender	Dead	non-citizen
2	Alexander Rennie (I.W.)	1897	Pickens	Mary M. Rennie	1897	Pickens
3	No. 1			No. 2		
4	No. 1			No. 2		

(NOTES)

No. 1 on Chickasaw roll as U.S. Allender
No. 2 "   "   "   " Annie   "
No. 3 "   "   "   " Dorrella   "
Nos. 2 and 3 Descendants of John McLish.
    See testimony of No. 1 taken Oct. 30, 1902.
No. 3 Birth affidavit filed Aug. 28, 1897
No. 4 "   "   " April 3, *(illegible)*

Nov. 25/98.
No. 4 April 27/99.

RESIDENCE: Pickens   COUNTY   CARD NO.

POST OFFICE: Duncan, I.T.   FIELD NO.

	NAME	RELATION-SHIP TO PERSON FIRST NAMED	AGE	SEX	BLOOD	TRIBAL ENROLLMENT		
						YEAR	COUNTY	PAGE
1	Minter, Willis H.	NAMED	25	M	I.W.			
2	" Agnes	Wife	22	F	1/16	1893	Pickens	P.R. #2 191

TRIBAL ENROLLMENT OF PARENTS

	NAME OF FATHER	YEAR	COUNTY	NAME OF MOTHER	YEAR	COUNTY
1	Jas. M. Minter	Dead	Non Citz	Martha Minter		Non Citz.
2	George Nesbit	"	" "	Sophie Nesbit	Dead	Tishomingo

(NOTES)

Nos. 1 - 2 were married March 8/99.   *(No. 1 Dawes' Roll No. 485)*
No. 2 on Chickasaw Roll as Agnes Rooks.

17

Chickasaw Enrollment Cards 1898-1914
Chickasaw by Blood   Volume III

Descendant of John McLish
See testimony of No. I taken October 17, 1902.

No. 2 enrolled Nov. 25/98.
No. I   "   Aug. 1/99.

P.O. Womack, I.T. Oct. 17, 1903.

RESIDENCE: Pickens COUNTY					CARD No.			
POST OFFICE: Pauls Valley, Ind. Ter.					FIELD No.			
NAME	RELATION-SHIP TO PERSON FIRST NAMED	AGE	SEX	BLOOD	TRIBAL ENROLLMENT			
					YEAR	COUNTY	PAGE	
1 Rennie, Alexander	NAMED	70	M	I.W.	1897	Pickens	79	
2 " Mary M	Wife	54	F	1/8	1897	"	38	
3 " Alexander Jr.	Son	27	M	1/16	1897	"	38	
4 " ~~John~~	~~"~~	~~21~~	~~"~~	~~1/16~~	~~1897~~	~~"~~	~~38~~	

TRIBAL ENROLLMENT OF PARENTS							
NAME OF FATHER	YEAR	COUNTY	NAME OF MOTHER	YEAR	COUNTY		
1 Alexander Rennie	Dead	non-citizen	Catherine Rennie	Dead	non citizen		
2 Richard Humphreys	"	" "	Sallie Humphreys	"	Chickasaw roll		
3 No. I			No. 2				
4 ~~No. I~~			~~No. 2~~				

(NOTES)

Nos. I and 2 married in 1861. No marriage license or certificate required.
All except No. I Descendants of John McLish.
No. I Died March 13, 1899; proof death filed April 2, 1902.
No. 3 on Chickasaw roll as A. Rennie, Jr.
No. 3 is now the husband of Lula D. Burris on Chickasaw Card #44, June 28, 1901.
Aug 7/99; No. 4 has been placed on Chick Card No. 4 with Wife

Nov. 25/98.

RESIDENCE: Pickens COUNTY					CARD No.			
POST OFFICE: Chickasha, I.T.					FIELD No.			
NAME	RELATION-SHIP TO PERSON FIRST NAMED	AGE	SEX	BLOOD	TRIBAL ENROLLMENT			
					YEAR	COUNTY	PAGE	
1 Minter, William H.	NAMED	43	M	I.W.				
2 " Sallie L.	Wife	46	F	1/8	1897	Pontotoc	66	
3 Campbell, Montfort T.	S.Son	20	M	1/16	1897	"	66	
4 " Holmes Colbert	"	18	"	1/16	1897	"	66	
5 " Lawrence	"	15	"	1/16	1897	"	66	

18

Chickasaw Enrollment Cards 1898-1914
Chickasaw by Blood   Volume III

6	" John	"	12	"	1/16	1897	"	66
7	" Rex	"	10	"	1/16	1897	"	66
8	Minter, Sinie L.	Dau	5mo	F	1/16			
9	Campbell, Charles T.	Son of No. 3	2wks	M	1/32			

TRIBAL ENROLLMENT OF PARENTS

	NAME OF FATHER	YEAR	COUNTY	NAME OF MOTHER	YEAR	COUNTY
1	William Minter	Dead	Non Citiz	Mary Minter	Dead	Non Citz.
2	Richd Humphreys	"	" "	Sallie Humphreys	"	Chick Roll
3	Chas L. Campbell	"	" "	No. 2		
4	Chas L. Campbell	"	" "	No. 2		
5	Chas L. Campbell	"	" "	No. 2		
6	Chas L. Campbell	"	" "	No. 2		
7	Chas L. Campbell	"	" "	No. 2		
8	No. 1			No. 2		
9	No. 3			Fannie Campbell		non citizen

(NOTES)

No. 1 Enrolled Aug. 1/99. All others enrolled nov. 25/98.   *(No. 1 Dawes' Roll No. 553)*
No. 2 then enrolled as Sallie L. Campbell.
No. 2 on Chickasaw roll as S.L. Campbell.
No. 3 "   "   " " M.P.   "
No. 4 "   "   " " Holmes "
       Descendants of John McLish.
No. 3 is now the husband of Fannie Campbell a non-citizen. Evidence of marriage filed Aug. 30, 1901.
No. 8 Enrolled 6/14/1900
No. 9 Enrolled Aug. 30, 1901.
See additional testimony of No. 1, taken Oct. 15, 1902.

P.O. Pocasset, I.T. 3-2-04
P.O. Chickasha, I.T.

RESIDENCE: Pickens COUNTY						CARD NO.		
POST OFFICE: Kingston, Ind. Ter.						FIELD NO.		
NAME	RELATION-SHIP TO PERSON FIRST NAMED	AGE	SEX	BLOOD	TRIBAL ENROLLMENT			
					YEAR	COUNTY	PAGE	
1 Escue, Walter	NAMED	19	M	1/32	1897	Pickens	12	
2 " Ida	Sister	15	F	1/32	1897	"	12	

TRIBAL ENROLLMENT OF PARENTS

	NAME OF FATHER	YEAR	COUNTY	NAME OF MOTHER	YEAR	COUNTY
1	John Escue	Dead	Non citizen	Phillippi Escue	Dead	Chickasaw roll

19

2	" "	"	" " "	" "	"	" "

(NOTES)

Sir name on Chickasaw roll as Askew
Dexcendants of John McLish.

Nov. 25/98.

RESIGENCE: Choctaw Nation   ~~COUNTY~~   CARD NO.
POST OFFICE: Antlers, Ind. Ter.   FIELD NO.

NAME	RELATION-SHIP TO PERSON	AGE	SEX	BLOOD	TRIBAL ENROLLMENT		
					YEAR	COUNTY	PAGE
1 Eyatubby, Ben	FIRST NAMED	30	M	Full	1897	Chick residing in Choctaw N. 3rd Dist.	73

TRIBAL ENROLLMENT OF PARENTS

NAME OF FATHER	YEAR	COUNTY	NAME OF MOTHER	YEAR	COUNTY
1 James Coheche	Dead	Chickasaw roll	Martha Ann	Dead	Chickasaw roll

(NOTES)

Properly belongs to 2nd District, Cedar Co.
No. 1 is now husband of Ceza Henderson on Chickasaw card #763. See
testimony taken in that case November 13, 1902.

Nov. 24/98.

RESIDENCE: Pontotoc   COUNTY   CARD NO.
POST OFFICE: Minco, Ind. Ter.   FIELD NO.

NAME	RELATION-SHIP TO PERSON	AGE	SEX	BLOOD	TRIBAL ENROLLMENT		
					YEAR	COUNTY	PAGE
1 Keno, Emily	FIRST NAMED	30	F	Full	1893	Pontotoc	P.R. #2 131
2 " Houston	Son	15	M	1/2	1893	"	"
3 " Martha	Dau	13	F	1/2	1893	"	"
4 " Mattie	"	10	"	1/2	1893	"	"
5 " Lizzie	"	9	"	1/2	1893	"	"
6 " Fannie	"	6	"	1/2	1893	"	"
7 " Frank	Son	4	M	1/2			
8 " Carrie	Dau	5mo	F	1/2			

TRIBAL ENROLLMENT OF PARENTS

NAME OF FATHER	YEAR	COUNTY	NAME OF MOTHER	YEAR	COUNTY
1 Columbus Nelson	1897	Pontotoc	Louvina Nelson	Dead	Pontotoc
2 Keno Monyose		Mexican	No. 1		

20

3	" "		"	No. 1		
4	" "		"	No. 1		
5	" "		"	No. 1		
6	" "		"	No. 1		
7	" "		"	No. 1		
8	Ehenio Keno		"	No. 1		

(NOTES)

No. 8 Enrolled May 24, 1900

on this card Nov. 24/98.
From white card No. D.201.

RESIDENCE: Pickens   COUNTY   CARD NO.

POST OFFICE: Sunon, Ind. Ter.   FIELD NO.

NAME	RELATION-SHIP TO PERSON FIRST NAMED	AGE	SEX	BLOOD	TRIBAL ENROLLMENT		
					YEAR	COUNTY	PAGE
1 Duroderigo, Columbus		22	M	3/8	1893	Pickens	P.R. #2 170

TRIBAL ENROLLMENT OF PARENTS

NAME OF FATHER	YEAR	COUNTY	NAME OF MOTHER	YEAR	COUNTY
1 Osavior Duroderigo	Dead	Mexican	Jane Duroderigo	Dead	Chickasaw roll

(Notes)

On Chickasaw roll as Columbus Osavier

No. 1 is a brother of the three Duroderigo sisters on Chickasaw card #555.

on this card Nov. 24/98.
From white card No. D.54.

RESIDENCE: Tishomingo   COUNTY   CARD NO.

POST OFFICE: Mill Creek, Ind. Ter.   FIELD NO.

NAME	RELATION-SHIP TO PERSON FIRST NAMED	AGE	SEX	BLOOD	TRIBAL ENROLLMENT		
					YEAR	COUNTY	PAGE
1 Tyson, Willie		24	M	1/2	1897	Tishomingo	29

TRIBAL ENROLLMENT OF PARENTS

NAME OF FATHER	YEAR	COUNTY	NAME OF MOTHER	YEAR	COUNTY
1 Cobush Tyson	Dead	Quasada Indian	Amanda Tyson	Dead	Chickasaw roll

(NOTES)

Nov. 24/98.

RESIDENCE: Choctaw Nation   *COUNTY*   *CARD NO.*

POST OFFICE: Lehigh, Ind. Ter.   *FIELD NO.*

NAME	RELATION-SHIP TO PERSON FIRST NAMED	AGE	SEX	BLOOD	TRIBAL ENROLLMENT		
					YEAR	COUNTY	PAGE
1 McIntosh, Thomas		15	M	1/4			
2 Robinson, Lee	1/2 Bro.	13	"	1/4			

TRIBAL ENROLLMENT OF PARENTS

	NAME OF FATHER	YEAR	COUNTY	NAME OF MOTHER	YEAR	COUNTY
1	Roach McIntosh		Creek Citz.	Mary Robinson	Dead	Chick residing in Choctaw N. 3rd Dist.
2	Jim Robinson		Kiamitia County Choctaw Roll	" "	"	" " " "

(NOTES)

No. 1 on Choctaw Census Record No. 2, Page 372, transferred to Chickasaw roll by Dawes Com.

No. 2 "   "   "   "   No. 2   " 414   "   "   "   "   "   "   "

　　　Both living with H.C. Wilson.

No. 1 on Choctaw Roll 1896, Blue County No. 9429.

No. 2 "   "   " 1896, "   "   " 10955

Nov. 24/98.

CANCELLED Stamped across card

RESIDENCE: Choctaw Nation   ~~COUNTY~~   *CARD NO.*

POST OFFICE: Kasomo, Ind. Ter.   *FIELD NO.*

NAME	RELATION-SHIP TO PERSON FIRST NAMED	AGE	SEX	BLOOD	TRIBAL ENROLLMENT		
					YEAR	COUNTY	PAGE
1 Yakamby, Willie		56	M	Full	1897	Chick residing in Choctaw N. 3rd Dist.	73

TRIBAL ENROLLMENT OF PARENTS

	NAME OF FATHER	YEAR	COUNTY	NAME OF MOTHER	YEAR	COUNTY
1	Yakamby	Dead	Chickasaw roll	Betsey Yakamby	Dead	Chickasaw Roll

(NOTES)

Now living in Cedar Co. 2nd Dist. Choctaw Nation.

Nov. 24/98.

RESIDENCE: Tishomingo COUNTY					CARD NO.			
POST OFFICE: Nineko, Ind. Ter.					FIELD NO.			

	NAME	RELATION-SHIP TO PERSON FIRST NAMED	AGE	SEX	BLOOD	TRIBAL ENROLLMENT		
						YEAR	COUNTY	PAGE
1	Chandler, Ellen E.		24	F	1/2	1897	Pickens	25
2	" Joseph B.	Son	2mo	M	1/4			

TRIBAL ENROLLMENT OF PARENTS							
	NAME OF FATHER	YEAR	COUNTY	NAME OF MOTHER	YEAR	COUNTY
1	James Edwards	Dead	Choctaw roll	Adeline Edwards	1897	Pickens
2	Bud Chandler		Mexican	No. 1		

(NOTES)

On Chickasaw roll as Ellen Edwards.
Wife of Bud Chandler, a Mexican.
No. 1 died Sept. 17, 1901; proof of death filed December 4, 1902.
No. 2 enrolled Mar. 6/99.
No. 2 died Oct. 16, 1900; proof of death filed December 4, 1902.

Nov. 23/98.

RESIDENCE: Tishomingo COUNTY					CARD NO.			
POST OFFICE: Anadarko, Ind. Ter.					FIELD NO.			

	NAME	RELATION-SHIP TO PERSON FIRST NAMED	AGE	SEX	BLOOD	TRIBAL ENROLLMENT		
						YEAR	COUNTY	PAGE
1	~~Collins, Adeline~~		~~45~~	~~F~~	~~Full~~	~~1897~~	~~Pickens~~	~~25~~
2	~~Conner, Norah Edwards~~	~~Dau~~	~~16~~	"	~~1/2~~	~~1897~~	"	~~25~~
3	~~Edwards, Liza~~	"	~~6~~	"	~~1/2~~	~~1897~~	"	~~25~~

TRIBAL ENROLLMENT OF PARENTS							
	NAME OF FATHER	YEAR	COUNTY	NAME OF MOTHER	YEAR	COUNTY
1	Levi Thomas	Dead	Chickasaw roll	Liza Thomas	Dead	Chickasaw roll
2	James Edwards	"	Choctaw roll	No. 1		
3	" "	"	" "	No. 1		

(NOTES)

(Some notations illegible)
No. 3 on Chickasaw roll as Lizzie Edwards.

Nov. 23/98.

Chickasaw Enrollment Cards 1898-1914
Chickasaw by Blood   Volume III

RESIDENCE: Pickens   COUNTY

POST OFFICE: Lebanon, Ind. Ter.

CARD NO.

FIELD NO.

NAME	RELATION-SHIP TO PERSON FIRST NAMED	AGE	SEX	BLOOD	TRIBAL ENROLLMENT		
					YEAR	COUNTY	PAGE
1 McLish, Frazier		36	M	Full	1897	Pickens	25

TRIBAL ENROLLMENT OF PARENTS

NAME OF FATHER	YEAR	COUNTY	NAME OF MOTHER	YEAR	COUNTY
1 Billy McLish	Dead	Chickasaw roll	Mollie McLish	Dead	Pickens

(NOTES)

Nov. 23/98.

RESIDENCE: Tishomingo   COUNTY

POST OFFICE: Nebo, Ind. Ter.

CARD NO.

FIELD NO.

NAME	RELATION-SHIP TO PERSON FIRST NAMED	AGE	SEX	BLOOD	TRIBAL ENROLLMENT		
					YEAR	COUNTY	PAGE
1 Wolfe, Nelson		23	M	Full	1897	Tishomingo	31
2 " Iva P.	Wife	17	F	I.W.			

TRIBAL ENROLLMENT OF PARENTS

NAME OF FATHER	YEAR	COUNTY	NAME OF MOTHER	YEAR	COUNTY
1 Murphy Wolfe	Dead	Pickens	Sun-mat-hoy-ye	Dead	Pickens
2 W.J. Preston		non citz.	Susie Preston		non cit.

(NOTES)

9/14/99
Nov. 23/98.

RESIDENCE: Choctaw Nation   ~~COUNTY~~

POST OFFICE: Goodland, Ind. Ter.

CARD NO.

FIELD NO.

NAME	RELATION-SHIP TO PERSON FIRST NAMED	AGE	SEX	BLOOD	TRIBAL ENROLLMENT		
					YEAR	COUNTY	PAGE
1 ~~Wachubbe, Rhoda~~		~~58~~	F	~~Full~~	~~1897~~	~~Chick residing in Choctaw N. 3rd Dist.~~	~~73~~
2 Roberts, Betsey	G.Dau	6	F	1/2			
3 Wachubbe, Lewis	Son	14	M	1/2			

TRIBAL ENROLLMENT OF PARENTS

NAME OF FATHER	YEAR	COUNTY	NAME OF MOTHER	YEAR	COUNTY
1 ~~Wm Garland~~	~~Dead~~	~~Chickasaw roll~~	~~Ah-lo-ag-gey or Liza~~	~~Dead~~	~~Chickasaw roll~~

2	Eastman Roberts		Kiamitia County Choctaw roll	Mollie Roberts	1897	Chick residing in Choctaw N. 3rd Dist.
3	Willie Wachubbe		Kiamitia Co Choctaw Roll	No. 1		

(NOTES)

No. 1 Died May 31, 1900. Enrollment cancelled by Dept. July 2, 1904.
No. 1 Wife of Willie Wochubbe, Choctaw Card No. 468.
No. 1 on Chickasaw roll as Rhoda Wachubbee
No. 1 Died May 31, 1900; proof of death filed Oct. 11, 1902.
No. 2 on Choctaw Census Record No. 2, Page 411, transferred to Chickasaw roll by Dawes Com.
Nos. 1, 2 and 3 transferred to Choctaw Card *(remainder illegible)*
No. 3 found on Kiamitia Co. 1893 Pay Roll (Marked Choctaw Roll No. 4) Page 105.
No. 3 Enrolled Mar. 21/99.

Nov. 23/98.

RESIDENCE: Choctaw Nation   ~~COUNTY~~   CARD NO.

POST OFFICE: Nelson, Ind. Ter.   FIELD NO.

	NAME	RELATION-SHIP TO PERSON FIRST NAMED	AGE	SEX	BLOOD	TRIBAL ENROLLMENT		
						YEAR	COUNTY	PAGE
1	Thompson, George W.	NAMED	40	M	I.W.			
2	" Mattie	Wife	30	F	3/8			
3	" Juanita	Dau	13	"	3/16			
4	" Eugene	"	12	"	3/16			
5	" Edgar	Son	10	M	3/16			
6	" Daisy	Dau	7	F	3/16			
7	" Grace	"	5	"	3/16			
8	" Atwood	Son	3	M	3/16			
9	" Georgie	Dau	2mo	F	3/16			

TRIBAL ENROLLMENT OF PARENTS

	NAME OF FATHER	YEAR	COUNTY	NAME OF MOTHER	YEAR	COUNTY
1	Alfred Thompson	Dead	non citizen	Eliza Thompson		non citizen
2	George Colbert	1897	Chick residing in Choctaw N. 3rd Dist.	Elizabeth Colbert	Dead	" "
3	No. 1			No. 2		
4	No. 1			No. 2		
5	No. 1			No. 2		
6	No. 1			No. 2		
7	No. 1			No. 2		
8	No. 1			No. 2		
9	No. 1			No. 2		

(NOTES)

No. 1   on Choctaw Intermarried Roll, Page 106; transferred to Chickasaw roll by Dawes Com.

All others "   "   Census Record No. 2, " 448,   "   "   "   "   "   "   "

No. 3 on Choctaw roll as Netta Thompson 1896, Kiamitia County, No. 12366

No. 8 "   "   "   " Etwood   "   1896   "   "   " 12371

No. 1 "   "   "   " George   "   1896   "   "   " 15108

No. 1 Died April 24, 1899. Proof of death filed Aug. 5, 1901.

No. 9 Enrolled Nov. 4/99.

No. 2 on Choctaw Roll 1896, Kiamitia Co., No. 12365

No. 4 "   "   " 1896   "   "   " 12367

No. 5 "   "   " 1896   "   "   " 12368

No. 6 "   "   " 1896   "   "   " 12369

No. 7 "   "   " 1896   "   "   " 12370

No. 22/98.

CANCELLED Stamped across card

RESIDENCE: Choctaw Nation ~~COUNTY~~					CARD NO.			
POST OFFICE: Nelson, Ind. Ter.					FIELD NO.			
NAME	RELATION-SHIP TO PERSON FIRST	AGE	SEX	BLOOD	TRIBAL ENROLLMENT			
					YEAR	COUNTY	PAGE	
1 Griggs, Dora	NAMED	33	F	1/2	1893	Choctaw Dist.		
2 " Thomas	Stepson	20	M	3/8				
NAME OF FATHER	YEAR	COUNTY		NAME OF MOTHER		YEAR	COUNTY	
1 Jim McCauley		non citizen		Susan McCauly[sic]		Dead	Chickasaw roll	
2 Thomas L. Griggs		Kiamitia County Choctaw Roll		Mary Griggs		"	" "	

(NOTES)

No. 1 on Maytubby Pay Roll, No. 2, as Mrs. Tom Griggs. Wife of Thomas L. Griggs, Choctaw roll, Card No. 456.

No. 2 on Choctaw Census Record No. 2, Page 207; transferred to Chickasaw roll by Dawes Com.

No. 2 on Choctaw Roll, 1896, Kiamitia County, No. 4829, as Thomas L. Griggs, Jr.

No. 2 transferred to Choctaw Card No. *(remainder illegible)*

Nov. 22/98.

RESIDENCE: Choctaw Nation ~~COUNTY~~					CARD NO.			
POST OFFICE: Kasoma, Ind. Ter.					FIELD NO.			
NAME	RELATION-SHIP TO PERSON FIRST	AGE	SEX	BLOOD	TRIBAL ENROLLMENT			
					YEAR	COUNTY	PAGE	
1 Davenport, George	NAMED	42	M	1/2				

TRIBAL ENROLLMENT OF PARENTS						
	NAME OF FATHER	YEAR	COUNTY	NAME OF MOTHER	YEAR	COUNTY
1	Barnett Davenport	Dead	Choctaw roll	*(Name Illegible)*	Dead	Chickasaw roll

(NOTES)

On Choctaw Census Record No. 2, Page 137, transferred to Chickasaw roll by Dawes Commission.
Husband of Betsey Davenport, Choctaw roll Card No. 454.
On Choctaw Roll, 1896, Cedar County, No. 3360.
No. 1 Died Dec. 15, 1898. proof of death filed Sept. 26, 1902.

Nov. 22/98.

CANCELLED Stamped across card
Died prior to Sept. 25, 1902

RESIDENCE: Choctaw Nation ~~COUNTY~~ CARD NO.
POST OFFICE: Caddo, Ind. Ter. FIELD NO.

	NAME	RELATION-SHIP TO PERSON FIRST NAMED	AGE	SEX	BLOOD	TRIBAL ENROLLMENT YEAR	COUNTY	PAGE
1	Arnold, Luther W.		9	M	1/4	1897	Chick residing in Choctaw N. 3rd Dist.	74

TRIBAL ENROLLMENT OF PARENTS						
	NAME OF FATHER	YEAR	COUNTY	NAME OF MOTHER	YEAR	COUNTY
1	John W. Arnold	Dead	non-citizen	Margaret Arnold	Dead	Chick residing in Choctaw N. 3rd Dist.

(NOTES)

No. 1 on Chickasaw roll as Luthur W. Arnold

Nov. 21/98.

RESIDENCE: Pickens COUNTY CARD NO.
POST OFFICE: Chickasha, Ind. Ter. FIELD NO.

	NAME	RELATION-SHIP TO PERSON FIRST NAMED	AGE	SEX	BLOOD	TRIBAL ENROLLMENT YEAR	COUNTY	PAGE
1	Sparks, Nellie Gaines		13	F	1/16	1897	Pickens	20
2	" J.B.	Father	42	M	I.W.			

TRIBAL ENROLLMENT OF PARENTS						
	NAME OF FATHER	YEAR	COUNTY	NAME OF MOTHER	YEAR	COUNTY
1	J.B. Sparks		non citizen	Nona Criner Sparks	1897	Pontotoc
2	Wm Sparks	Dead	" "	Hannah Sparks	Dead	Non Citizen

(NOTES)

No. 1 is admitted *(remainder illegible)*
No. 1 is daughter of Nos. 1 and 2 on Chickasaw Court Card #C.11.

" 1 admitted by Dawes Com. in 1896, case 266 affirmed by *(remainder illegible)*

" 2 " " " " " " " " " " " *(No. 2 Dawes' Roll No. 352)*

(2 notations illegible)

Nos. 1 and 2 admitted by U.S. Court Decr 22/99, Southern District Case # *(illegible)*

No. 2 is admitted as a citizen by intermarriage by C.C.C.C. June 30/04

No. 2 transferred to this card July 20 '04 from Chickasaw C.N. Case *(illegible)*

No. 21/98.

						TRIBAL ENROLLMENT		
RESIDENCE: Choctaw Nation ~~COUNTY~~			CARD NO.					
POST OFFICE: Silo, Ind. Ter.			FIELD NO.					
NAME	RELATION-SHIP TO PERSON FIRST NAMED	AGE	SEX	BLOOD	YEAR	COUNTY	PAGE	
1 Cooper, Uriah M.		47	M	I.W.	1897	Chick residing in Choctaw N. 3rd Dist.	82	

	TRIBAL ENROLLMENT OF PARENTS						
NAME OF FATHER	YEAR	COUNTY	NAME OF MOTHER	YEAR	COUNTY		
1 Lina Cooper	Dead	non-citizen	Winnie Cooper	Dead	non-citizen		

(NOTES)

On Chickasaw roll as N.M. Cooper.

Nov. 21/98.

RESIDENCE: Choctaw Nation ~~COUNTY~~					CARD NO.			
POST OFFICE: Antlers, Ind. Ter.					FIELD NO.			
NAME	RELATION-SHIP TO PERSON FIRST NAMED	AGE	SEX	BLOOD	TRIBAL ENROLLMENT			
					YEAR	COUNTY	PAGE	
1 Stevens, Ellen	NAMED	38	F	3/8				
2 " Samuel	Son	16	M	3/16				
3 " Eva	Dau	13	F	3/16				
4 " Mary	"	8	"	3/16				
5 " Martha	"	6	"	3/16				
6 " John D.	Son	5	M	3/16				

	TRIBAL ENROLLMENT OF PARENTS						
NAME OF FATHER	YEAR	COUNTY	NAME OF MOTHER	YEAR	COUNTY		
1 Samuel Colbert	Dead	Chickasaw roll	Loucina Colbert	Dead	Chickasaw roll		
2 Alexander Stevens	"	non citizen	No. 1				
3 " "	"	" "	No. 1				
4 " "	"	" "	No. 1				
5 " "	"	" "	No. 1				

6	" "	"	" "	No. I		

(NOTES)

All on Choctaw Census Record No. 2, Kiamitia Co., Page 428; transferred to Chickasaw roll by Dawes Com.

No. I on Choctaw roll as Ella Stevens, 1896, Kiamitia Co., No. 11535

No. 2 " " " " Dan " 1896 " " " 11536

No. 6 " " " " Dexter " 1896 " " " 11540

No. 3 " " " 1896 Kiamitia County, No. 11537

No. 4 " " " 1896 " " " 11538

No. 5 " " " 1896 " " " 11539

Nov. 21/98.

CANCELLED Stamped across card

RESIGNCE: Choctaw Nation	COUNTY				CARD NO.		
POST OFFICE: Antlers, Ind. Ter.					FIELD NO.		

NAME	RELATION-SHIP TO PERSON FIRST NAMED	AGE	SEX	BLOOD	TRIBAL ENROLLMENT		
					YEAR	COUNTY	PAGE
1 Sharp, Elba		29	F	3/16			
2 " Leo C.	Son	6	M	3/32			

TRIBAL ENROLLMENT OF PARENTS

NAME OF FATHER	YEAR	COUNTY	NAME OF MOTHER	YEAR	COUNTY
1 Geo. W. Colbert	1897	Chick residing in Choctaw N. 2nd Dist.	Lizzie Colbert	Dead	non-citizen
2 John Sharp	Dead	non-citizen	No. I		

(NOTES)

On Page 432 Choctaw Census Record No. 2 Jack Fork Co., transferred to Chickasaw roll by Dawes Com.

No. 2 on Choctaw roll as Leo B. Sharp

No. I on Choctaw roll 1896 Jacks Fork County, No. 11699 as Elbie Sharp

No. 2 " " " 1896 " " " " 11700 " Leo B. "

Nov. 21/98.

CANCELLED Stamped across card

RESIGNCE: Choctaw Nation	COUNTY				CARD NO.		
POST OFFICE: Antlers, Ind. Ter.					FIELD NO.		

NAME	RELATION-SHIP TO PERSON FIRST NAMED	AGE	SEX	BLOOD	TRIBAL ENROLLMENT		
					YEAR	COUNTY	PAGE
1 Colbert, George W.		61	M	3/8	1897	Chick residing in Choctaw N. 2nd Dist.	72
2 " Dora	Wife	29	F	I.W.	1897	" " " "	82
3 " Geo. W. Jr.	Son	6	M	3/16	1897	" " " "	72

4	" Henry C.		"	4	"	3/16	1897	"	" "	"	72
5	" Rufus		"	1 1/2	"	3/16					
6	" Ruth		Dau	1 1/2	F	3/16					

TRIBAL ENROLLMENT OF PARENTS

	NAME OF FATHER	YEAR	COUNTY	NAME OF MOTHER	YEAR	COUNTY
1	Samuel Colbert	Dead	Chickasaw roll	Loucina Colbert	Dead	Chickasaw roll
2	Wm McCarty		non-citizen	P.A. McCarty		non-citizen
3	No. 1			No. 2		
4	No. 1			No. 2		
5	No. 1			No. 2		
6	No. 1			No. 2		

(NOTES)

No. 1 on 1896 Choctaw Roll Page 72 No. 3053 Jacks Fork Co., as G.W. Colbert
No. 2 " 1896 " " " 384 " 14428 " " "
No. 3 " 1896 " " " 72 " 3054 " " " as G.W. Colbert
No. 4 " 1896 " " " 72 " 3055 " " " *(No. 4 Dawes' Roll No. 693)*
No. 4 on Chickasaw roll as W.C. Colbert
Nos. 5 and 6 Affidavits of attending physician to be supplied. Received Dec. 13/98. *(No. 5 Dawes' Roll No. 694)*
No. 2 admitted by Dawes Com. Case No. 987, as a Choctaw and no appeal taken. *(No. 6 Dawes' Roll No. 695)*
No. 2 on Chickasaw roll as G.W. Colbert, Jr.
No. 1 " " " " George W. Colbert, Sr.
No. 1 Died November 26, 1899. Evidence of death filed March 26, 1901.
No. 3 died Aug. 20, 1901; proof of death filed *(illegible)*

Nov. 21/98.

RESIDENCE: Choctaw Nation	~~COUNTY~~					CARD NO.			
POST OFFICE: Phillips, Ind. Ter.						FIELD NO.			

NAME	RELATION-SHIP TO PERSON FIRST NAMED	AGE	SEX	BLOOD	TRIBAL ENROLLMENT		
					YEAR	COUNTY	PAGE
1 James, Nellie		25	F	I.W.			

TRIBAL ENROLLMENT OF PARENTS

	NAME OF FATHER	YEAR	COUNTY	NAME OF MOTHER	YEAR	COUNTY
1	Abner Hill		non-citizen	Mary E. Hill		non-citizen

(NOTES)

Widow of Thomas James 1/4 Chickasaw Indian.
On Choctaw Intermarried Roll, Atoka Co., Page 53, transferred to Chickasaw Roll by Dawes Com.
    Married as a Choctaw
On Choctaw Roll, 1896, Atoka County, No. 14708.

Oct. 14/98.

CANCELLED Stamped across card

RESIDENCE: House of Correction   ~~COUNTY~~   **CARD NO.**

POST OFFICE: Detroit, Mich.   **FIELD NO.**

NAME	RELATION-SHIP TO PERSON FIRST NAMED	AGE	SEX	BLOOD	TRIBAL ENROLLMENT		
					YEAR	COUNTY	PAGE
1 Jacobs, John B.	NAMED	29	M	1/2	1897	Tishomingo	31

TRIBAL ENROLLMENT OF PARENTS

NAME OF FATHER	YEAR	COUNTY	NAME OF MOTHER	YEAR	COUNTY
1 Thomas Jacobs	Dead	Choctaw roll	Tennessee Jacobs	Dead	Chickasaw roll

(NOTES)

Born May 28, 1869.

On Chickasaw roll as John Jacob

In penitentiary for life at Detroit, Mich. 2/24/99 Granted a full pardon by the President Feb. 18/99.

Nephew of Ex. Gov. Jonas Wolfe and half brother of Ex. Gov. Palmer Moseby of Chickasaw Nation.

On Chickasaw card #D.142, Oct. 5, 1898; transferred to this card Oct. 29, 1898.

Oct. 29/98.

RESIDENCE: Pickens   **COUNTY**   **CARD NO.**

POST OFFICE: Ninnekah, Ind. Ter.   **FIELD NO.**

NAME	RELATION-SHIP TO PERSON FIRST NAMED	AGE	SEX	BLOOD	TRIBAL ENROLLMENT		
					YEAR	COUNTY	PAGE
1 Miller, Dora	NAMED	7	F	1/2	1893	Pickens	150
2 " Laura	Sister	6	"	1/2	1893	"	150
3 Sturges, Louise	1/2 "	15	"	1/2	1893	"	200

TRIBAL ENROLLMENT OF PARENTS

NAME OF FATHER	YEAR	COUNTY	NAME OF MOTHER	YEAR	COUNTY
1 J.C. Miller		white man	Zylphie Miller	Dead	Pickens
2 " " "		" "	" "	"	"
3 Charlie Sturges	Dead	Non citizen	" "	"	"

(NOTES)

All admitted by Dawes Com., Case No. 102 and no appeal taken.

~~No. 3 on Chickasaw roll as Louisa Sturgis~~

Nos. 1 & 2 on 1893 Chick Pay Roll Page 150

No. 3   "   "   "   "   " Page 200

Oct. 22/98.

Chickasaw Enrollment Cards 1898-1914
Chickasaw by Blood   Volume III

RESIDENCE: Pontotoc COUNTY					CARD NO.		
POST OFFICE: Minco, Ind. Ter.					FIELD NO.		

	NAME	RELATION-SHIP TO PERSON FIRST NAMED	AGE	SEX	BLOOD	TRIBAL ENROLLMENT		
						YEAR	COUNTY	PAGE
1	Campbell, Charles B.	NAMED	37	M	1/8	1897	Pontotoc	65
2	" Annie Belle	Dau	13	F	1/16	1897	"	65
3	" Charles W.W.	Son	11	M	1/16	1897	"	65
4	" Mary Ellen	Dau	9	F	1/16	1897	"	65
5	" Milton Bryant	Son	6	M	1/16	1897	"	65
6	" Stella Bernard	Dau	4	F	1/16	1897	"	65
7	" Frances B.	"	5mo	"	1/16			
8	" Effie May	Dau	1mo	F	1/16			

TRIBAL ENROLLMENT OF PARENTS

	NAME OF FATHER	YEAR	COUNTY	NAME OF MOTHER	YEAR	COUNTY
1	Michael Campbell	Dead	Non-citizen	Adelaide Campbell now Bond	1897	Pontotoc
2	No. 1			Margaret J. Campbell		non citizen
3	No. 1			" " "		" "
4	No. 1			" " "		" "
5	No. 1			" " "		" "
6	No. 1			" " "		" "
7	No. 1			" " "		" "
8	No. 1			" " "		" "

(NOTES)

No. 1 On Chickasaw roll as C.B. Campbell.
No. 2 "   "   " " Annie   " . Born Feb. 3, 1886
No. 3 "   "   " " W.W.   "   " Sept. 6, 1887
No. 4 "   "   " " M.E.   "   " Nov. 6, 1889
No. 5 "   "   " " M.B.   "   " Sept. 15, 1892
No. 6 "   "   " " S.B.   "   " Feb. 16, 1895
No. 7 Enrolled Nov. 4/99.
No. 8 Born July 1, 1902; Enrolled Feb. 3, 1902[sic].

Oct. 22/98.

RESIDENCE: Pickens COUNTY					CARD NO.		
POST OFFICE: Purdy, Ind. Ter.					FIELD NO.		

	NAME	RELATION-SHIP TO PERSON FIRST NAMED	AGE	SEX	BLOOD	TRIBAL ENROLLMENT		
						YEAR	COUNTY	PAGE
1	Gibson, Emily	NAMED	21	F	Full	1897	Pickens	24

Chickasaw Enrollment Cards 1898-1914
Chickasaw by Blood   Volume III

2	" Nancy	Dau	2lmo	F	1/2				
3	" Hickman	Son	2mo	M	1/2				
4	" Millenda	Dau	19mo	F	1/2				

TRIBAL ENROLLMENT OF PARENTS

	NAME OF FATHER	YEAR	COUNTY	NAME OF MOTHER	YEAR	COUNTY
1	Tecumseh Loman	Dead	Chickasaw roll	Linda Loman	1897	Pickens
2	Joseph Gibson		Choctaw residing in Chickasaw Dist.	No. 1		
3	" "		" "	No. 1		
4	" "		" "	No. 1		

(NOTES)

No. 1 on Chickasaw roll as Emly Lomen
No. 1 Wife of Joseph Gibson, Choctaw roll, Card No. 447
No. 4 Born Sept. 26, 1900; enrolled May 10, 1902.

RESIDENCE: Pickens COUNTY   CARD NO.
POST OFFICE: Chickasha, Ind. Ter.   FIELD NO.

	NAME	RELATION-SHIP TO PERSON FIRST NAMED	AGE	SEX	BLOOD	TRIBAL ENROLLMENT		
						YEAR	COUNTY	PAGE
1	Fillmore, Benjamin Franklin	NAMED	25	M	Full	1897	Pickens	19
2	" Robert	Son	2	"	1/2	1897	"	19
3	" Frank	"	1	"	1/2			
4	" Emly Labell	Dau	1mo	F	1/2			
5	" Sallie	Wife	13	F	I.W.			

TRIBAL ENROLLMENT OF PARENTS

	NAME OF FATHER	YEAR	COUNTY	NAME OF MOTHER	YEAR	COUNTY
1	Nut-a-kin-cha Fillmore	Dead	Chickasaw roll	Louisa Scarlett	1897	Pickens
2	No. 1			Sallie Fillmore		non citizen
3	No. 1			" "		" "
4	No. 1			" "		" "
5	(Name Illegible)			Emily Brown		non citizen

(NOTES)

No. 1 On Chickasaw roll as Ben F. Filmore
No. 4 Enrolled Sept. 4, 1901
    Sallie Fillmore, wife of No. 1 on Chickasaw D.283
No. 5 transferred from Chickasaw card #D.283, March 20, 1903.   (No. 5 Dawes' Roll No. 64)
    See decision of March 13, 1903.

P.O. Ninnekah, I.T. 10/17/02.   Oct. 21/98.

33

RESIDENCE: Pontotoc COUNTY					CARD NO.			
POST OFFICE: Minco, Ind. Ter.					FIELD NO.			
NAME	RELATION-SHIP TO PERSON FIRST NAMED	AGE	SEX	BLOOD	TRIBAL ENROLLMENT			
					YEAR	COUNTY		PAGE
1 McLish, Henry F.	NAMED	34	M	5/8	1897	Pontotoc		65
2 " Cora	Wife	30	F	I.W.	1897	"		81
3 " Nina	Dau	6	F	5/16	1897	"		65
4 " Lena	"	4	"	5/16	1897	"		65
5 " Clara	"	3	"	5/16	1897	"		65
6 " Glenn	Son	1mo	M	5/16				

TRIBAL ENROLLMENT OF PARENTS

	NAME OF FATHER	YEAR	COUNTY	NAME OF MOTHER	YEAR	COUNTY
1	Frazier McLish	Dead	Chickasaw roll	Julia Foutubby	Dead	Tishomingo
2	John Aber		non citizen	Lizzie Aber		non citizen
3	No. 1			No. 2		
4	No. 1			No. 2		
5	No. 1			No. 2		
6	No. 1			No. 2		

(NOTES)

No. 1 on Chickasaw roll as H.F. McLish   *(No. 2 Dawes' Roll No. 484)*
No. 4 "   "   "   " Sena   "
No. 6 Born Sept. 6, 1902. enrolled Oct. 23, 1902.   *(No. 6 Dawes' Roll No. 4214)*
     See testimony of No. 1 taken October 16, 1902.

Oct. 21/98.

RESIDENCE: Pontotoc COUNTY					CARD NO.			
POST OFFICE: Waldon, Ind. Ter.					FIELD NO.			
NAME	RELATION-SHIP TO PERSON FIRST NAMED	AGE	SEX	BLOOD	TRIBAL ENROLLMENT			
					YEAR	COUNTY		PAGE
1 Gray, Lon	NAMED	42	M	Full	1897	Pontotoc		65
2 " Amanda	Wife	25	F	I.W.	1897	"		81
3 " Robert	Son	7	M	1/2	1897	"		65
4 " Vidi	Dau	4	F	1/2	1897	"		65
5 " Elsie	"	4mo	"	1/2				

TRIBAL ENROLLMENT OF PARENTS

	NAME OF FATHER	YEAR	COUNTY	NAME OF MOTHER	YEAR	COUNTY
1	Adam Gray	Dead	Chickasaw roll	Elsie Gray	Dead	Tishomingo
2	Abb Start	"	non citizen	Viney Start	"	non citizen

3	No. 1			No. 2		
4	No. 1			No. 2		
5	No. 1			No. 2		

(NOTES)

No. 2 Affidavit of witness to marriage to be supplied - Received Jan. 4/99.
No. 5 Proof of birth received and filed Sept. 30, 1902.
    Evidence of marriage between Nos. 1 and 2 in accordance with tribal laws received and filed Oct. 21, 1902.
    See testimony of No. 2 taken October 17, 1902.
    See testimony of No. 1 taken Oct. 21, 1902

P.O. Naples, I.T. 9/30/02.   Oct. 21/98.

RESIDENCE: Pontotoc COUNTY				CARD NO.		
POST OFFICE: Minco. Ind. Ter.				FIELD NO.		

NAME	RELATION-SHIP TO PERSON FIRST NAMED	AGE	SEX	BLOOD	TRIBAL ENROLLMENT		
					YEAR	COUNTY	PAGE
1 Connaway, Philip K.	NAMED	34	M	I.W.	1897	Pontotoc	81

TRIBAL ENROLLMENT OF PARENTS

NAME OF FATHER	YEAR	COUNTY	NAME OF MOTHER	YEAR	COUNTY
1 Dennis H. Connaway	Dead	Non-citizen	Serena Connaway	Dead	non-citizen

(NOTES)

On Chickasaw roll as Phillip K. Conway   *(No. 1 Dawes 'Roll No. 483)*
No. 1 was formerly husband of Stella Johnson to whom he was married January 10, 1894 and he lived
    with her until her death in May 1896.
    Her name appears on Page 121 of Chickasaw 1893 Pay Roll No. 2

                                                                 Oct. 21/98.

RESIDENCE: Pontotoc COUNTY				CARD NO.		
POST OFFICE: Minco, Ind. Ter.				FIELD NO.		

NAME	RELATION-SHIP TO PERSON FIRST NAMED	AGE	SEX	BLOOD	TRIBAL ENROLLMENT		
					YEAR	COUNTY	PAGE
1 Johnson, Tilford Thomas	NAMED	22	M	1/8	1897	Pontotoc	65
2 " Minnie	Wife	22	F	I.W.			

TRIBAL ENROLLMENT OF PARENTS

NAME OF FATHER	YEAR	COUNTY	NAME OF MOTHER	YEAR	COUNTY
1 Montford T. Johnson	Dead	Pontotoc	Mary E. Johnson (I.W.)	Dead	Pontotoc
2 Jim Fitch		Non-citz	Anna Fitch		Non-citz

(NOTES)

On Chickasaw roll as T.T. Johnson   *(No. 2 Dawes' Roll No. 198)*

No. 1 is now the husband of Minnie Johnson, Chick. Card D.365.
Evidence of marriage filed Sept. 9, 1902.
No. 1 transferred from Chickasaw Card #D.365
See decision of May , 1902

Oct. 21/98.

	NAME	RELATION-SHIP TO PERSON FIRST NAMED	AGE	SEX	BLOOD	TRIBAL ENROLLMENT		
						YEAR	COUNTY	PAGE
1	Johnson, Robert Miller	NAMED	24	M	1/8	1897	Pontotoc	65
2	" Virgie	Wife	24	F	1/8	1897	"	39
3	" William Montfort	Son	7mo	M	1/8			

RESIDENCE: Pontotoc   COUNTY   CARD NO.
POST OFFICE: Minco, Ind. Ter.   FIELD NO.

TRIBAL ENROLLMENT OF PARENTS

	NAME OF FATHER	YEAR	COUNTY	NAME OF MOTHER	YEAR	COUNTY
1	Montford T. Johnson	Dead	Pontotoc	Mary E. Johnson (I.W.)	Dead	Pontotoc
2	John D. Molette	"	non citizen	Hattie Love	1897	Pickens
3	No. 1			No. 2		

(NOTES)

No. 1 on Chickasaw Roll as R.M. Johnson
No. 2 "   "   " " Virgie Molette

Oct. 21/98.

RESIDENCE: Pontotoc   COUNTY   CARD NO.
POST OFFICE: Minco, Ind. Ter.   FIELD NO.

	NAME	RELATION-SHIP TO PERSON FIRST NAMED	AGE	SEX	BLOOD	TRIBAL ENROLLMENT		
						YEAR	COUNTY	PAGE
1	Johnson, Henry Belton	NAMED	29	M	1/8	1897	Pontotoc	65
2	" Effie M.	Wife	22	F	I.W.	1897	"	81
3	" Mary Margaret	Dau	5	F	1/16	1897	"	65
4	" Effie Maurine	"	3	"	1/16	1897	"	65
5	" Stella Bernadine	"	1	"	1/16			

TRIBAL ENROLLMENT OF PARENTS

	NAME OF FATHER	YEAR	COUNTY	NAME OF MOTHER	YEAR	COUNTY
1	Montford T. Johnson	Dead	Pontotoc	Mary Johnson (I.W.)	Dead	Pontotoc
2	Geo. W. Merchant	"	Non citizen	Alice Merchant		non citizen
3	No. 1			No. 2		
4	No. 1			No. 2		

5	No. 1			No. 2		

(NOTES)

No. 1 on Chickasaw roll as H.B. Johnson   *(No. 2 Dawes' Roll No. 169)*

No. 3 "   "   "   "   M.M.   "

No. 4 "   "   "   "   Effie M. "   , Jr.

No. 3 Died Jany. 21, 1901. proof of death filed June 9, 1902.

No. 4 Died Jany. 23, 1901. proof of death filed June 9, 1902.

No. 5 Died Jany. 26, 1901. proof of death filed June 9, 1902.

P.O. Chickasha, I.T. 12/17/02   Oct. 21/98.

RESIDENCE: Pontotoc   **COUNTY**   **CARD NO.**

POST OFFICE: Minco, Ind. Ter.   **FIELD NO.**

	NAME	RELATION-SHIP TO PERSON FIRST NAMED	AGE	SEX	BLOOD	TRIBAL ENROLLMENT		
						YEAR	COUNTY	PAGE
1	Reynolds, Ida	NAMED	6	F	3/8	1897	Pontotoc	96
2	" Charles	Bro	4	M	3/8			

TRIBAL ENROLLMENT OF PARENTS

	NAME OF FATHER	YEAR	COUNTY	NAME OF MOTHER	YEAR	COUNTY
1	Jack Reynolds	1897	Pontotoc	Edna Reynolds		
2	" "	"	"	" "		

(NOTES)

No. 1 See decision of June 13 '04   *(No. 1 Dawes' Roll No. 4867)*

     Father Jack Reynolds on Chickasaw Card #388 on final roll #1170

     On Choctaw Census Record No. 2, Page 417, transferred to Chickasaw Roll by Dawes Com

Nos. 1 and 2 are the children of Edna F. Henley on Choctaw card #D.97.

     Citizenship of Edna Reynolds not determined.

No. 1 on 1893 Chickasaw Pay Roll No. 2, Page 192

No. 1 on Choctaw Roll, 1896, Chickasaw Dist., No. 11069, as Ida Raynolds

No. 2 "   "   "   1896   "   "   "   11070 as Charlie   "

No. 2 transferred to Choc. card #5486, Oct. 20, 1902.

2/6/03. Affidavit of election filed *(remainder illegible)*

           Oct. 21/98.

RESIDENCE: Pickens   **COUNTY**   **CARD NO.**

POST OFFICE: Chickasha, Ind. Ter.   **FIELD NO.**

	NAME	RELATION-SHIP TO PERSON FIRST NAMED	AGE	SEX	BLOOD	TRIBAL ENROLLMENT		
						YEAR	COUNTY	PAGE
4	~~Vaughn, Edward A.~~	NAMED	~~16~~	M	~~1/8~~	~~1897~~	~~Pickens~~	~~19~~

2	"	Grover Cleveland	Bro	14	"	1/8	1897	"	19
3	"	Benjamin C.	"	10	"	1/8	1897	"	19
4	"	Oscar S.	"	8	"	1/8	1897	"	19

TRIBAL ENROLLMENT OF PARENTS

	NAME OF FATHER	YEAR	COUNTY	NAME OF MOTHER	YEAR	COUNTY
1	~~B.J. Vaughn~~		~~non-citizen~~	~~Emily Vaughn~~	~~Dead~~	~~Pickens~~
2	" " "		" "	" "	"	"
3	" " "		" "	" "	"	"
4	" " "		" "	" "	"	"

(NOTES)

No. 1 On Chickasaw roll as Edward Vaughn
No. 2 "   "   " " Grover   "
No. 3 "   "   " " Ben   "
No. 4 "   "   " " Oscar   "

Nos. 1, 2, 3 and 4 admitted as Chickasaws by blood by U.S. Court, Southern district I.T. December 22, 1897
    Court Case #43: B.J. Vaughan et. al. vs. Chickasaw Nation.
    Surname in judgement is Vaughan.
No. 3 Died Nov. 10, 1900; Proof of death filed Oct. 18-1902.

Oct. 21/98.

RESIDENCE: Tishomingo COUNTY							CARD NO.			
POST OFFICE: Mill Creek, Ind. Ter.							FIELD NO.			

NAME	RELATION- SHIP TO PERSON FIRST	AGE	SEX	BLOOD	TRIBAL ENROLLMENT		
					YEAR	COUNTY	PAGE
1 Tushawaha, Willie	NAMED	28	M	Full	1897	Tishomingo	31

TRIBAL ENROLLMENT OF PARENTS

	NAME OF FATHER	YEAR	COUNTY	NAME OF MOTHER	YEAR	COUNTY
1	Tushawaha	Dead	Tishomingo	Katsie Ontiubby	Dead	Tishomingo

(NOTES)

Oct. 21/98.

RESIDENCE: Pickens COUNTY							CARD NO.			
POST OFFICE: Chickasha, Ind. Ter.							FIELD NO.			

NAME	RELATION- SHIP TO PERSON FIRST	AGE	SEX	BLOOD	TRIBAL ENROLLMENT		
					YEAR	COUNTY	PAGE
1 Baker, Frank Elmer	NAMED	36	M	I.W.	1897	Pickens	78
2 " Mary V.	Wife	24	F	1/8	1897	"	18
3 " Charles Wesley	Son	5	M	1/16	1897	"	18

4	"	Ada Gertrude	Dau	3	F	1/16	1897	"	18
5	"	Franklin Bryan	Son	2	M	1/16	1897	"	18
6	"	John Garland	"	3mos	"	1/16			
7	"	William Lee	"	1wk	"	1/16			
8	"	Flora Dell	Dau	1wk	F	1/16			

TRIBAL ENROLLMENT OF PARENTS

	NAME OF FATHER	YEAR	COUNTY	NAME OF MOTHER	YEAR	COUNTY
1	John W. Baker	Dead	non citizen	Barbara Ann Baker	Dead	non citizen
2	L.L. Woods	"	" "	Frances E. Woods	"	Pickens
3	No. 1			No. 2		
4	No. 1			No. 2		
5	No. 1			No. 2		
6	No. 1			No. 2		
7	No. 1			No. 2		
8	No. 1			No. 2		

(NOTES)

First four admitted by Dawes Com., Case No. 10, and no appeal taken.

Marriage papers on filed in office of Dawes Com, Muskogee, Ind. Ter.

See additional testimony of No. 1, taken Oct. 15, 1902.

No. 1 on Chickasaw roll as F.E. Baker   *(No. 1 Dawes' Roll No. 443)*

No. 2 "   "   "   " Mary V. Barker

No. 3 "   "   "   " Chas W.   "

No. 4 "   "   "   " Ada G.   "

No. 5 "   "   "   " Frank   "

No. 7 enrolled December 3, 1900.

No. 8 Born Sept. 16, 1902. enrolled Sept. 22, 1902

No. 1 See decision of June 13 '04.

Oct. 20/98.

RESIDENCE: Pickens   COUNTY   CARD NO.

POST OFFICE: Ninnekah, Ind. Ter.   FIELD NO.

	NAME	RELATION-SHIP TO PERSON FIRST NAMED	AGE	SEX	BLOOD	TRIBAL ENROLLMENT		
						YEAR	COUNTY	PAGE
1	Beeler, George R.	NAMED	45	M	I.W.	1897	Pickens	77
2	" Georgia A	Wife	31	F	1/8	1897	"	22
3	Thomson, Della May	Dau	16	"	1/16	1897	"	22
4	Beeler, Fred Grant	Son	14	M	1/16	1897	"	22
5	" Melton	"	12	"	1/16	1897	"	22
6	" Julia	Dau	6	F	1/16	1897	"	22
7	" George R., Jr.	Son	9mos	M	1/16			

39

8	Thomson, William Paul	Son of No. 3	4mo	M	1/32				
9	Beeler, Sarah Louise	Dau	2mo	F	1/16				
10	Thomson, William H.	Hus of No. 3	29	M	I.W.				

TRIBAL ENROLLMENT OF PARENTS

	NAME OF FATHER	YEAR	COUNTY	NAME OF MOTHER	YEAR	COUNTY
1	John S. Beeler		non-citizen	Martha Beeler		non citizen
2	Dan Collins (I.W.)	1897		Sarah Collins	1897	Panola
3	No. 1			Mollie Beeler	Dead	Pickens
4	No. 1			" "	"	"
5	No. 1			" "	"	"
6	No. 1			No. 2		
7	No. 1			No. 2		
8	William H. Thomson		non-citizen	No. 3		
9	No. 1			No. 2		
10	John T. Thomson		non citizen	Lizzie J. Thomson		non citizen

(NOTES)

No. 1 Certified copy of marriage license and certificate to be supplied.   *(No. 1 Dawes' Roll No. 293)*

No. 3 On Chickasaw roll as May Beeler

No. 4   "   "   "   " Fred   "

No. 3 now wife of William H. Thomson non-citizen; Evidence of marriage filed June 27, 1902.
  Affidavit of Guy Keel as to marriage and license received Nov. 11/98.

No. 8 Born Feb. 19, 1902; enrolled June 27, 1902.

No. 9 Born June 6, 1902; enrolled Aug. 25, 1902.

No. 3 Husband is on Chickasaw card #D.373 Sept. 24, 1902.
  See testimony of No. 1 taken October 16, 1902.

No. 10 transferred from Chick Card D.373 August 1, 1903. See decision of July 16, 1903.

Certified copy of certificate of marriage between No. 1 and Mary Grant, his first Chickasaw wife, filed May 27, 1903.

Affidavit of No. 1, stating that Mary Grant Beeler, was never married previous to her marriage to him,
  filed July 15, 1903.

Oct. 20/98.

RESIDENCE:	Tishomingo	COUNTY			CARD NO.			
POST OFFICE:	Tishomingo, Ind. Ter.				FIELD NO.			

	NAME	RELATIONSHIP TO PERSON FIRST NAMED	AGE	SEX	BLOOD	TRIBAL ENROLLMENT		
						YEAR	COUNTY	PAGE
1	Nesbit, Arthur H.		21	M	1/16	1897	Tishomingo	32

TRIBAL ENROLLMENT OF PARENTS						
NAME OF FATHER	YEAR	COUNTY	NAME OF MOTHER	YEAR	COUNTY
1 George Nesbit	Dead	non citizen	Sophia Nesbet	Dead	non-citizen

(NOTES)

On Chickasaw roll as Arthur D. Nesbit   *(No. I Dawes' Roll No. 4758)*
   Descendant of John McLish.
(Notation illegible)

Oct. 20/98.

RESIDENCE: Pickens COUNTY						CARD NO.		
POST OFFICE: Chickasha, Ind. Ter.						FIELD NO.		
NAME	RELATION-SHIP TO PERSON FIRST NAMED	AGE	SEX	BLOOD	TRIBAL ENROLLMENT			
					YEAR	COUNTY	PAGE	
1 Cawdell, Jay	FIRST NAMED	16	M		1893	Pickens	P.R. #1 30	

TRIBAL ENROLLMENT OF PARENTS						
NAME OF FATHER	YEAR	COUNTY	NAME OF MOTHER	YEAR	COUNTY
1 Joe Cawdell		non citizen	Hattie Cawdell	Dead	Pickens

(NOTES)

   Admitted by Dawes Com. Case No. 9 and no appeal taken.
   Attending school in Ft. Smith, Ark., and residing at 802 N. 8th St. that city.
No. I is now the husband of Ethel D. White on Chickasaw card #778, Nov. 12, 1902.

P.O. Tishomingo, I.T.   Oct. 20/98.

RESIDENCE: Pickens COUNTY						CARD NO.		
POST OFFICE: Alex, Ind. Ter.						FIELD NO.		
NAME	RELATION-SHIP TO PERSON FIRST NAMED	AGE	SEX	BLOOD	TRIBAL ENROLLMENT			
					YEAR	COUNTY	PAGE	
1 Chitwood, Mary	NAMED	28	F	1/8	1897	Pickens	24	
2 " Emil	Son	8	M	1/16	1897	"	24	
3 " Silas	"	5	"	1/16	1897	"	24	
4 " Lena	Dau	3	F	1/16	1897	"	24	
5 " William Tolbert	Son	2	M	1/16	1897	"	24	
6 " Walter Belvin	"	10mo	"	1/16				
7 " David P.	"	4mo	"	1/16				
8 " Lee	Son	1mo	M	1/16				

41

Chickasaw Enrollment Cards 1898-1914
Chickasaw by Blood   Volume III

	TRIBAL ENROLLMENT OF PARENTS						
	NAME OF FATHER	YEAR	COUNTY	NAME OF MOTHER	YEAR	COUNTY
1	W. V. Alexander		Non-citizen	Jennie Alexander	Dead	Chickasaw roll
2	David Chitwood		" "	No. 1		
3	" "		" "	No. 1		
4	" "		" "	No. 1		
5	" "		" "	No. 1		
6	" "		" "	No. 1		
7	" "		" "	No. 1		
8	" "		" "	No. 1		

(NOTES)

No. 2 on Chickasaw roll as Annie Chitwood
No. 5 "   "   "   " Tolbert   "
No. 6 affidavit of midwife to be supplied, Received Nov. 7/98.
No. 8 Enrolled May 8, 1901.   *(No. 8 Dawes' Roll No. 761)*
No. 8 Died Oct. 2, 1902. proof of death filed Oct. 22, 1902.
No. 7 Enrolled Nov. 4/99.

Oct. 20/98.

RESIDENCE: Pickens   COUNTY   CARD NO.
POST OFFICE: Chickasha, Ind. Ter.   FIELD NO.

	NAME	RELATIONSHIP TO PERSON FIRST NAMED	AGE	SEX	BLOOD	TRIBAL ENROLLMENT		
						YEAR	COUNTY	PAGE
1	Sturdivant, Isabella		65	F	1/8	1897	Pickens	18

	TRIBAL ENROLLMENT OF PARENTS						
	NAME OF FATHER	YEAR	COUNTY	NAME OF MOTHER	YEAR	COUNTY
1	Christopher Moore	Dead	non-citizen	Kittie Moore	Dead	Chickasaw roll

(NOTES)

On Chickasaw roll as Isabell Studvant.

Oct. 20/98.

RESIDENCE: Pickens   COUNTY   CARD NO.
POST OFFICE: Purdy, Ind. Ter.   FIELD NO.

	NAME	RELATIONSHIP TO PERSON FIRST NAMED	AGE	SEX	BLOOD	TRIBAL ENROLLMENT		
						YEAR	COUNTY	PAGE
1	Gibson, Thomas		26	M	1/2			
2	" Laura	Wife	20	F	I.W.			
3	" Ada	Dau	3	"	1/4			

42

4	" Verda	"	1	"	1/4				
5	" Jesse	Son	3mo	M	1/4				
6	" Etta	Dau	7mo	F	1/4				

TRIBAL ENROLLMENT OF PARENTS

	NAME OF FATHER	YEAR	COUNTY	NAME OF MOTHER	YEAR	COUNTY
1	Reuben Gibson		Choctaw residing in Chickasaw Dist.	Nicey Gibson	1897	Pickens
2	Newt Hale	Dead	non citizen	Mollie Hale		non citizen
3	No. 1			No. 2		
4	No. 1			No. 2		
5	No. 1			No. 2		
6	No. 1			No. 2		

(NOTES)

Nos. 1, 3 & 4 on Choctaw Census Record No. 2, Page 213; transferred to Chickasaw roll by Dawes Com.
  No. 2 " " Intermarried Roll " 39 " " " " " " "
  No. 1 on Choctaw Roll, 1896, Jacks Fork County, No. 4990
  No. 2 " " " 1896 " " " " 14583
  No. 3 " " " 1896 " " " " 4991 as Eda Gibson.
  No. 6 Enrolled Aug. 6th, 1900.
  No. 6 Born Jany. 8, 1902; enrolled Aug. 23, 1902.

Oct. 20/98.

CANCELLED Stamped across card

| *RESIDENCE:* Tishomingo *COUNTY* | | | | | | *CARD NO.* | | | |
| *POST OFFICE:* Tishomingo, Ind. Ter. | | | | | | *FIELD NO.* | | | |

	NAME	RELATION-SHIP TO PERSON FIRST NAMED	AGE	SEX	BLOOD	TRIBAL ENROLLMENT		
						YEAR	COUNTY	PAGE
1	Folsom, David	NAMED	29	M	3/4	1897	Tishomingo	33
2	" Myrtle	Dau	7	F	3/8	1897	"	33
3	" Nora	"	5	"	3/8	1897	"	33
4	" Agnes	"	2	"	3/8	1897	"	88
5	" Virgil	"	2	"	3/8	1897	"	88
6	" Rosa	Wife	29	F	I.W.			

TRIBAL ENROLLMENT OF PARENTS

	NAME OF FATHER	YEAR	COUNTY	NAME OF MOTHER	YEAR	COUNTY
1	Gus Folsom	Dead	Chickasaw roll	Eliza Folsom	Dead	Chickasaw roll
2	No. 1			Rosa Folsom		white woman
3	No. 1			" "		" "
4	No. 1			" "		" "

5	No. 1			" "		" "
6	Thomas Swadley		non citizen	Minerva Swadley		non citizen

(NOTES)

No. 1 on Chickasaw roll as Dave Fulsom
No. 4 "   "   " " Agnes Fulsome   *(No. 4 Dawes' Roll No. 4209)*
No. 5 "   "   " " Virgil   "   *(No. 5 Dawes' Roll No. 4210)*
    Evidence of marriage of No. 1 and Rosa Folsom attqached to Card No. D.196
Nos. 4 & 5   Proof of birth filed Oct. 14, 1902.
No. 6 transferred from Chickasaw card #D.196 Oct. 31, 1904. See decision of Oct. 15, 1904.

                                          Oct. 20/98.

RESIDENCE: Pontotoc   **COUNTY**   **CARD NO.**
POST OFFICE: Minco, Ind. Ter.   **FIELD NO.**

	NAME	RELATION-SHIP TO PERSON FIRST NAMED	AGE	SEX	BLOOD	TRIBAL ENROLLMENT		
						YEAR	COUNTY	PAGE
1	Tuttle, James H.		38	M	I.W.	1897	Pontotoc	81
2	" Carrie M.	Wife	25	F	1/16	1897	"	65
3	" Virginia Molette	Dau	6	"	1/32	1897	"	65
4	" Nora Alma	"	4	"	1/32	1897	"	65
5	" James Bond	Son	2	M	1/32	1897	"	65
6	" Charles Campbell	"	1mo	"	1/32			
7	" Barbara Ann	Dau	3mo	F	1/32			

TRIBAL ENROLLMENT OF PARENTS

	NAME OF FATHER	YEAR	COUNTY	NAME OF MOTHER	YEAR	COUNTY
1	James H. Tuttle	Dead	non citizen	Virginia A. Tuttle	Dead	non-citizen
2	Charles L. Campbell	"	" "	Sallie L. Campbell	1897	Pontotoc
3	No. 1			No. 2		
4	No. 1			No. 2		
5	No. 1			No. 2		
6	No. 1			No. 2		
7	No. 1			No. 2		

(NOTES)

No. 1 marriage certificate - first marriage to be supplied. Affidavit of witness rec'd 3/24/99
    (No. 1 Dawes' Roll No. 168)
No. 3 on Chickasaw roll as G.M. Tuttle
No. 4 "   "   " " N.A.   "
No. 5 "   "   " " J.B.   "
No. 6 named in physician's affidavit as Charles Lawrence Tuttle.
No. 7 enrolled December 22, 1900.
All except No. 1 are descendants of John McLish.

Chickasaw Enrollment Cards 1898-1914
Chickasaw by Blood   Volume III

See additional testimony of No. 1, dated Oct. 15, '02.

No. 1 enrolled Oct. 20/98.
all others   Nov. 25/98.

RESIDENCE: Pickens COUNTY   CARD NO.
POST OFFICE: Chickasha, Ind. Ter.   FIELD NO.

NAME	RELATION-SHIP TO PERSON FIRST NAMED	AGE	SEX	BLOOD	TRIBAL ENROLLMENT		
					YEAR	COUNTY	PAGE
1 Edwards. Pocahontas	NAMED	5	F	1/4	1897	Pontotoc	61

TRIBAL ENROLLMENT OF PARENTS

NAME OF FATHER	YEAR	COUNTY	NAME OF MOTHER	YEAR	COUNTY
1 W.A. Edwards		non-citizen	Susie Edwards, now McCrummer	1897	Pontotoc

(NOTES)

On Chickasaw roll as Polk Edwards
Admitted by Dawes Com. Case No. 250, as Pokahauntas Edwards, and no appeal taken.
Mother of No. 1 on Chick Card #40.

Oct. 20/98.

RESIDENCE: Tishomingo COUNTY   CARD NO.
POST OFFICE: Davis, Ind. Ter.   FIELD NO.

NAME	RELATION-SHIP TO PERSON FIRST NAMED	AGE	SEX	BLOOD	TRIBAL ENROLLMENT		
					YEAR	COUNTY	PAGE
1 Thomas, Charley	NAMED	32	M	3/4	1897	Tishomingo	28
2 " Wm Montgomery	Son	14	"	3/8	1897	"	28
3 " Lillie Asley	Dau	11	F	3/8	1897	"	28
4 " Jefferson	Son	8	M	3/8	1897	"	28
5 " Jessie May	Dau	7	F	3/8	1897	"	28
6 " Callie Ray	"	5	"	3/8	1897	"	28
7 " Donnie Eveline	"	2	"	3/8	1897	"	28
8 " Charles N.D.	Son	9mo	M	3/8			

TRIBAL ENROLLMENT OF PARENTS

NAME OF FATHER	YEAR	COUNTY	NAME OF MOTHER	YEAR	COUNTY
1 Gabe Thomas	Dead	Chickasaw roll	Caroline Thomas	Dead	Chickasaw roll
2 No. 1			Nancy Thomas		
3 No. 1			" "		
4 No. 1			" "		
5 No. 1			" "		
6 No. 1			" "		

45

7	No. 1			" "		
8	No. 1			Nancy Thomas		

(NOTES)

No. 2 on Chickasaw roll as William Thomas
No. 3 "   "   "   " Lillie   "
No. 4 "   "   "   " Jeff   "
No. 5 "   "   "   " Jessie   "
No. 6 "   "   "   " Celier   "
No. 7 "   "   "   " Dona   "
No. 8 Enrolled Jany. 17/00
    Citizenship of Nancy Thomas wife of No. 1 is undetermined
Post office of parties is now Purcell, I.T. June 4, 1900.
Wife Nancy Thomas on Choctaw card R #485

P.O. Lindsay, I.T. 12/16/02   Oct. 20/98.

RESIDENCE: Pontotoc COUNTY						CARD NO.		
POST OFFICE: Purcell, Ind. Ter.						FIELD NO.		

NAME	RELATION-SHIP TO PERSON FIRST NAMED	AGE	SEX	BLOOD	TRIBAL ENROLLMENT		
					YEAR	COUNTY	PAGE
1 Goins, Susan		40	F	Full	1897	Pontotoc	63
2 " Charles Calvin	Son	16	M	1/2	1897	"	63
3 " Melinda Alzina	Dau	13	F	1/2	1897	"	63
4 " Vaney Dixon	Son	12	M	1/2	1897	"	63
5 " Ludie Napoleon	"	8	"	1/2	1897	"	63
6 " Susie Alice	Dau	2	F	1/2	1897	"	63

TRIBAL ENROLLMENT OF PARENTS

	NAME OF FATHER	YEAR	COUNTY	NAME OF MOTHER	YEAR	COUNTY
1	Robert Thomas	Dead	Chickasaw roll	Caroline Thomas	Dead	Chickasaw roll
2	Reuben Goins			No. 1		
3	" "			No. 1		
4	" "			No. 1		
5	" "			No. 1		
6	" "			No. 1		

(NOTES)

No. 2 on Chickasaw roll as C.C. Goins
No. 3 "   "   "   " M.A. "
No. 4 "   "   "   " V.D. "
No. 5 "   "   "   " L.N. "
No. 6 "   "   "   " S.A. "

Chickasaw Enrollment Cards 1898-1914
Chickasaw by Blood   Volume III

Reuben Goins, husband of No. 1 on Choctaw Card #5165.
No. 3 now married Sept 23, 1901 to John L. *(Illegible)*

Oct. 20/98.

RESIDENCE: Pontotoc   **COUNTY**   **CARD NO.**
POST OFFICE: Purcell, Ind. Ter.   **FIELD NO.**

	NAME	RELATION-SHIP TO PERSON FIRST NAMED	AGE	SEX	BLOOD	TRIBAL ENROLLMENT		
						YEAR	COUNTY	PAGE
1	Criner, Frank		11	F[sic]	1/32	1893	Pontotoc	P.R.#2 53

TRIBAL ENROLLMENT OF PARENTS

	NAME OF FATHER	YEAR	COUNTY	NAME OF MOTHER	YEAR	COUNTY
1	Frank A. Criner	Dead	Pontotoc	Zula J. Story		non-citizen

(NOTES)

On Chickasaw Pay Roll No. 2 as Frank A. Criner.

P.O. Story, I.T. 10/24/02   On Colored card Oct. 20/98.

RESIDENCE: Pontotoc   **COUNTY**   **CARD NO.**
POST OFFICE: Chickasha, Ind. Ter.   **FIELD NO.**

	NAME	RELATION-SHIP TO PERSON FIRST NAMED	AGE	SEX	BLOOD	TRIBAL ENROLLMENT		
						YEAR	COUNTY	PAGE
1	Walthall, George O.		38	M	I.W.	1897	Pickens	82
2	" Malinda	Wife	38	F	Full	1897	"	18
3	" Nicholas Mondavis	Son	14	M	1/2	1897	"	18
4	" Samuel Dixon	"	12	"	1/2	1897	"	18
5	" Bruce Love	"	6	"	1/2	1897	"	19
6	Hawkins, William	Ward	17	"	Full	1897	"	19
7	Walthall, George B.	Son	1mo	"	1/2			

TRIBAL ENROLLMENT OF PARENTS

	NAME OF FATHER	YEAR	COUNTY	NAME OF MOTHER	YEAR	COUNTY
1	J.F. Walthall	Dead	non citizen	Terressa A. Brown		non citizen
2	Robert Thomas	"	Chickasaw roll	Caroline Thomas	Dead	Chickasaw roll
3	No. 1			No. 2		
4	No. 1			No. 2		
5	No. 1			No. 2		

6	Fred Waite	Dead	Pickens	Patsey Hawkins	Dead	Pontotoc
7	No. 1			No. 2		

(NOTES)

No. 2 Died April 5, 1899; Evidence of death filed Sept. 9, 1901   *(No. 1 Dawes' Roll No. 482)*

No. 3 On Chickasaw roll as Nicholas Walthall   *(No. 3 Dawes' Roll No. 4840)*

No. 4 "   "   " " Samuel D. "   *(No. 4 Dawes' Roll No. 4814)*

No. 5 "   "   " " Bruce L. "   *(No. 5 Dawes' Roll No. 4812)*

No. 7 Died June 25, 1899; Evidence of death filed Sept. 9, 1901.

    Nos. 1, 3, 4 & 5 admitted by Dawes Com., Cae No. 212, and appeal dismissed.

    See sworn statement as to marriage hereto attached.

    See additional testimony of No. 1 taken October 17, 1902.

Note: an appeal was taken in this case to U.S. Court, Southern district, I.T., but case was dismissed May 8, 1897

                                                     Oct. 20/98.

RESIDENCE: Pickens   **COUNTY**   **CARD NO.**

POST OFFICE: Bailey, Ind. Ter.   **FIELD NO.**

NAME	RELATION-SHIP TO PERSON FIRST NAMED	AGE	SEX	BLOOD	TRIBAL ENROLLMENT		
					YEAR	COUNTY	PAGE
1 Story, Lotta Estella	NAMED	3	F	1/2			

TRIBAL ENROLLMENT OF PARENTS

	NAME OF FATHER	YEAR	COUNTY	NAME OF MOTHER	YEAR	COUNTY
1	Sam Story	1897	Pickens	Bettie Story		non citizen

(NOTES)

    See sworn statements hereto attached.

    See testimony of J.F. *(Illegible)* taken October 17, 1902.

No. 1 Evidence of marriage between parents received and filed Nov. 1, 1902.   *(No. 1 Dawes' Roll No. 4298)*

No. 1 Affidavit of attending nurse as to birth received and filed Nov. 1, 1901.

P.O. Naples, I.T.   On Colored Card Oct. 20/98.

RESIDENCE: Pickens   **COUNTY**   **CARD NO.**

POST OFFICE: Chickasha, Ind. Ter.   **FIELD NO.**

	NAME	RELATION-SHIP TO PERSON FIRST NAMED	AGE	SEX	BLOOD	TRIBAL ENROLLMENT		
						YEAR	COUNTY	PAGE
1	Burney, Edward Sehon	NAMED	38	M	1/4	1897	Pickens	17
2	" Ada	Wife	34	F	I.W.	1897	"	78
3	" Wessie Ella	Dau	15	F	1/8	1897	"	18
4	" Joseph Calhoun	Son	12	M	1/8	1897	"	18

5	"	Edward Everett	"	8	"	1/8	1897	"	18
6	"	Overton Love	"	4	"	1/8	1897	"	18
7	"	Effie Sudye	Dau	2	F	1/8	1897	"	18
8	"	Ada Bessie	Dau	4mo	F	1/8	1897	"	85

TRIBAL ENROLLMENT OF PARENTS

	NAME OF FATHER	YEAR	COUNTY	NAME OF MOTHER	YEAR	COUNTY
1	David D. Burney	Dead	Pickens	Emily Burney	Dead	Pickens
2	J.P. Cross		non citizen	Martha A. Cross		non citizen
3	No. 1			No. 2		
4	No. 1			No. 2		
5	No. 1			No. 2		
6	No. 1			No. 2		
7	No. 1			No. 2		
8	No. 1			No. 2		

(NOTES)

No. 1 See decision of June 13 '04   *(No. 2 Dawes' Roll No. 412)*
No. 1 on Chickasaw roll as Ed Burney
No. 3 "   "   " " Wessie E. "
No. 4 "   "   " " Joe C. "
No. 5 "   "   " " Ed. E. "
No. 6 "   "   " " Overton L. "
No. 7 "   "   " " Effie "
No. 7 Died June 24, 1899; Evidence of death filed March 27, 1901.
No. 8 Enrolled Aug. 30, 1901
      See testimony of No. 1 as to enrollment of No. 2, taken Oct. 22, 1902.

Oct. 20/98.

RESIDENCE:	Pickens	COUNTY					CARD NO.		
POST OFFICE:	Chickasha, Ind. Ter.						FIELD NO.		

NAME	RELATION-SHIP TO PERSON FIRST NAMED	AGE	SEX	BLOOD	TRIBAL ENROLLMENT		
					YEAR	COUNTY	PAGE
1	Brown, Stella M.		38	F	1/4	1897	Pontotoc	65
2	"	Mattie	Dau	1	"	1/8			
3	"	John W.	husband	45	M	I.W.			

	NAME OF FATHER	YEAR	COUNTY	NAME OF MOTHER	YEAR	COUNTY
1	Colbert Carter	Dead	Chickasaw roll	Elizabeth Carter	Dead	Chickasaw roll
2	John W. Brown		white man	No. 1		
3	*(Illegible)* Brown	Dead	non citz	Martha Brown now Lawrence		non citz

(NOTES)

No. 2 Died June 18, 1899; Evidence of death filed March 27, 1904

Chickasaw Enrollment Cards 1898-1914
Chickasaw by Blood   Volume III

Husband of No. 1 on Chickasaw D.194
No. 3 transferred from Chickasaw Card #D.194 April 1, 1903
See decision of March , 1903.

Oct. 20/98.

	NAME	RELATION-SHIP TO PERSON FIRST NAMED	AGE	SEX	BLOOD	TRIBAL ENROLLMENT		
	RESIDENCE: Pickens COUNTY					CARD NO.		
	POST OFFICE: Chickasha, Ind. Ter.					FIELD NO.		
						YEAR	COUNTY	PAGE
1	Earl, William	NAMED	20	M	1/32	1897	Pickens	11
2	" Katie Ethel	Dau	6mo	F	1/64			
3	" Edith May	Dau	6wks	F	1/64			

TRIBAL ENROLLMENT OF PARENTS

	NAME OF FATHER	YEAR	COUNTY	NAME OF MOTHER	YEAR	COUNTY
1	Henry Earl	Dead	non citizen	Kate O'Brien	1897	Panola
2	No. 1			Sarah Earl		non citizen
3	No. 1			" "		

(NOTES)

On Chickasaw roll as Willie Earl
No. 1 is now the husband of Sarah F. Earl, a non-citizen. Evidence of marriage Aug. 3, 1901.
No. 2 Enrolled Aug. 2, 1901.
No. 3 Born June 24, 1902; enrolled Aug. 14, 1902.

P.O. Ninnekah, I.T.

Oct. 20/98.

	NAME	RELATION-SHIP TO PERSON FIRST NAMED	AGE	SEX	BLOOD	TRIBAL ENROLLMENT		
	RESIDENCE: Pickens COUNTY					CARD NO.		
	POST OFFICE: Ninnekah, Ind. Ter.					FIELD NO.		
						YEAR	COUNTY	PAGE
1	Sturdivant, Luke Love	NAMED	40	M	1/16	1897	Pickens	18
2	" Minnie	Wife	22	F	I.W.			

TRIBAL ENROLLMENT OF PARENTS

	NAME OF FATHER		YEAR	COUNTY	NAME OF MOTHER	YEAR	COUNTY
1	Joel A. Sturdivant	I.W.	Dead	Pickens	Isabella Sturdivant	1897	Pickens
2	Jacob Mutz			non citz	Maggie Mutz	Dead	Non Citz

(NOTES)

On Chickasaw roll as Log Studvant

50

Husband of Minnie Sturdivant, Chickasaw Card No. D. 193
No. 2 married to No. 1 in 1895 under U.S. law, and again married to him under Chickasaw law July 11, 1895.
No. 2 transferred from Chickasaw Card #D.193. See decision of Aug. 17, 1904. Sept. 1, 1904.

Oct. 20/98.

RESIDENCE: Pickens COUNTY					CARD NO.			
POST OFFICE: Chickasha, Ind. Ter.					FIELD NO.			
NAME	RELATION-SHIP TO PERSON FIRST	AGE	SEX	BLOOD	TRIBAL ENROLLMENT			
					YEAR	COUNTY	PAGE	
1 Feland, Maggie	NAMED	24	F	1/16	1897	Pickens	18	
2 " Hattie	Dau	5	"	1/32	1897	"	18	
3 " Lucretia Graham	"	4	"	1/32	1897	"	18	
4 " Columbus Scott	Son	2	M	1/32	1897	"	18	
5 " William Thomas	"	3wks	"	1/32				

	TRIBAL ENROLLMENT OF PARENTS						
NAME OF FATHER	YEAR	COUNTY	NAME OF MOTHER	YEAR	COUNTY		
1 Judge Sturdevant	Dead	non citizen	Isabella Sturdivant	1897	Pickens		
2 Columbus Feland	"	" "	No. 1				
3 " "	"	" "	No. 1				
4 " "	"	" "	No. 1				
5 " "	"	" "	No. 1				

(NOTES)

No. 3 on Chickasaw roll as Lucita G. Feland
No. 4 "   "   " " Cohenbuz S "
Nos. 1, 2, 3 and 4 admitted by Dawes Commission in 1896 as citizens by blood;
        Chickasaw Case #44; no appeal.
No. 5 Enrolled Nov. 19/98.

Oct. 20/98

RESIDENCE: Pickens COUNTY					CARD NO.			
POST OFFICE: Burt, Ind. Ter.					FIELD NO.			
NAME	RELATION-SHIP TO PERSON FIRST	AGE	SEX	BLOOD	TRIBAL ENROLLMENT			
					YEAR	COUNTY	PAGE	
1 Cochran, Lynch Bailey	NAMED	53	M	I.W.				

NAME OF FATHER	YEAR	COUNTY	NAME OF MOTHER	YEAR	COUNTY		
1 A.D. Cochran	Dead	Non-Citizen	Frances Cochran	Dead	Non Citizen		

(NOTES)

(Notation illegible)

On Choctaw Intermarried roll, Page 19; transferred to Chickasaw roll by Dawes Com.

Husband of Viola Cochran, Choctaw roll, Card No. 423

On Choctaw Roll, 1896, Chickasaw District, No. 14448 as L.B. Cochran

12/6/99 See Dawes Commission record 1896, Cae No. 984

No. 1 On 1885 Choctaw Roll, Tobucksy County, as Lynch B. Cochran

Note: he was married under a Chickasaw license to Susan Burris, a Chickasaw *(illegible)* 1878 and after her death married Viola Toole, a Choctaw, May 9, 1883, in 1896 he applied to Dawes Commission fo Choctaw Intermarried Citizenship in case #984 by reason of his marriage to his Choctaw wife and was denied. No appeal.

Question: is said judgment adverse to his rights as an intermarried Chickasaw or has he married out

P.O. Bailey   Oct. 19/98.

	NAME	RELATIONSHIP TO PERSON FIRST NAMED	AGE	SEX	BLOOD	TRIBAL ENROLLMENT		
						YEAR	COUNTY	PAGE
1	Tussy, Henry B.	NAMED	43	M	I.W.	1897	Pickens	77
2	" Lila	Wife	30	F	1/2	1897	"	21
3	" Mary Elizabeth	Dau	11	"	1/4	1897	"	21
4	" Martha Jane	"	9	"	1/4	1897	"	21
5	" Lucy Lee	"	7	"	1/4	1897	"	21
6	" Lola May	"	4	"	1/4	1897	"	21
7	" Alex Hugh	Son	11/2	M	1/4			
8	" Lilla F.	Dau	2mo	F	1/4			
9	" Minnie Edna	Dau	6wks	F	1/4			

RESIDENCE: Pickens COUNTY   CARD NO.

POST OFFICE: Tissy, Ind. Ter.   FIELD NO.

TRIBAL ENROLLMENT OF PARENTS

	NAME OF FATHER	YEAR	COUNTY	NAME OF MOTHER	YEAR	COUNTY
1	Jake Tussy	Dead	Non citizen	Mary Tussy	Dead	Non citizen
2	Jim Colbert	"	Chickasaw roll	Lizzie Colbert	"	Pickens
3	No. 1			No. 2		
4	No. 1			No. 2		
5	No. 1			No. 2		
6	No. 1			No. 2		
7	No. 1			No. 2		
8	No. 1			No. 2		
9	No. 1			No. 2		

(NOTES)

No. 1 on Chickasaw roll as Henry B. Tussay
No. 2 "   "   "   " Lela Tussy
No. 3 "   "   "   " Mary E. "
No. 4 "   "   "   " Martha J. "
No. 9 Born Feby. 12, 1902; enrolled March 24, 1902.
    See testimony of No. 1 taken Oct. 20, 1902
No. 8 enrolled Nov. 4/99.
(Notation illegible)

Oct. 19/98.

| RESIDENCE: Pickens COUNTY | | | | | CARD NO. | | |
| POST OFFICE: Petersburg, I.T. | | | | | FIELD NO. | | |

NAME	RELATION-SHIP TO PERSON FIRST NAMED	AGE	SEX	BLOOD	TRIBAL ENROLLMENT		
					YEAR	COUNTY	PAGE
1 Bourland, William Howard		51	M	1/8	1897	Pickens	21

TRIBAL ENROLLMENT OF PARENTS

NAME OF FATHER		YEAR	COUNTY	NAME OF MOTHER	YEAR	COUNTY
1 Reuben R. Bourland	(I.W.)	1897	Chick residing in Choctaw N. 1st Dist.	Eliza Bourland	Dead	Chickasaw roll

(NOTES)

On Chickasaw roll as W.H. Bourland
Husband of Louinda Melvina Bourland, Choctaw roll, Card No. 419.

Oct. 18/98.

| RESIDENCE: Pickens COUNTY | | | | | CARD NO. | | |
| POST OFFICE: Duncan, Ind. Ter. | | | | | FIELD NO. | | |

NAME	RELATION-SHIP TO PERSON FIRST NAMED	AGE	SEX	BLOOD	TRIBAL ENROLLMENT		
					YEAR	COUNTY	PAGE
1 Chisholm, William F.		18	M	1/2	1897	Pickens	44

TRIBAL ENROLLMENT OF PARENTS

NAME OF FATHER	YEAR	COUNTY	NAME OF MOTHER	YEAR	COUNTY
1 Bill Chisholm	Dead	Pickens	Eliza Chisholm	Dead	Pickens

(NOTES)

No. 1 On Chickasaw roll as William F. Chisolm.

Oct. 18/98.

Chickasaw Enrollment Cards 1898-1914
Chickasaw by Blood   Volume III

RESIDENCE: Pickens   COUNTY   CARD NO.

POST OFFICE: Hope, Ind. Ter.   FIELD NO.

NAME	RELATION-SHIP TO PERSON FIRST NAMED	AGE	SEX	BLOOD	TRIBAL ENROLLMENT		
					YEAR	COUNTY	PAGE
1 Jones, Frank W.	NAMED	38	M	I.W.	1897	Pickens	77
2 " Carrie	Wife	28	F	1/4	1897	"	21
3 " Frankie Velma	Dau	10	"	1/8	1897	"	21
4 " Mattie	"	8	"	1/8	1897	"	21
5 " Neoma	"	5	"	1/8	1897	"	21
6 " Ruth	"	3	"	1/8	1897	"	21
7 " Vera Nelson	"	3mo	"	1/8			

TRIBAL ENROLLMENT OF PARENTS

	NAME OF FATHER	YEAR	COUNTY	NAME OF MOTHER	YEAR	COUNTY
1	Manson Jones	Dead	Non citizen	Sarah Manion		non citizen
2	Christopher C. Colbert	"	Pickens	Nancy Colbert	1897	Pickens
3	No. 1			No. 2		
4	No. 1			No. 2		
5	No. 1			No. 2		
6	No. 1			No. 2		
7	No. 1			No. 2		

(NOTES)

No. 1 See decision of June 13 '04.   *(No. 1 Dawes' Roll No. 411)*

No. 1 Admitted as an intermarried citizen and Nos. 5 and 6 as citizens by blood; Chickasaw Case #56; no appeal

No. 3 on Chickasaw roll as Frankie Jones

No. 5 "   "   " " Nannie   "

No. 7 Born Dec. 7, 1901; enrolled March 25, 1902

P.O. Duncan, I.T.   Oct. 18/98.

RESIDENCE: Pickens   COUNTY   CARD NO.

POST OFFICE: Terral, Ind. Ter.   FIELD NO.

NAME	RELATION-SHIP TO PERSON FIRST NAMED	AGE	SEX	BLOOD	TRIBAL ENROLLMENT		
					YEAR	COUNTY	PAGE
1 Colbert, Albert D.	NAMED	43	M	3/4	1897	Pickens	21
2 " Mary	Wife	43	F	I.W.	1897	"	77
3 " David Ward	Son	3wks	M	3/8			

TRIBAL ENROLLMENT OF PARENTS						
NAME OF FATHER	YEAR	COUNTY	NAME OF MOTHER	YEAR	COUNTY
1	Joseph Colbert	Dead	Pickens	Elzira Colbert	Dead	Pickens
2	Allan McCasland	"	non citizen	Tellitha McCasland	"	non citizen
3	No. 1			No. 2		

(NOTES)

No. 1 On Chickasaw roll as Albert Colbert   *(No. 2 Dawes' Roll No. 480)*
No. 3 Enrolled Dec. 13/98.
No. 3 Died May 4, 1899; proof of death filed Oct. 22, 1902.

Oct. 18/98.

RESIDENCE: Pickens COUNTY						CARD NO.		
POST OFFICE: Terral, Ind. Ter.						FIELD NO.		

NAME	RELATIONSHIP TO PERSON FIRST NAMED	AGE	SEX	BLOOD	TRIBAL ENROLLMENT		
					YEAR	COUNTY	PAGE
1	Wray, Samuel L.	NAMED	34	M	I.W.			
2	" Serena Belle	Wife	21	F	1/4	1893	Pickens	P.R. #2 192
3	" Lester W.	Son	3	M	1/8	1897	"	20
4	" David Walker	"	11mos	"	1/8			
5	" Carrie E.	Dau	2mo	F	1/8			
6	" William Thomas	Son	1mo	M	1/8			

TRIBAL ENROLLMENT OF PARENTS						
NAME OF FATHER	YEAR	COUNTY	NAME OF MOTHER	YEAR	COUNTY
1	David Wray	Dead	non-citizen	Violet R. Wray	Dead	Non citizen
2	S.W. Ryan		" "	Carrie Cheadle Ryan	"	Pickens
3	No. 1			No. 2		
4	No. 1			No. 2		
5	No. 1			No. 2		
6	No. 1			No. 2		

(NOTES)

No. 1 Marriage license and certificate filed with Dawes Com. in 1897   *(No. 1 Dawes' Roll No. 167)*
No. 2 On 1893 Pay roll as Bell Wray
No. 3 " Chickasaw roll as Lester W. Roy
No. 5 Enrolled Mar. 24/99
No. 6 Born March 26, 1902; enrolled April 17, 1902
        See additional testimony of No. 1, taken Oct. 15, 1902.

Oct. 18/98.

RESIDENCE: Pickens   COUNTY   CARD NO.
POST OFFICE: Duncan, Ind. Ter.   FIELD NO.

NAME	RELATION-SHIP TO PERSON FIRST	AGE	SEX	BLOOD	TRIBAL ENROLLMENT		
					YEAR	COUNTY	PAGE
1 Colbert, James Beldon	NAMED	30	M	1/4	1897	Pickens	20
2 " Gladdes	Dau	9mo	F	1/8			
3 " Ida	Wife	28	F	I.W.			
4 Colbert, Holmes B.	Son	6	M	1/8			

TRIBAL ENROLLMENT OF PARENTS

NAME OF FATHER	YEAR	COUNTY	NAME OF MOTHER	YEAR	COUNTY
1 Christopher C. Colbert	Dead	Pickens	Nancy Colbert	1897	Pickens
2	No. 1		Ida Colbert		intermarried
3 J.M. Wall		non citizen	Lou Wall		non citz
4	No. 1		No. 3		

(NOTES)

For child of Nos. 1 & 3, see *(remainder illegible)*
On Chickasaw roll as Belton Colbert.
No. 1 is husband of Ida Colbert on Chickasaw card #D.269
No. 1 has resided in Arizona for 3 years on account of health. See hs letter in Gen. off. files #17304-1902.
No. 2 Born Jan'y 21, 1902, enrolled Oct. 11/1902.   *(No. 2 Dawes' Roll No. 4757)*
    Evidence of marriage *(remainder illegible)*
No. 3 transferred from Chickasaw card #E.269 Oct. 31, 1904. See decision oct. 15, 1904.
No. 4 placed hereon under order Commission to Five Civilized Tribes of Feb'y. 26, 1906, holding that
    application was made for his enrollment within the time provided by the Act of Congress,
    approved July 1, 1902.

P.O. Pearce, Cohise[sic] Co, Arizona. 10/11/02.   Oct. 18/98.

RESIDENCE: Pickens   COUNTY   CARD NO.
POST OFFICE: Duncan, Ind. Ter.   FIELD NO.

NAME	RELATION-SHIP TO PERSON FIRST	AGE	SEX	BLOOD	TRIBAL ENROLLMENT		
					YEAR	COUNTY	PAGE
1 Colbert, Nancy	NAMED	53	F	I.W.	1897	Pickens	20
2 " Sam Tilden	Son	21	M	1/4	1897	"	21
3 " Thomas Rutherford	"	20	M	1/4	1897	"	21
4 Barnes, Mary Eliza	Dau	18	F	1/4	1897	"	21
5 ~~Williams, Lillie Katinka~~	"	~~15~~	"	~~1/4~~	~~1897~~	"	~~21~~

Chickasaw Enrollment Cards 1898-1914
Chickasaw by Blood   Volume III

	Name	Relationship	Age	Sex	Blood			
6	Barnes, Samuel Paul	Gr. Son	1mo	M	1/8			
7	Williams, Nelson O.	Husband of No. 5	27	N	I.W.			
8	Colbert, Lillie	Wife of No. 3	21	F	I.W.			

TRIBAL ENROLLMENT OF PARENTS

	NAME OF FATHER	YEAR	COUNTY	NAME OF MOTHER	YEAR	COUNTY
1	John M. Bourland	Dead	non-citizen	Nancy M. Bourland	Dead	non-citizen
2	Christopher C. Colbert	"	Pickens	No. 1		
3	" " "	"	"	No. 1		
4	" " "	"	"	No. 1		
5	~~" " "~~	~~"~~	~~"~~	~~No. 1~~		
6	Birton A. Barnes		non-citizen	No. 4		
7	J.W. Williams		non "	Cynthia Williams	Dead	non-citz
8	G. Stubblefield		non citz	Sallie Stubblefield		non citizen

(NOTES)

No. 1 on Chickasaw roll by blood through error.   *(No. 1 Dawes' Roll No. 551)*
No. 2 "   "   " as Sam Colbert   *(No. 7 Dawes' Roll No. 59)*
No. 3 "   "   "   " Ed   "
No. 4 "   "   "   " Eliza   "
No. 5 "   "   "   " Lillia   "
No. 5 is wife of Nelson C. Williams on Chickasaw card #D.271
No. 5 Died July 23, 1900; proof of death filed May 16, 1902
No. 4 is now the wife of Birton A. Barnes on Chickasaw card #E.357 June 3, 1902
No. 6 Born Aug. 1, 1902; enrolled Sept. 3, 1902.
No. 8 placed on this card under order of the Commission to the Five Civilized Tribes of January 11, 1906, holding
    that application was *(illegible)* for her enrollment within the time prescribed by the Act of Congress,
    approved July 1, 1902 (32 Stats 641)
No. 1 formerly wife of Christopher C. Colbert, a recognized Chickasaw by blood, who died on Mar. 25, 1883.

Oct. 18/98.

RESIDENCE: Pickens   **COUNTY**   **CARD NO.**
POST OFFICE: Berwyn, Ind. Ter.   **FIELD NO.**

	NAME	RELATION-SHIP TO PERSON FIRST NAMED	AGE	SEX	BLOOD	TRIBAL ENROLLMENT		
						YEAR	COUNTY	PAGE
1	Reynolds, Ben F.		25	M	1/8	1897	Pickens	12

TRIBAL ENROLLMENT OF PARENTS

	NAME OF FATHER	YEAR	COUNTY	NAME OF MOTHER	YEAR	COUNTY
1	Sam Reynolds	Dead	non citizen	Mary Colbert Reynolds	Dead	Panola

57

(NOTES)

In Troop "M". Rough Rider regiment, U.S.V.
On Chickasaw roll as Ben Reynolds.

Oct. 18/98.

RESIDENCE: Pickens COUNTY					CARD NO.			
POST OFFICE: Hennepin, Ind. Ter.					FIELD NO.			
NAME	RELATION-SHIP TO PERSON FIRST	AGE	SEX	BLOOD	TRIBAL ENROLLMENT			
					YEAR	COUNTY		PAGE
1 Pytchlyn, George	NAMED	36	M	3/4	1897	Tishomingo		31

TRIBAL ENROLLMENT OF PARENTS							
NAME OF FATHER	YEAR	COUNTY	NAME OF MOTHER	YEAR	COUNTY		
1 Jeff Pitchlyn	Dead	Tishomingo	Judy Pitchlyn	Dead	Tishomingo		

(NOTES)

Oct. 17/98.

RESIDENCE: Pickens COUNTY					CARD NO.			
POST OFFICE: Duncan, Ind. Ter.					FIELD NO.			
NAME	RELATION-SHIP TO PERSON FIRST	AGE	SEX	BLOOD	TRIBAL ENROLLMENT			
					YEAR	COUNTY		PAGE
1 Leftwich, James	NAMED	28	M	I.W.	1897	Pickens		77
2 " Minnie C.	Wife	23	F	1/16	1893	"		120
3 " Velma	Dau	3 1/2	"	1/32				
4 " George C.	Son	2	M	1/32	1897	Pickens		21
5 " Dewey	"	4mos	"	1/32				
6 " James Brooks	Son	5mo	M	1/32				

TRIBAL ENROLLMENT OF PARENTS							
NAME OF FATHER	YEAR	COUNTY	NAME OF MOTHER	YEAR	COUNTY		
1 John S. Leftwich	Dead	Non Citizen	Sarah E. Leftwich		Non Citizen		
2 James Jones	"	Pickens	Olive Morris (I.W.)	1897	Pickens		
3	No. 1			No. 2			
4	No. 1			No. 2			
5	No. 1			No. 2			
6	No. 1			No. 2			

(NOTES)

Nos. 1 to 6 incl. See decision of March 15, 1904.   *(No. 1 Dawes' Roll No. 410)*
No. 2 on 1893 Chick Pay Roll, No. 2, Page 120 as Minnie Jones   *(No. 2 Dawes' Roll No. 4805)*
   Marriage papers on file in office of Dawes Com, Muskogee I.T.   *(No. 3 Dawes' Roll No. 4806)*
   Sir name on Chickasaw roll as Lefwich.   *(No. 4 Dawes' Roll No. 4807)*
   All except Dewey, admitted by Dawes Com, Case No. 72. No information from US Court as to status
   Appeal taken to U.S. Court, Ardmore. Case dismissed.
No. 3 Admitted as Elina Leftwick.   *(No. 5 Dawes' Roll No. 4808)*
No. 3 Proof of birth - received and filed Nov. 1, 1902.   *(No. 6 Dawes' Roll No. 4809)*
   Full name of No. 2 is Minnie Clementine Leftwich. See letter of No. 1 filed July 3, 1901.
No. 6 Enrolled June 24, 1901.

P.O. Loco, IT 12/29/02   Oct. 17/98.

RESIDENCE: Pickens   COUNTY   CARD NO.
POST OFFICE: Comanche, Ind. Ter.   FIELD NO.

	NAME	RELATIONSHIP TO PERSON FIRST NAMED	AGE	SEX	BLOOD	TRIBAL ENROLLMENT		
						YEAR	COUNTY	PAGE
1	Wilson, John D.	NAMED	34	M	1/16	1897	Pickens	21
2	" Lillie Louella	Wife	30	F	I.W.	1897	Pickens	77
3	" Augusta Jessie	Dau	10	"	1/32	1897	"	21
4	" Gracie Ethel	"	8	"	1/32	1897	"	21
5	" Laura Lee	"	4	"	1/32	1897	"	21
6	" Clara May	"	2	"	1/32			
7	" J.D.	Son	1mo	M	1/32			
8	" Frankie Florence	Dau	5mo	F	1/32			

TRIBAL ENROLLMENT OF PARENTS

	NAME OF FATHER	YEAR	COUNTY	NAME OF MOTHER	YEAR	COUNTY
1	Philip Wilson	Dead	non citz.	Susan Mayes	1897	Pontotoc
2	Henry L. Mann		" "	Rhoda Mann	Dead	non citizen
3	No. 1			No. 2		
4	No. 1			No. 2		
5	No. 1			No. 2		
6	No. 1			No. 2		
7	No. 1			No. 2		
8	No. 1			No. 2		

(NOTES)
All except Nos. 6 and 7 admitted by Dawes Com., Case No. 213, and no appeal taken.
Marriage papers on file in office of Dawes Com., Muskogee, Ind. Ter.
No. 1 admitted by Dawes Com. as John C. Wilson
No. 2   "   "   "   "   " Millie L.   "   *(No. 2 Dawes' Roll No. 479)*

No. 3 "   "   "   "   " Augustus "

No. I on Chickasaw roll as John C. Wilson
No. 3 "   "   "   " Jessie A. "
No. 4 "   "   "   " Grace   "
No. 5 "   "   "   " Laura   "

Oct. 17/98.

RESIDENCE: Pickens COUNTY					CARD NO.			
POST OFFICE: Velma, Ind. Ter.					FIELD NO.			
NAME	RELATION-SHIP TO PERSON FIRST	AGE	SEX	BLOOD	TRIBAL ENROLLMENT			
					YEAR	COUNTY		PAGE
1 Payne, Thomas B.	NAMED	45	M	I.W.	1897	Pickens		77
2 " Thomas H.	Son	5	"	1/32	1897	"		20

	TRIBAL ENROLLMENT OF PARENTS						
NAME OF FATHER	YEAR	COUNTY	NAME OF MOTHER	YEAR	COUNTY		
1 Thomas H. Payne	Dead	non-citizen	Martha J. Payne		non citizen		
2 No. I			Mollie Payne	Dead	Pickens		

(NOTES)

No. I on Chickasaw roll as Thomas Payne   *(No. I Dawes' Roll No. 478)*
No. 2 "   "   "   " Tom H. Paine

10/15/02 P.O. Arthur, I.T.   Oct. 17/98.

RESIDENCE: Pickens COUNTY					CARD NO.			
POST OFFICE: Bailey, Ind. Ter.					FIELD NO.			
NAME	RELATION-SHIP TO PERSON FIRST	AGE	SEX	BLOOD	TRIBAL ENROLLMENT			
					YEAR	COUNTY		PAGE
1 Miller, John M.	NAMED	26	M	1/4	1897	Pontotoc		61
2 " James	Son	Imo	"	1/8				
3 " Willie G.	Son	2m	M	1/8				

	TRIBAL ENROLLMENT OF PARENTS						
NAME OF FATHER	YEAR	COUNTY	NAME OF MOTHER	YEAR	COUNTY		
1 John Miller		non citizen	Kittie Howard	1897	Pickens		
2 No. I			Virginia P. Miller		non citizen		
3 No. I			" " "		" "		

(NOTES)

No. 3 Enrolled February 5, 1901.

Evidence of marriage of No. 1 and Virginia P. Miller Filed Feby. 5, 1901.   Oct. 17/98.

RESIDENCE: Pickens **COUNTY**   **CARD NO.**

POST OFFICE: Marlow, Ind. Ter.   **FIELD NO.**

	NAME	RELATION-SHIP TO PERSON FIRST NAMED	AGE	SEX	BLOOD	TRIBAL ENROLLMENT		
						YEAR	COUNTY	PAGE
1	Percival, Taylor	NAMED	49	M	I.W.	1897	Pickens	78
2	" Kate	Wife	42	F	1/4	1897	"	13
3	" Edward H.	Son	17	M	1/8	1897	"	13
4	Short, Effie Jane	Dau	15	F	1/8	1897	"	13
5	Percival, Lela	"	13	"	1/8	1897	"	13
6	" Fred	Son	11	M	1/8	1897	"	13
7	" Claude	"	5	"	1/8	1897	"	13
8	" Brit	"	2	"	1/8			
9	" Ottis	"	1mo	"	1/8			
10	Short, Ode	GrandSon	1mo	M	1/16			
11	" Holmes	Gr.Son	3wks	M	1/16			
12	*(Line blank on microfilm)*							
13	Short, John C.	Hus. of No. 4	22	M	I.W.			

TRIBAL ENROLLMENT OF PARENTS

	NAME OF FATHER	YEAR	COUNTY	NAME OF MOTHER	YEAR	COUNTY
1	Edward Percival	Dead	non citizen	Sarah Percival	Dead	non citizen
2	Wm H. Bourland	"	" "	Caroline Bourland, now Ayers	1897	Pickens
3	No. 1			No. 2		
4	No. 1			No. 2		
5	No. 1			No. 2		
6	No. 1			No. 2		
7	No. 1			No. 2		
8	No. 1			No. 2		
9	No. 1			No. 2		
10	John C. Short			No. 4		
11	" " "			No. 4		
12	*(Line blank on microfilm)*					
13	Jim Short		non citizen	Mary Short		non citizen

(NOTES)

No. 2 on Chickasaw roll as Katie Percival

No. 4 "   "   "   " Effy J. "

No. 4 is now the wife of John C. Short on Chickasaw card D.326

No. 9 Enrolled Mar. 27/99

No. 10 Enrolled Sept. 18, 1900

No. 11 Born July 7, 1902, enrolled July 31, 1902.

No. 13 transferred from Chick. Card D.326 August 1, 1903. See decision of July 16, 1903.

  Certified copy of divorce proceedings between No. 2 and her former husband, also affidavits

  of Ellen Moore and others relative to divorce filed April 20, 1902.

Oct. 17/98.

RESIDENCE: Pickens COUNTY					CARD NO.			
POST OFFICE: Newport, Ind. Ter.					FIELD NO.			
NAME	RELATION-SHIP TO PERSON FIRST NAMED	AGE	SEX	BLOOD	TRIBAL ENROLLMENT			
					YEAR	COUNTY	PAGE	
1 Jones, Amelia	NAMED	28	F	1/4	1897	Pickens	20	
2 " Hettie L	Dau	3	"	1/8	1897	"	20	
3 " James Pate	Husband	30	M	I.W.				

TRIBAL ENROLLMENT OF PARENTS

NAME OF FATHER	YEAR	COUNTY	NAME OF MOTHER	YEAR	COUNTY
1 James McCauley (I.W.)	1897	Pickens	Susan McCauley	Dead	Chickasaw roll
2 James Pate Jones		white man	No. 1		
3 Woody Jones	Dead	Non Citizen	Martha J. Jones		Non Citizen

(NOTES)

No. 2 admitted by Dawes Com. Case No. 57 and no appeal taken. *(No. 2 Dawes' Roll No. 4207)*

  Husband of No. 1 on Chickasaw D.183

No. 3 first married No. 1 under U.S. license Dec. 18, 1894, then under Chickasaw license Sept.. 23, 1898

No. 3 admitted by Dawes Com. in 1896 in case No. 57 no appeal *(No. 3 Dawes' Roll No. 440)*

No. 3 transferred from Chickasaw Card #D.183, See decision of August 17, 1904. Sept. 1, 1904.

P.O. Purcell, I.T. Oct. 17/98.

RESIDENCE: Pickens COUNTY					CARD NO.			
POST OFFICE: Doyle, Ind. Ter.					FIELD NO.			
NAME	RELATION-SHIP TO PERSON FIRST NAMED	AGE	SEX	BLOOD	TRIBAL ENROLLMENT			
					YEAR	COUNTY	PAGE	
1 Sadler, James	NAMED	20	M	1/2	1897	Pickens	22	
2 " Jane	Wife	21	F	I.W.				
3 " Williams	Son	5mo	M	1/4				
4 " Joseph	Son	1wk	M	1/4				

TRIBAL ENROLLMENT OF PARENTS

Chickasaw Enrollment Cards 1898-1914
Chickasaw by Blood   Volume III

	NAME OF FATHER	YEAR	COUNTY	NAME OF MOTHER	YEAR	COUNTY
1	Joe Sadler (I.W.)	1897	Pickens	Jane Sadler	1897	Pickens
2	Dave Sullivan	Dead	Non Citizen	Cass Burton		Non Citizen
3	No. 1			No. 2		
4	No. 1			No. 2		

(NOTES)

No. 1 on Chickasaw roll as James Saddler   *(No. 2 Dawes' Roll No. 477)*
No. 3 enrolled Nov. 4/99
No. 4 Born Aug. 21, 1902; enrolled Aug. 27, 1902

Oct. 17/98.

RESIDENCE: Pickens   COUNTY   CARD NO.
POST OFFICE: Duncan, Ind. Ter.   FIELD NO.

	NAME	RELATION-SHIP TO PERSON FIRST NAMED	AGE	SEX	BLOOD	TRIBAL ENROLLMENT		
						YEAR	COUNTY	PAGE
1	Doak, Lulu E.		15	F	1/2	1897	Pickens	25

TRIBAL ENROLLMENT OF PARENTS

	NAME OF FATHER	YEAR	COUNTY	NAME OF MOTHER	YEAR	COUNTY
1	J.T. Doak		white man	Lena Doak	Dead	Tishomingo

(NOTES)

On Chickasaw roll as Lula Doak.
No. 1 Admitted by U.S. Court; Southern District, I.T. Ardmore, I.T. Dec. 22, 1897 in Court case No. 21
No. 1 is a duplicate enrollment of No. 2 on Chickasaw Card #C.106.

Oct. 17/98.

CANCELLED Stamped across card

RESIDENCE: Panola   COUNTY   CARD NO.
POST OFFICE: Colbert, Ind. Ter.   FIELD NO.

	NAME	RELATION-SHIP TO PERSON FIRST NAMED	AGE	SEX	BLOOD	TRIBAL ENROLLMENT		
						YEAR	COUNTY	PAGE
1	Colbert, Holmes		35	M	1/4	1897	Panola	2
2	" Frank Overton	Son	3	"	3/16	1897	"	2
3	" Janie Estelle	Dau	5m	F	1/8			
4	" Marion Estelle	Dau	5m	F	1/8			
5	" Bessie	Wife	26	F	I.W.			

TRIBAL ENROLLMENT OF PARENTS

	NAME OF FATHER	YEAR	COUNTY	NAME OF MOTHER	YEAR	COUNTY

1	Frank Colbert	Dead	Panola	Georgeann Colbert	Dead	Panola
2	No. 1			Ella Overton	"	Pickens
3	No. 1			Bessie Colbert		
4	No. 1			" "		
5	R.W. Hobson		non citizen	Jane Hobson		non citizen

(NOTES)

No. 1 is now the husband of Bessie Colbert Chickasaw card D.242 June 16, 1900

No. 2 on Chickasaw roll as Frank O. Colbert

No. 3 Enrolled June 16, 1900

No. 4 Born June 6, 1901. Enrolled Nov. 14, 1902.   *(No. 4 Dawes' Roll No. 4206)*

No. 5 transferred from Chickasaw card D.242, April 7, 1904.   *(No. 5 Dawes' Roll No. 342)*
      See decision of March 15, 1904.

No. 3 died 7th day July 1900, Proof of death fowarded to Muskogee, 1/3-05.

Oct. 13/98.

RESIDENCE: Choctaw Nation (1st Dist.)   ~~COUNTY~~   **CARD NO.**

POST OFFICE: South Canadian, Ind. Ter.   **FIELD NO.**

NAME	RELATION-SHIP TO PERSON FIRST NAMED	AGE	SEX	BLOOD	TRIBAL ENROLLMENT		
					YEAR	COUNTY	PAGE
1 Atkinson, Clarence E.		27	M	I.W.	1897	Chick residing in Choctaw N. 1st Dist.	82
2 " Mattie	Wife	22	F	1/32	1893	Chickasaw residing in Choctaw Nation leashatubby roll	#
3 " Susan B.	Dau	2	F	1/64			
4 " Thos. James	Son	7mo	M	1/64			

TRIBAL ENROLLMENT OF PARENTS

	NAME OF FATHER	YEAR	COUNTY	NAME OF MOTHER	YEAR	COUNTY
1	James M. Atkinson		non citizen	Martha Atkinson		non citizen
2	Thos. J. Phillips (I.W.)	1897	Chick residing in Choctaw N. 1st Dist.	Mary E. Phillips	Dead	Chick residing in Choctaw N. 1st Dist.
3	Clarence E. Atkinson (I.W.)	1897	" " " "	No. 2		
4	No. 1			No. 2		

(NOTES)

No. 1 See decision of June 13 '04   *(No. 1 Dawes' Roll No. 409)*

(Notation illegible)

No. 2 on leashatubby Roll, June 26, 1903 as child of Mary E. Phillips

No. 3 affidavit of attending physician to be supplied. Received Oct. 20/98.

No. 4 affidavit showing date of birth May 2/99, received, but irregular and returned for correction Dec. 13/99.
      Rec'd and filed Jany. 17, 1900.

No. 1 was admitted as an intermarried citizen by the Commission in 1896, Chickasaw case #175 as C.E. Atkinson,
      no appeal.

64

P.O. Chickasha, I.T.   Oct. 14/98.

RESIDENCE:	Choctaw Nation ~~COUNTY~~				CARD NO.			
POST OFFICE:	Atoka, Ind. Ter.				FIELD NO.			

	NAME	RELATION-SHIP TO PERSON FIRST NAMED	AGE	SEX	BLOOD	TRIBAL ENROLLMENT		
						YEAR	COUNTY	PAGE
1	Downing, Sam	NAMED	26	M	1/4			
2	" Mose	Bro	21	"	1/4			
3	" Maud	Wife	27	F	I.W.			
4	" Gordon S.	Son	3wks	M	1/8			
5	" Mary Mozelle	Dau of No. 2	1mo	F	1/8			
6	" George Todd	Son	6mo	M	1/8			

TRIBAL ENROLLMENT OF PARENTS

	NAME OF FATHER	YEAR	COUNTY	NAME OF MOTHER	YEAR	COUNTY
1	George Downing	Dead	non citizen	Malissa Downing	Dead	Chickasaw roll
2	" "	"	" "	" "	"	" "
3	D.M. Miller		" "	Wilda S. Miller		non citz.
4	No. 1			No. 3		
5	No. 2			Mattie Downing on Chickasaw Card #	D.361	
6	No. 1			No. 3		

(NOTES)

Both on Choctaw Census Record No. 2, Atoka Co., Page 148, transferred to Chickasaw roll by Dawes Com.
No. 1 on Choctaw Roll, 1896, Atoka County, No. 3586
No. 2 "   "   " 1896,   "   "   " 3587
No. 3 Evidence of marriage to be supplied. Filed Nov. 4/99.
No. 3 enrolled Sept. 1/99
No. 4 enrolled January 2, 1901
No. 5 Born June 5- 1902, enrolled July 17, 1902.
No. 6 Born March 29, 1902, enrolled Oct. 2, 1902.
    Wife of #2 on Chickasaw D.361. July 17, 1902.

                                                                Oct. 14/98.

CANCELLED Stamped across card

65

Chickasaw Enrollment Cards 1898-1914
Chickasaw by Blood   Volume III

RESIDENCE: Choctaw Nation ~~COUNTY~~					CARD NO.			
POST OFFICE: Boggy Depot, Ind. Ter.					FIELD NO.			

NAME	RELATION-SHIP TO PERSON FIRST NAMED	AGE	SEX	BLOOD	TRIBAL ENROLLMENT		
					YEAR	COUNTY	PAGE
1 Byington, Joel	NAMED	32	M	Full			

TRIBAL ENROLLMENT OF PARENTS

NAME OF FATHER	YEAR	COUNTY	NAME OF MOTHER	YEAR	COUNTY
1 Wallace Byington	Dead	Chickasaw roll	Sibbey Byington	Dead	Chickasaw roll

(NOTES)
Husband of Emma Byington Choctaw roll Card No. 403,
On Choctaw Census Record No. 2, Blue Co., Page 66, transferred to Chickasaw roll by Dawes Com.
On Choctaw Roll, 1896, Blue County, No. 1591.

Oct. 14/98.

CANCELLED Stamped across card

RESIDENCE: Pontotoc COUNTY					CARD NO.			
POST OFFICE: Stonewall, Ind. Ter.					FIELD NO.			

NAME	RELATION-SHIP TO PERSON FIRST NAMED	AGE	SEX	BLOOD	TRIBAL ENROLLMENT		
					YEAR	COUNTY	PAGE
1 Perry, Amy	NAMED	20	F	Full	1893	Pontotoc	P.R. #2 142
2 Lewis, Cornelia	Dau	5mo	"	"			
3 Perry, Coleman	Son	4mo	M	"			

TRIBAL ENROLLMENT OF PARENTS

NAME OF FATHER	YEAR	COUNTY	NAME OF MOTHER	YEAR	COUNTY
1 Wilson Lewis	Dead	Pontotoc	Dinah Lewis	Dead	Pontotoc
2 Illegitimate			No. 1		
3 Houston Perry	1897	Pontotoc	No. 1		

(NOTES)
Also on 1897 Chickasaw roll, Page 95 as Annie Lewis
No. 1 is now the wife of Houston Perry on Chickasaw Card #353, May 7, 1901.
No. 2 Enrolled Mar. 22/99
No. 3 Enrolled May 7, 1901.

Oct. 14/98.

Chickasaw Enrollment Cards 1898-1914
Chickasaw by Blood   Volume III

RESIDENCE: Choctaw Nation ~~COUNTY~~   CARD NO.

POST OFFICE: Wall, Ind. Ter.   FIELD NO.

	NAME	RELATION-SHIP TO PERSON FIRST NAMED	AGE	SEX	BLOOD	TRIBAL ENROLLMENT		
						YEAR	COUNTY	PAGE
1	McCoy, Parthenia	FIRST NAMED	25	F	1/2	1897	Chick residing in Choctaw N. 1st Dist.	71
2	Campbell, Lewis	Son	4	M	1/4	1897	" " " "	71
3	McCoy, Athen Elonzo	Son	3mo	M	1/4			

TRIBAL ENROLLMENT OF PARENTS

	NAME OF FATHER	YEAR	COUNTY	NAME OF MOTHER	YEAR	COUNTY
1	Jonas Brown		Chick Freedman	Tennessee Brown	Dead	Chickasaw roll
2	Richmond Campbell		Choctaw "	No. 1		
3	W.M. McCoy		Choc. Freedman	No. 1		

(NOTES)

No. 1 on Chickasaw roll as Bathine Campbell

No. 3 Enrolled Aug. 10, 1901.

Husband is on Choctaw freedman card #1152.

See his affidavit filed in Choctaw freedman Cae #1152, Aug. 21, 1901.

Oct. 14/98.

RESIDENCE: Choctaw Nation ~~COUNTY~~   CARD NO.

POST OFFICE: Atoka, Ind. Ter.   FIELD NO.

	NAME	RELATION-SHIP TO PERSON FIRST NAMED	AGE	SEX	BLOOD	TRIBAL ENROLLMENT		
						YEAR	COUNTY	PAGE
1	Fronterhouse, William	NAMED	41	M	I.W.			
2	" Dick	Son	20	"	1/4			
3	" Lucinda	Dau	17	F	1/4			
4	" Addie	"	14	"	1/4			
5	" Willie	Son	12	M	1/4			
6	" Ward	"	7	"	1/4			
7	Scroggins, Alvin	Grand Son	6wks	M	1/8			

TRIBAL ENROLLMENT OF PARENTS

	NAME OF FATHER	YEAR	COUNTY	NAME OF MOTHER	YEAR	COUNTY
1	John T. Fronterhouse	Dead	non citizen	Cynda Fronterhouse		non citizen
2	No. 1			Lucy Fronterhouse	Dead	Chick residing in Choctaw N. 3rd Dist.
3	No. 1			" "	"	" " " "
4	No. 1			" "	"	" " " "

67

5	No. 1			"	"		"	"	"	"	"
6	No. 1			"	"		"	"	"	"	"
7	G.W. Scroggins		non citizen	No. 3							

(NOTES)

No. 1 on Choctaw Intermarried roll, Atoka Co., Page 32; transferred to Chickasaw roll by Dawes Com.
Others "   "   Census Record No. 2 " "   "   191,   "   "   "   "   "   "   "
No. 1 on Choctaw roll, 1896, Atoka County, No. 14544
No. 2 "   "   "   1896   "   "   "   4497
No. 3 "   "   "   1896   "   "   "   4498
No. 4 "   "   "   1896   "   "   "   4499
No. 5 "   "   "   1896   "   "   "   4501
No. 3 is now the wife of G.W. Scroggins, a non-citizen. Evidence of marriage filed October 16, 1901.
No. 7 Born August 28, 1901 - Enrolled Oct. 16, 1901.

Oct. 14/98.

CANCELLED Stamped across card

RESIDENCE: Choctaw Nation ~~COUNTY~~   CARD NO.

POST OFFICE: Tuskahoma, Ind. Ter.   FIELD NO.

NAME	RELATION-SHIP TO PERSON FIRST NAMED	AGE	SEX	BLOOD	TRIBAL ENROLLMENT		
					YEAR	COUNTY	PAGE
1 Morris, Nehota		40	F	Full	1897	Chick residing in Choctaw N. 3rd Dist.	73

TRIBAL ENROLLMENT OF PARENTS

NAME OF FATHER	YEAR	COUNTY	NAME OF MOTHER	YEAR	COUNTY
1 Ewing Moore	Dead	Chickasaw roll	(Name Illegible)	Dead	Chickasaw roll

(NOTES)

Wife of Joel Morris, Choctaw roll, Card No. 402.
No. 1 died Nov. 30, 1898; proof of death filed Dec. 15. 1902.

Oct. 14/98.

RESIDENCE: Choctaw Nation ~~COUNTY~~   CARD NO.

POST OFFICE: Cameron, Ind. Ter.   FIELD NO.

	NAME	RELATION-SHIP TO PERSON FIRST NAMED	AGE	SEX	BLOOD	TRIBAL ENROLLMENT		
						YEAR	COUNTY	PAGE
1	Coffee, I.B.		44	M	I.W.			
2	" Laura	Wife	30	F	1/8			
3	" Edwin	Son	10	M	1/16			
4	" Ada	Dau	6	F	1/16			
5	" Ruby Addie	Dau	5mo	F	1/16			

68

	TRIBAL ENROLLMENT OF PARENTS						
	NAME OF FATHER	YEAR	COUNTY	NAME OF MOTHER	YEAR	COUNTY
1	Itey Coffee		non citizen	*(Name Illegible)*	Dead	non citizen
2	John Pierson	Dead	" "	Nancy Osborne	1897	Chick residing in Choctaw N. 1st Dist.
3	No. 1			No. 2		
4	No. 1			No. 2		
5	No. 1			No. 2		

(NOTES)

No. 1   on Choctaw Intermarried roll, Page 12, transferred to Chickasaw roll by Dawes Com.
Nos. 2, 3, & 4 "   " Census Record No. 2 " 88,   "   "   "   " "   "   "
No. 1 admitted by Dawes Com Case No. 960, as a Choctaw, and no appeal taken;
        marriage papers on file in office of Dawes Com, Muskogee, Ind. Ter.
No. 1 on Choctaw Roll 1896, Skullyville Co., No. 14374
No. 2 "   "   "   "   "   " " 2175
No. 3 "   "   "   "   "   " " 2176
No. 4 "   "   "   "   "   " " 2177
No. 5 Enrolled May 24, 1900.

Oct. 14/98.

CANCELLED Stamped across card

RESIDENCE: Choctaw Nation   ~~COUNTY~~   CARD NO.
POST OFFICE: Tucker, Ind. Ter.   FIELD NO.

NAME	RELATION-SHIP TO PERSON FIRST NAMED	AGE	SEX	BLOOD	TRIBAL ENROLLMENT		
					YEAR	COUNTY	PAGE
1 Osborne, Nancy		53	F	1/4			

	TRIBAL ENROLLMENT OF PARENTS						
	NAME OF FATHER	YEAR	COUNTY	NAME OF MOTHER	YEAR	COUNTY
1	Stephen Krebs	Dead	non citizen	Peggy Krebs	Dead	Chickasaw roll

(NOTES)

On Choctaw Census Record No. 2 Skullyville Co., Page 389; transfered[sic] to Chickasaw roll by Dawes Com
On Choctaw Roll, 1896, Skullyville County, No. 9898.

Oct. 14/98.

CANCELLED Stamped across card

Chickasaw Enrollment Cards 1898-1914
Chickasaw by Blood   Volume III

RESIDENCE: Panola   COUNTY   CARD NO.
POST OFFICE: Kemp, Ind. Ter.   FIELD NO.

	NAME	RELATION-SHIP TO PERSON FIRST NAMED	AGE	SEX	BLOOD	TRIBAL ENROLLMENT		
						YEAR	COUNTY	PAGE
1	Duckworth, Thomas	NAMED	21	M	1/2	1897	Panola	3
2	" Lauson	Son	5mo	"	1/4			
3	" Raymond	Son	5mo	"	1/4			

TRIBAL ENROLLMENT OF PARENTS

	NAME OF FATHER	YEAR	COUNTY	NAME OF MOTHER	YEAR	COUNTY
1	Berry Duckworth (I.W.)	1897	Panola	Louisa Duckworth	1897	Panola
2	No. 1			Josephine "		Non citizen
3	No. 1			" "		" "

(NOTES)

No. 1 on Chickasaw roll as Tom Duckworth
No. 3 Enrolled June 15, 1900
    Evidence of marriage of No. 1 and Josephine Ducksorth to be supplied, filed 7/23/1900

Oct. 14/98.

RESIDENCE: Panola   COUNTY   CARD NO.
POST OFFICE: Kemp, Ind. Ter.   FIELD NO.

	NAME	RELATION-SHIP TO PERSON FIRST NAMED	AGE	SEX	BLOOD	TRIBAL ENROLLMENT		
						YEAR	COUNTY	PAGE
1	Tabor, Rhoda	NAMED	25	F	7/8	1897	Panola	3
2	" Frances	Dau	5	"	7/16	1897	"	3
3	" Juanita	"	16mo	"	7/16			
4	" Electer	Dau	3mo	"	7/16			
5	" Agness Retta	Dau	2mo	"	7/16			

TRIBAL ENROLLMENT OF PARENTS

	NAME OF FATHER	YEAR	COUNTY	NAME OF MOTHER	YEAR	COUNTY
1	John Lewis	Dead	Panola	Jennie Lewis	Dead	Panola
2	T.M. Tabor		non citizen	No. 1		
3	" " "		" "	No. 1		
4	" " "		" "	No. 1		
5	" " "		" "	No. 1		

(NOTES)

No. 2 on Chickasaw roll as Francis Tabor
No. 4 Enrolled May 24, 1900
No. 5 Born Aug. 7, 1902; enrolled Oct. 9, 1902

Oct. 14/98.

Chickasaw Enrollment Cards 1898-1914
Chickasaw by Blood   Volume III

RESIDENCE: Panola   COUNTY   CARD NO.
POST OFFICE: Kemp, Ind. Ter.   FIELD NO.

NAME	RELATION-SHIP TO PERSON FIRST NAMED	AGE	SEX	BLOOD	TRIBAL ENROLLMENT		
					YEAR	COUNTY	PAGE
1 Kemp, Frank	NAMED	30	M	3/4	1897	Panola	4
2 " Annie	Wife	25	F	1/2	1897	"	4
3 " Estella	Dau	3	"	5/8	1897	"	4
4 " Lillie	"	11mo	"	5/8			
5 " Walton C.	Son	1mo	M	5/8			
6 " Frankie	Dau	2wks	F	5/8			

TRIBAL ENROLLMENT OF PARENTS

	NAME OF FATHER	YEAR	COUNTY	NAME OF MOTHER	YEAR	COUNTY
1	Walton Kemp	Dead	Panola	Elsie Kemp	Dead	Panola
2	Jesse Cho-mut-te	"	Tishomingo	Mary Cho-mut-te	"	non citizen
3	No. 1			No. 2		
4	No. 1			No. 2		
5	No. 1			No. 2		
6	No. 1			No. 2		

(NOTES)

Nos. 2, 3 and 4 are on Creek roll card #3642
No. 2 on 1890 Creek roll, Thlopthloccolown, as Annie Chumaittee
No. 2 " 1895 " " No. 117 as Annie Barnett
    Enroll as Chickasaws; not on final Creek roll
No. 5 enrolled Nov. 4/99.
No. 6 Born July 24, 1902; enrolled Aug. 9, 1902.

P.O. Alhambra, I.T. 8/9/02   Oct. 14/98.

RESIDENCE: Panola   COUNTY   CARD NO.
POST OFFICE: Colbert, Ind. Ter.   FIELD NO.

NAME	RELATION-SHIP TO PERSON FIRST NAMED	AGE	SEX	BLOOD	TRIBAL ENROLLMENT		
					YEAR	COUNTY	PAGE
1 Kemp, Jackson	NAMED	53	M	1/2	1897	Panola	3
2 " Martha	Dau	3mo	F	1/4			

TRIBAL ENROLLMENT OF PARENTS

	NAME OF FATHER	YEAR	COUNTY	NAME OF MOTHER	YEAR	COUNTY
1	Jackson Kemp	Dead	Panola	Patsey Kemp	1897	Panola
2	No. 1			Annie Kemp		non citizen

(NOTES)
No. 1 is now the husband of Annie Kemp a non-citizen. Evidence of marriage filed April 8, 1902.
No. 2 Born Dec. 29, 1901; enrolled April 8, 1902.

P.O. Kemp, I.T.   Oct. 14/98.

RESIDENCE: Choctaw Nation	~~COUNTY~~				CARD NO.			
POST OFFICE: South McAlester, Ind. Ter.					FIELD NO.			
NAME	RELATION-SHIP TO PERSON FIRST NAMED	AGE	SEX	BLOOD	TRIBAL ENROLLMENT			
					YEAR	COUNTY	PAGE	
1 McLish, Israel		41	M	1/2				

	TRIBAL ENROLLMENT OF PARENTS						
NAME OF FATHER	YEAR	COUNTY	NAME OF MOTHER	YEAR	COUNTY		
1 John McLish	Dead	Choctaw roll	Shim-o-te-cha	Dead	Chickasaw roll		

(NOTES)
On Choctaw Census Record No. 2 Tobucksy Co, Page 365; transferred to Chickasaw roll by Dawes Com.
On Choctaw Roll 1896, Tobucksy County, No. 9184, as Israel McClish

Oct. 14/98.

RESIDENCE: Choctaw Nation	~~COUNTY~~				CARD NO.			
POST OFFICE: Durant, Ind. Ter.					FIELD NO.			
NAME	RELATION-SHIP TO PERSON FIRST NAMED	AGE	SEX	BLOOD	TRIBAL ENROLLMENT			
					YEAR	COUNTY	PAGE	
1 Colbert, Harley Eugene		17	M	1/4	1897	Panola	2	
2 " Richard G.	Bro	15	"	1/4	1897	"	2	

	TRIBAL ENROLLMENT OF PARENTS						
NAME OF FATHER	YEAR	COUNTY	NAME OF MOTHER	YEAR	COUNTY		
1 Frank Colbert	Dead	Panola	Anna Louise Winter	1893	Panola		
2 " "	"	"	" " "	"	"		

(NOTES)
No. 1 on Chickasaw roll as Harley Colbert
No. 2 "   "   " " Richard   "
No. 1 is now husband of Pearl Potts, Chicasaw[sic] Roll Card No. 1131
    Evidence of marriage filed Dec. 22, 1902.

Oct. 14/98.

RESIDENCE: Choctaw Nation ~~COUNTY~~   **CARD NO.**

POST OFFICE: Bennington, Ind. Ter.   **FIELD NO.**

NAME	RELATION-SHIP TO PERSON FIRST NAMED	AGE	SEX	BLOOD	TRIBAL ENROLLMENT		
					YEAR	COUNTY	PAGE
1 Jones, Ellen	NAMED	50	F	1/4			
2 " Osborne	Son	21	M	1/8			
3 " Billy	"	18	"	1/8			
4 " Minnie	Dau	10	F	1/8			
5 " John	Son	9	M	1/8			
6 " Pearl	Dau	7	F	1/8			

TRIBAL ENROLLMENT OF PARENTS

	NAME OF FATHER	YEAR	COUNTY	NAME OF MOTHER	YEAR	COUNTY
1	*(Name Illegible)*	Dead	Choctaw roll	Eliza Impson	1897	Chick residing in Choctaw N. 1st Dist.
2	Jacob Jones		" "	No. 1		
3	" "		" "	No. 1		
4	" "		" "	No. 1		
5	" "		" "	No. 1		
6	" "		" "	No. 1		

(NOTES)

Also on Choctaw census Record No. 2, Jackson Co, Page 299, transferred to Chickasaw roll by Dawes Com.
No. 1 on Choctaw Roll 1896, Jackson County, No. 7128
No. 2 "   "   " 1896   "   "   " 7129
No. 3 "   "   " 1896   "   "   " 7130
No. 4 "   "   " 1896   "   "   " 7131
No. 5 "   "   " 1896   "   "   " 7132
No. 6 "   "   " 1896   "   "   " 7133

Oct. 14/98.

CANCELLED Stamped across card

RESIDENCE: Choctaw Nation ~~COUNTY~~   **CARD NO.**

POST OFFICE: Atoka, Ind. Ter.   **FIELD NO.**

NAME	RELATION-SHIP TO PERSON FIRST NAMED	AGE	SEX	BLOOD	TRIBAL ENROLLMENT		
					YEAR	COUNTY	PAGE
1 Armstrong, Wallace	NAMED	60	M	1/2			
2 Carnes, Jackson	Step Gr. Son	14	"	1/2			

73

	TRIBAL ENROLLMENT OF PARENTS						
	NAME OF FATHER	YEAR	COUNTY	NAME OF MOTHER	YEAR	COUNTY
1	Wm Armstrong	Dead	Choctaw roll	Oh-ko-wi-ke	Dead	Chickasaw roll
2	Tillis Carnes	"	" "	Phoebe Carnes	"	Chick residing in Choctaw N. 3rd Dist.

(NOTES)

No. 1 on Choctaw Census Record No. 2, Atoka Co, Page 18, transferred to Chick roll by Dawes Com.

No. 2 "   "   "   " No. 2 "   "   " 118 "   "   "   "   "   " "   "

No. 1 on Choctaw Roll 1896, Atoka County, No. 427

No. 2 "   "   " 1896   Blue   "   " 2907   Oct. 14/98.

CANCELLED Stamped across card

RESIGNDENCE: Choctaw Nation ~~COUNTY~~		CARD NO.
POST OFFICE: Atoka, Ind. Ter.		FIELD NO.

	NAME	RELATION- SHIP TO PERSON FIRST	AGE	SEX	BLOOD	TRIBAL ENROLLMENT		
						YEAR	COUNTY	PAGE
1	Folsom, Ida	NAMED	20	F	1/8			
2	" Nellie	Sister	15	"	1/8			

	TRIBAL ENROLLMENT OF PARENTS						
	NAME OF FATHER	YEAR	COUNTY	NAME OF MOTHER	YEAR	COUNTY
1	Alfred E. Folsom		Atoka County Choctaw roll	Margaret Folsom	Dead	Chick residing in Choctaw N. 3rd Dist.
2	" " "		" "	" "	"	" " " "

(NOTES)

Both on Choctaw Census Record, No. 2, Atoka Co, Page 189; transferred to Chickasaw roll by Dawes Com.

No. 1 on Choctaw Roll 1896 Atoka County, No. 4438

No. 2 "   " 1896 "   " 4439

Father of Nos. 1 and 2 is Alfred Emerson Folsom, on Choctaw card #400.

Oct. 14/98.

CANCELLED Stamped across card

RESIDENCE: Choctaw Nation ~~COUNTY~~		CARD NO.
POST OFFICE: Atoka, Ind. Ter.		FIELD NO.

	NAME	RELATION- SHIP TO PERSON FIRST	AGE	SEX	BLOOD	TRIBAL ENROLLMENT		
						YEAR	COUNTY	PAGE
1	Anglin, Charles Roberts	NAMED	48	M	I.W.			
2	" Mary	Wife	27	F	1/4			

Chickasaw Enrollment Cards 1898-1914
Chickasaw by Blood   Volume III

TRIBAL ENROLLMENT OF PARENTS

	NAME OF FATHER	YEAR	COUNTY	NAME OF MOTHER	YEAR	COUNTY
1	Hezekiah Anglin	Dead	non citizen	Kate Anglin	Dead	Non citizen
2	George Downing (I.W.)		Chickasaw roll	Melissa Downing	"	Chick residing in Choctaw N. 3rd Dist.

(NOTES)

No. 1 on Choctaw Intermarried roll, Page 3, transferred to Chickasaw roll by Dawes Com.
No. 2 "   "   Census Record, No. 2, " 18   "   "   "   " "   "   "
No. 1 on Choctaw Roll 1896, Atoka County, No. 14264. as C.R. Anglen
No. 2 "   "   " 1896   "   "   " 426

Oct. 14/98.

CANCELLED Stamped across card

RESIDENCE: Choctaw Nation ~~COUNTY~~				CARD NO.			
POST OFFICE: Caddo, Ind. Ter.				FIELD NO.			

	NAME	RELATION-SHIP TO PERSON FIRST NAMED	AGE	SEX	BLOOD	TRIBAL ENROLLMENT		
						YEAR	COUNTY	PAGE
1	Long, LeRoy	NAMED	30	M	I.W.			
2	" Martha	Wife	24	F	1/4			
3	" LeRoy D.	Son	11/2	M	1/8			
4	" Wendell McLean	"	3mo	"	1/8			

TRIBAL ENROLLMENT OF PARENTS

	NAME OF FATHER	YEAR	COUNTY	NAME OF MOTHER	YEAR	COUNTY
1	W.T. Long		non citizen	Mary E. Long		non citizen
2	Geore Downing (I.W.)	Dead	Chickasaw roll	Melissa Downing	Dead	Chick residing in Choctaw N. 3rd Dist.
3	No. 1			No. 2		
4	No. 1			No. 2		

(NOTES)

No. 1   on Choctaw Intermarried Roll, Page 64, transferred to Chickasaw roll by Dawes Com.
Nos. 2 & 3 "   "   Census Record No. 2 " 339   "   "   "   " "   "   "
No. 1 on Choctaw Roll, 1896, Blue County, No. 14774, as Dr. Leroy Long
No. 2 "   "   " 1896   "   "   " 8209 " Mrs. Martha Long.
        Evidence of birth of No. 3 filed Jan. 29, 1902.

Oct. 14/98.
No. 4 April 29/99.

CANCELLED Stamped across card

Chickasaw Enrollment Cards 1898-1914
Chickasaw by Blood   Volume III

RESIDENCE: Choctaw Nation   ~~COUNTY~~   CARD NO.

POST OFFICE: Simpson, Ind. Ter.   FIELD NO.

NAME	RELATION-SHIP TO PERSON FIRST NAMED	AGE	SEX	BLOOD	TRIBAL ENROLLMENT		
					YEAR	COUNTY	PAGE
1 Tuskatonnubby, James	FIRST NAMED	26	M	1/2	1893	Tishomingo	P.R. #1 132

TRIBAL ENROLLMENT OF PARENTS

NAME OF FATHER	YEAR	COUNTY	NAME OF MOTHER	YEAR	COUNTY
1 Tuskatonnubby	Dead	Tishomingo	Lottie Wilson	Dead	non citizen

(NOTES)

On Chickasaw roll as Jim Tuskatomby.
Additional testimony taken June 7,

Oct. 14/98

CANCELLED Stamped across card

RESIDENCE: Choctaw Nation   ~~COUNTY~~   CARD NO.

POST OFFICE: Durant, Ind. Ter.   FIELD NO.

NAME	RELATION-SHIP TO PERSON FIRST NAMED	AGE	SEX	BLOOD	TRIBAL ENROLLMENT		
					YEAR	COUNTY	PAGE
1 Wilkinson, Ada	NAMED	16	F	1/2			
2 " Albert L.	Son	3mo	M	1/4			
3 " Durward Arthur	Son	3wks	M	1/4			

TRIBAL ENROLLMENT OF PARENTS

NAME OF FATHER	YEAR	COUNTY	NAME OF MOTHER	YEAR	COUNTY
1 John Vails		non citizen	Louvina Vails	Dead	
2 Henry Wilkinson		" "	No. 1		
3 " "		" "	No. 1		

(NOTES)

On Choctaw Census Record No. 1, Blue Co, Page 331; transferred to Chickasaw roll by Dawes Com.
On Chickasaw Roll, 1896, Blue County, No. 12606, as Ada Vail.
No. 2 enrolled Nov. 4/99
No. 3 Enrolled Oct. 1, 1901.

Sept. 14/98.

CANCELLED Stamped across card

RESIDENCE: Choctaw Nation ~~COUNTY~~   CARD NO.

POST OFFICE: South McAlester, Ind. Ter.   FIELD NO.

	NAME	RELATION-SHIP TO PERSON	AGE	SEX	BLOOD	TRIBAL ENROLLMENT		
						YEAR	COUNTY	PAGE
1	Anderson, Hagen	FIRST NAMED	30	M	Full	1897	Chick residing in Choctaw N. 1st Dist.	69
2	" Minnie	Wife	24	F	I.W.	1897	" " " "	82
3	" Frank	Son	8	M	1/2	1897	" " " "	69
4	" Edward	"	6	"	1/2	1897	" " " "	69
5	" Ralph	"	2	"	1/2	1897	" " " "	69
6	" John	"	4mo	"	1/2			
7	" Edith	Dau	4mo	F	1/2			

TRIBAL ENROLLMENT OF PARENTS

	NAME OF FATHER	YEAR	COUNTY	NAME OF MOTHER	YEAR	COUNTY
1	John Anderson	Dead	Chickasaw Roll	Asie Anderson	Dead	Chickasaw Roll
2	(Name Illegible)		non citizen	Elizabeth (Illegible)		non citizen
3	No. 1			No. 2		
4	No. 1			No. 2		
5	No. 1			No. 2		
6	No. 1			No. 2		
7	No. 1			No. 2		

(NOTES)

No. 2 See decision of June 13, '04

No. 2 Marriage license and certificate to be supplied, Marriage certificate received Oct. 20/98.

No. 6 Enrolled March 24/99

No. 7 Born Aug. 24, 1901, enrolled Jan 14, 1902.

Oct. 14/98.

RESIDENCE: Choctaw Nation ~~COUNTY~~   CARD NO.

POST OFFICE: South McAlester   FIELD NO.

	NAME	RELATION-SHIP TO PERSON	AGE	SEX	BLOOD	TRIBAL ENROLLMENT		
						YEAR	COUNTY	PAGE
1	Anderson, Joe	FIRST NAMED	37	M	Full	1897	Chick residing in Choctaw N. 1st Dist.	69
2	" Leona	Wife	30	F	I.W.	1897	" " " "	82
3	Carney, Willie	Nephew	11	M	1/2	1897	" " " "	69

Chickasaw Enrollment Cards 1898-1914
Chickasaw by Blood   Volume III

	TRIBAL ENROLLMENT OF PARENTS						
	NAME OF FATHER	YEAR	COUNTY	NAME OF MOTHER	YEAR	COUNTY
1	John Anderson	Dead	Chickasaw Roll	Asie Anderson	Dead	Chickasaw Roll
2	John *(Illegible)*		non citizen	Elizabeth *(Illegible)*		non citizen
3	William Carney	Dead	Choctaw Roll	Jennie Carney	Dead	Chick residing in Choctaw N. 1st Dist.

(NOTES)

No. 2 Marriage license/certificate to be supplied. Marriage certificate received Oct. 21/98
    (No. 2 Dawes' Roll No. 166)
No. 3 *(Entry illegible)*
No. 3 Died July 12, 1899; Proof of death filed *(illegible)*

Oct. 14/98

RESIDENCE:	Choctaw Nation	~~COUNTY~~				CARD NO.			
POST OFFICE:	South McAlester, Ind. Ter.					FIELD NO.			

	NAME	RELATION-SHIP TO PERSON FIRST NAMED	AGE	SEX	BLOOD	TRIBAL ENROLLMENT		
						YEAR	COUNTY	PAGE
1	Lester, Preston Sydney		38	M	I.W.			
2	" Alice	Wife	25	F	1/2			
3	" Mr Curtain	Son	5	M	1/4			
4	" Lucile	Dau	3	F	1/4			
5	" Wynema	"	10mo	"	1/4			
6	Pitchlynn, Josephine	Sister in Law	20	"	1/2			
7	Lester, Louise A.	Dau	6mo	"	1/4			
8	" Preston S. Jr.	Son	2mo	M	1/4			
9	Jones, William B.	Son of No. 6	8da	"	1/4			
10	" Capitola	Dau of No. 6	2	F	1/4			

	TRIBAL ENROLLMENT OF PARENTS						
	NAME OF FATHER	YEAR	COUNTY	NAME OF MOTHER	YEAR	COUNTY
1	Preston Lester		non citizen	Carrie Lester		non citizen
2	Wm Pitchlynn	Dead	Choctaw Roll	Elsie Pitchlynn	Dead	Chick residing in Choctaw N. 1st Dist.
3	No. 1			No. 2		
4	No. 1			No. 2		
5	No. 1			No. 2		
6	Wm Pitchlynn	Dead	Choctaw Roll	Elsie Pitchlynn	Dead	Chick residing in Choctaw N. 1st Dist.
7	No. 1			No. 2		
8	No. 1			No. 2		

78

9	John W. Jones	Choctaw Card 4727	No. 6		
10	" " "	" " "	No. 6		

(NOTES)

No. 1   on Choctaw Intermarried Roll Page 61 transferred to Chickasaw Roll by Dawes Com.

No. 2, 3 & 4 "   "   Census Record No. 2 "   331   "   "   "   "   "   "   "

No. 3 on Choctaw Roll as Green the Curtain Lester

No. 2 "   "   "   "   Alice P.   "

No. 5 Affidavit of attending physician to be supplied. Received *(Illegible)* 21/98

No. 6 on Choctaw Census Record No. 2, Tobucksy Co, Page 395 transferred to Chickasaw Roll by Dawes Com

All except No. 5 on Choctaw Roll 1896 Tobucksy Co. She is *(remainder illegible)*

No. 7 Enrolled Nov. 4/99

No. 8 Enrolled July 12, 1901

No. 9 Born Aug. 4, 1902, Enrolled Aug. 7, 1902

No. 10 Born Jan 2, 1900. Enrolled Oct. 18, 1902

Evidence of marriage between parents of 9 & 10 filed Oct. 18, 1902.

Oct. 14/98.

CANCELLED Stamped across card

RESIDENCE: Choctaw Nation   ~~COUNTY~~   **CARD NO.**

POST OFFICE: Atoka, Ind. Ter.   **FIELD NO.**

	NAME	RELATION-SHIP TO PERSON FIRST NAMED	AGE	SEX	BLOOD	TRIBAL ENROLLMENT		
						YEAR	COUNTY	PAGE
1	Frinzell, Amelia		38	F	1/2			
2	" John	Son	22	M	1/4			
3	" Lena	Dau	7	F	1/4			
4	" Irene	Niece	12	"	1/4			
5	McMurtrey, John	Husband	45	M	I.W.			
6	" Clyde	Son	2mo	"	1/4			
7	" Glenn	Gr.Nephew	1mo	"	1/8			

TRIBAL ENROLLMENT OF PARENTS

	NAME OF FATHER	YEAR	COUNTY	NAME OF MOTHER	YEAR	COUNTY
1	Banj. Smallwood	Dead	Choctaw Roll	Annie Smallwood	Dead	Chickasaw roll
2	John Frinzell	"	non citizen	No. 1		
3	" "	"	" "	No. 1		
4	Harry Cox		" "	*(Illegible)* Cox	Dead	Chick residing in Choctaw N. 3rd Dist.
5	Joe McMurtrey	Dead	" "	Martha McMurtrey		non citz
6	No. 5			No. 1		
7	Lora McMurtrey		non-citizen	No. 4		

(NOTES)

All on Choctaw Census Record No. 2 Atoka Co, Page 190, transferred to Chickasaw Roll by Dawes Com.

No. 1 On Chickasaw Roll 1896 Atoka County, No. 4448

No. 2 "   "   " 1896 "   "   " 4449

No. 3 "   "   " 1896 "   "   " 4451

No. 4 "   "   " 1896 "   "   " 4450

No. 4 is now the wife of Lora McMurtrey, a non citizen Jan 23, 1902

No. 5 Enrolled Aug. 29/99

No. 6 Enrolled December 15, 1900

No. 7 Born Dec. 12, 1901 Enrolled Jany 23, 1902.

Oct. 14/98.

CANCELLED Stamped across card

RESIDENCE: Choctaw Nation ~~COUNTY~~						CARD NO.		
POST OFFICE: Bennington, Ind. Ter.						FIELD NO.		
NAME	RELATION-SHIP TO PERSON	AGE	SEX	BLOOD	TRIBAL ENROLLMENT			
					YEAR	COUNTY	PAGE	
1 Kepo, Cephus	FIRST NAMED	30	M	Full	1897	Chick residing in Choctaw N. 3rd Dist.	74	
NAME OF FATHER	YEAR	COUNTY		NAME OF MOTHER		YEAR	COUNTY	
1 James Kapo[sic]	Dead	Chickasaw Roll		Margaret Kepo		Dead	Chickasaw Roll	

(NOTES)

Husband of Mary Kepo, Choctaw Census Record No. 2, Jackson Co, Page 401

On Chickasaw Roll as Cephus Polk

Oct. 14/98.

RESIDENCE: Choctaw Nation ~~COUNTY~~						CARD NO.		
POST OFFICE: Tuskahoma, Ind. Ter.						FIELD NO.		
NAME	RELATION-SHIP TO PERSON	AGE	SEX	BLOOD	TRIBAL ENROLLMENT			
					YEAR	COUNTY	PAGE	
1 McGee, Fulsome	FIRST NAMED	54	M	Fi"	1897	Chick residing in Choctaw N. 3rd Dist.	73	
TRIBAL ENROLLMENT OF PARENTS								
NAME OF FATHER	YEAR	COUNTY		NAME OF MOTHER		YEAR	COUNTY	
1 (Name Illegible)	Dead	Chickasaw Roll		Stim-ma-(illegible)		Dead	Chickasaw Roll	

(NOTES)

Husband of Mollie McGee, Choctaw Roll Card No. 399.

Oct. 14/98.

Chickasaw Enrollment Cards 1898-1914
Chickasaw by Blood   Volume III

RESIDENCE: Choctaw Nation   ~~COUNTY~~   CARD NO.

POST OFFICE: Bennington, Ind. Ter.   FIELD NO.

NAME	RELATION- SHIP TO PERSON FIRST NAMED	AGE	SEX	BLOOD	TRIBAL ENROLLMENT		
					YEAR	COUNTY	PAGE
1 Jackson, Louisa E.		32	F	1/2			

TRIBAL ENROLLMENT OF PARENTS

NAME OF FATHER	YEAR	COUNTY	NAME OF MOTHER	YEAR	COUNTY
1 Alfred Fulsom		Blue County Choctaw Roll	(Name Illegible)	1897	Chick residing in Choctaw N. 3rd Dist.

(NOTES)

On Choctaw Census Record No. 1 Blue Co, Page 177 Transferred to Chickasaw Roll by Dawes Com
"   "   Roll 1896 Blue County, No. 7197

Oct. 14/98.

CANCELLED Stamped across card

RESIDENCE: Choctaw Nation   ~~COUNTY~~   CARD NO.

POST OFFICE: McAlester, Ind. Ter.   FIELD NO.

NAME	RELATION- SHIP TO PERSON FIRST NAMED	AGE	SEX	BLOOD	TRIBAL ENROLLMENT		
					YEAR	COUNTY	PAGE
1 Pusley, James		24	M	1/2	1897	Chick residing in Choctaw N. 3rd Dist.	69
2 " Mary J	Wife	20	F	I.W.			
3 " Mattie Jewell	Dau	6mo	"	1/4			

TRIBAL ENROLLMENT OF PARENTS

NAME OF FATHER	YEAR	COUNTY	NAME OF MOTHER	YEAR	COUNTY
1 George Pusley	Dead	Choctaw Roll	Julie Pusley	Dead	Chick residing in Choctaw N. 3rd Dist.
2 Jeff Cagle		Non Citizen	Amanda Cagle		Non Citizen
3 No. 1			No. 2		

(NOTES)

On Chickasaw Roll as Jimmie Pusley
No. 2 Enrolled March 20/99   (No. 2 Dawes' Roll No. 165)
No. 3 Born Decr. 15, 1901; Enrolled May 27, 1902

Oct. 14/98.

CANCELLED Stamped across card

RESIDENCE: Choctaw Nation ~~COUNTY~~   CARD NO.

POST OFFICE: Caddo, Ind. Ter.   FIELD NO.

#	NAME	RELATION-SHIP TO PERSON	AGE	SEX	BLOOD	TRIBAL ENROLLMENT		
						YEAR	COUNTY	PAG
1	Maytubby, Peter	FIRST NAMED	61	M	Full	1897	Chick residing in Choctaw N. 3rd Dist.	74
2	" ~~Tabitha~~	~~Wife~~	42	F	~~I.W.~~	~~1897~~	" " " "	74
3	" ~~Sophia~~	~~Dau~~	17	"	1/2	~~1897~~	" " " "	74
4	Pitchlynn, Sudie	"	15	"	12	1897	" " " "	74
5	Maytubby, Jesse D.Y.	Son	13	M	1/2	1897	" " " "	74
6	" Bessie	Dau	11	F	1/2	1897	" " " "	74
7	" Elihu Bennett	Son	6	M	1/2	1897	" " " "	74
8	" Lillie	Dau	4	F	1/2	1897	" " " "	74
9	Pitchlynn, Sophia M.	Dau of No. 4	4days	"	3/8			

TRIBAL ENROLLMENT OF PARENTS

#	NAME OF FATHER	YEAR	COUNTY	NAME OF MOTHER	YEAR	COUNTY
1	She-an-no	Dead	Chickasaw Roll	*(Name Illegible)*	Dead	Chickasaw Roll
2	~~Wm Bailey~~	"	~~Non-Citizen~~	*(Name Illegible)*	"	~~Non-citizen~~
3	~~No. 1~~			~~No. 2~~		
4	No. 1			No. 2		
5	No. 1			No. 2		
6	No. 1			No. 2		
7	No. 1			No. 2		
8	No. 1			No. 2		
9	Edward C. Pitchlynn		Choctaw Card 3757	No. 4		

(NOTES)

No. 3 transferred to Chickasaw Card # *(illegible)*

No. 2 Not on Page 74 *(remainder illegible)*   *(No. 2 Dawes' Roll No. 53)*

No. 4 is now the wife of Edward E. Pitchlynn, on Choctaw Card #3757; Evidence of marriage of No. 4 to Ed Pitchlynn filed 8/21/01

No. 5 on Chickasaw Roll as Jessie D.Y. Maytubby

No. 7 "   "   " " Elime B.   "

No. 9 Born June 21st 1902; Enrolled June 25th 1902

Oct. 14/98.

RESIDENCE: Choctaw Nation   ~~COUNTY~~   CARD NO.

POST OFFICE: Antler, Ind. Ter.   FIELD NO.

NAME	RELATION-SHIP TO PERSON FIRST NAMED	AGE	SEX	BLOOD	TRIBAL ENROLLMENT		
					YEAR	COUNTY	PAGE
1 Colbert, Lamon	FIRST NAMED	45	M	Full	1897	Chick residing in Choctaw N. 3rd Dist.	73

NAME OF FATHER	YEAR	COUNTY	NAME OF MOTHER	YEAR	COUNTY
1 Po-yo-ka Colbert	Dead	Chickasaw Roll	Shue-ma-ta-cha	Dead	Chickasaw Roll

(NOTES)

No. 1 husband of Ima Colbert, Choc. 1785.

Oct. 13/98.

RESIDENCE: Choctaw Nation   ~~COUNTY~~   CARD NO.

POST OFFICE: Tuskahoma, Ind. Ter.   FIELD NO.

NAME	RELATION-SHIP TO PERSON FIRST NAMED	AGE	SEX	BLOOD	TRIBAL ENROLLMENT		
					YEAR	COUNTY	PAGE
1 Potts, Judy	NAMED	38	F	1/2			
2 " Sarah	Dau	17	"	1/4			
3 " Joshua	Son	12	M	1/4			
4 " Allie	Dau	10	F	1/4			
5 " Willie	Son	8	M	1/4			
6 " Lillie	Dau	6	F	1/4			
7 " Eli	Son	5	M	1/4			
8 " Horace, Jr.	"	3	"	1/4			
9 " Laura	Dau	1	F	1/4			
10 " Rebecca	"	5mo	"	1/4			
11 " Margaret Susan	Dau of No. 2	2 1/2	"	1/4			

TRIBAL ENROLLMENT OF PARENTS

NAME OF FATHER	YEAR	COUNTY	NAME OF MOTHER	YEAR	COUNTY
1 Billie King	Dead	Choctaw Roll	Leth-ha-ke	Dead	Chickasaw Roll
2 Horace Potts		Wade Co. Choctaw Roll	No. 1		
3 " "		" "	No. 1		
4 " "		" "	No. 1		
5 " "		" "	No. 1		
6 " "		" "	No. 1		
7 " "		" "	No. 1		
8 " "		" "	No. 1		

9	" "		" "	No. 1		
10	" "		" "	No. 1		
11	(Illegitimate Archie Heath	on Choc	taw Card #2059	No. 2		

(NOTES)

No. 1 wife of Horace Potts Choctaw Roll Card No. 356.

All except No. 9 on Choctaw Census Record No. 2, Wade Co, Page 397 transferred to Chickasaw Roll by Dawes Com
" " " " " " Roll 1896, Wade Co. See list of names/numbers hereto attached.

No. 10 Enrolled Nov. 4/99

No. 11 (Illegitimate) Born Feb. 9, 1900; Enrolled July 22, 1902

Oct. 13/98.

RESIDENCE: Panola   COUNTY   CARD NO.

POST OFFICE: Mead, Ind. Ter.   FIELD NO.

NAME	RELATIONSHIP TO PERSON FIRST NAMED	AGE	SEX	BLOOD	TRIBAL ENROLLMENT		
					YEAR	COUNTY	PAGE
1 Love, Edward Davis	NAMED	38	M	1/4	Sept 22 1896	Panola No. 11	8
2 " Mary Caroline	Wife	30	F	I.W.	1897	Panola	76
3 " Hercules Martin	Son	13	M	1/8	1897	"	2
4 " Caryann Edna	Dau	11	F	1/8	1897	"	2
5 " Dolceny	"	8	"	1/8	1897	"	2
6 " Samuel	Son	7	M	1/8	1897	"	2
7 " Edward Davis, Jr.	"	5	"	1/8	1897	"	2
8 " Felix Theodore	"	3	"	1/8	1897	"	2
9 " Ula	Dau	1wk	F	1/8			
10 " Fula	"	1wk	"	1/8			
11 " Francis Marion	Son	7wks	M	1/8			

TRIBAL ENROLLMENT OF PARENTS

	NAME OF FATHER	YEAR	COUNTY	NAME OF MOTHER	YEAR	COUNTY
1	Sam Love	Dead	Panola	C.A.E. Love	Dead	Non-citizen
2	John Finch		Non-citizen	(Illegible) Finch		" "
3	No. 1			No. 2		
4	No. 1			No. 2		
5	No. 1			No. 2		
6	No. 1			No. 2		
7	No. 1			No. 2		
8	No. 1			No. 2		
9	No. 1			No. 2		
10	No. 1			No. 2		

11	No. 1			No. 2		

(NOTES)

No. 2 See decision of June 13 '04   *(No. 2 Dawes' Roll No. 407)*
No. 1 On Chickasaw Roll as Ed Love
No. 2 "   "   "   " M.C. " ; Evidence of license taken by stenographer to be attached Filed Oct. 14/98.
No. 3 "   "   "   " Hirk "
No. 4 "   "   "   " Cary "
No. 5 "   "   "   "Clemmy "
No. 7 "   "   "   " Ed, " Jr,
No. 8 "   "   "   " Felix "
Nos. 9 & 10 Enrolled Nov. 23/98
No. 10 Died July 20 1899, Proof of death filed Nov. 8, 1902
No. 11 Enrolled July 2, 1901.

Oct. 13/98.

RESIDENCE: Panola   **COUNTY**   **CARD NO.**
POST OFFICE: Kemp, Ind. Ter.   **FIELD NO.**

	NAME	RELATION-SHIP TO PERSON FIRST	AGE	SEX	BLOOD	TRIBAL ENROLLMENT		
						YEAR	COUNTY	PAGE
1	Dillingham, Nathan Thomas	NAMED	34	M	I.W.			
2	" Amanda	Wife	56	F	3/4	1897	Panola	4
3	Skinner, Permelia	StepDau	18	"	3/4	1897	"	4
4	" Russell F.	G.St.Son	4mo	M	3/8			
5	" Mollie Vernon	G.St.Dau	4mo	F	3/8			

TRIBAL ENROLLMENT OF PARENTS

	NAME OF FATHER	YEAR	COUNTY	NAME OF MOTHER	YEAR	COUNTY
1	W.M. Dillingham	Dead	Non Citizen	Mary Dillingham	Dead	Non Citizen
2	Lem Colbert	Dead	Chickasaw Roll	Susan Colbert	"	Chickasaw Roll
3	Jim Reynolds	"	Panola	No. 2		
4	W.L. Skinner		Non Citizen	No. 3		
5	" " "		" "	No. 3		

(NOTES)

No. 2 On Chickasaw Roll as Amanda Reynolds   *(No. 1 Dawes' Roll No. 476)*
No. 3 is now the wife of W.L. Skinner
No. 4 Enrolled Aug. 6, 1900
No. 5 Enrolled July 16, 1901

Oct. 13/98.

RESIDENCE: Choctaw Nation   ~~COUNTY~~   CARD NO.

POST OFFICE: Tuskahoma, Ind. Ter.   FIELD NO.

NAME	RELATION-SHIP TO PERSON FIRST NAMED	AGE	SEX	BLOOD	TRIBAL ENROLLMENT		
					YEAR	COUNTY	PAGE
1 ~~Muckintubby, Eton~~	FIRST NAMED	42	M	~~Full~~	~~1897~~	~~Chick residing in Choctaw N. 3rd Dist.~~	~~73~~
2 " Katie	Wife	33	F	"	1897	" " " "	73
3 " ~~Elizabeth~~	~~Dau~~	~~2mo~~	"	"			
4 Moore, Nathaniel	St.Son	2	M	1/2			
5 Muckintubby, Ada	Dau No. 2	3	F	Full			

TRIBAL ENROLLMENT OF PARENTS

NAME OF FATHER	YEAR	COUNTY	NAME OF MOTHER	YEAR	COUNTY
1 ~~Muckintubby~~	~~Dead~~	~~Chickasaw Roll~~	~~(Name Illegible)~~	~~Dead~~	~~Chickasaw Roll~~
2 Folsom McGee	1897	Chick residing in Choctaw N. 3rd Dist.	Susan McGee	"	" " "
3 ~~No. 1~~			~~No. 2~~		
4 Jonas Moore	Dead	Choctaw Roll	No. 2		
5 No. 1			No. 2		

(NOTES)

No. 2 on Chickasaw Roll as Katie McGee   *(No. 3 Dawes' Roll No. 3604)*

Nos. 3 & 4 Enrolled May 24, 1899   *(No. 5 Dawes' Roll No. 4866)*

No. 4 on Choctaw Roll Page 222 No. 886 as Nathaniel Moore, Jacks Fork Co, transferred to Chickasaw Roll by Dawes Com

(Entry illegible)

No. 1 died Dec, 1901; proof of death filed Dec. 16, 1902.

No. 3 " Oct, 1898; " " " " " " "

No. 2 is now wife of John Baker on Choctaw Card #3100 12/12/02

No. 5 born Dec. 5, 1900; app. made Dec. 12/02 *(remainder illegible)*

Oct. 13/98,

RESIDENCE: Panola   COUNTY   CARD NO.

POST OFFICE: Cole, Ind. Ter.   FIELD NO.

NAME	RELATION-SHIP TO PERSON FIRST NAMED	AGE	SEX	BLOOD	TRIBAL ENROLLMENT		
					YEAR	COUNTY	PAGE
1 Folsom, Mollie	NAMED	29	F	Full	1897	Panola	6
2 " Basey	Dau	9	"	1/2	1897	"	6
3 " Daisy	"	7	"	1/2	1897	"	6
4 " Minnie	"	5	"	1/2	1897	"	6

| 5 | " | Alice | " | 2 | " | 1/2 | 1897 | | " | 6 |
| 6 | " | Israel R. | Son | 11mo | M | 1/2 | | | | |

TRIBAL ENROLLMENT OF PARENTS

	NAME OF FATHER	YEAR	COUNTY	NAME OF MOTHER	YEAR	COUNTY
1	Gibson Kemp	Dead	Panola	Mary Ann Kemp	Dead	Panola
2	Tandy Folsom		Choctaw residing in Chickasaw Dist	No. 1		
3	" "		" "	No. 1		
4	" "		" "	No. 1		
5	" "		" "	No. 1		
6	" "		" "	No. 1		

(NOTES)

Sirname on Chickasaw Roll as Fulsome
No. 2   "   "   "   " Bessie Fulsome
No. 6 Enrolled Nov. 4/99
Father of children on this card and husband of No. 1 is Tandy W. Folsom on Choctaw Card #3214

Oct. 13/98.

| *RESIDENCE:* | Choctaw Nation | ~~COUNTY~~ | | | | *CARD NO.* | | | |
| *POST OFFICE:* | Tuskahoma, Ind. Ter. | | | | | *FIELD NO.* | | | |

	NAME	RELATION-SHIP TO PERSON FIRST NAMED	AGE	SEX	BLOOD	TRIBAL ENROLLMENT		
						YEAR	COUNTY	PAGE
1	Colbert, Martha	NAMED	22	F	3/4			
2	" Frances	Dau	4mo	F	3/8			
3	" Aaron	Son	1	M	3/8			

TRIBAL ENROLLMENT OF PARENTS

	NAME OF FATHER	YEAR	COUNTY	NAME OF MOTHER	YEAR	COUNTY
1	Calvin Gibson	Dead	Choctaw Roll	Nancy Gibson	Dead	Chickasaw Roll
2	Alexander Colbert	1896	Jacks Fork Co. Choctaw Roll	No. 1		
3	" "	1896	" "	No. 1		

(NOTES)

On Choctaw Census Record No. 2, Jacks Fork Co Page 124 transferred to Chickasaw Roll by Dawes Com.
"   "   Roll   1896   "   "   " No. 3047
Wife of Alexander Colbert, Choctaw Roll Card No. 395
No. 2 Enrolled March 21/99
No. 2 Affidavit of mother to be supplied 3/21/99
No. 3 Born Sept. 3, 1901; Enrolled Sept. 4, 1902

Oct. 13/98

CANCELLED Stamped across card

RESIDENCE: Panola COUNTY					CARD NO.			
POST OFFICE: Kemp, Ind. Ter.					FIELD NO.			
	NAME	RELATION-SHIP TO PERSON FIRST NAMED	AGE	SEX	BLOOD	TRIBAL ENROLLMENT		
						YEAR	COUNTY	PAGE
1	Kemp, Simon Burney		56	M	3/4	1897	Panola	4
2	" Mary Eliza	Wife	45	F	3/4	1897	"	4

TRIBAL ENROLLMENT OF PARENTS

	NAME OF FATHER	YEAR	COUNTY	NAME OF MOTHER	YEAR	COUNTY
1	Joel Kemp	Dead	Chickasaw Roll	Maria Kemp	Dead	Chickasaw Roll
2	Samuel Colbert	"	" "	Parthena Colbert	"	

(NOTES)

No. 1 On Chickasaw Roll as Simon Kemp
No. 2 " " " M.E. "
No. 1 Died April 25/1900; See testimony of J.M. Webb taken at Colbert *(illegible)* date 6/13/1900

Oct. 13/98.

RESIDENCE: Choctaw Nation ~~COUNTY~~					CARD NO.			
POST OFFICE: Kiowa, Ind. Ter.					FIELD NO.			
	NAME	RELATION-SHIP TO PERSON FIRST NAMED	AGE	SEX	BLOOD	TRIBAL ENROLLMENT		
						YEAR	COUNTY	PAGE
1	Thompson, Henry		23	M	1/4	1897	Chickasaw residing in Choctaw N. 1st Dist.	71

TRIBAL ENROLLMENT OF PARENTS

	NAME OF FATHER	YEAR	COUNTY	NAME OF MOTHER	YEAR	COUNTY
1	Alex Thompson	Dead	Non Citizen	Martha Thompson	1897	Chick residing in Choctaw N. 1st Dist.

(NOTES)

Oct. 13/98.

RESIDENCE: Panola COUNTY					CARD NO.			
POST OFFICE: Colbert, Ind. Ter.					FIELD NO.			
	NAME	RELATION-SHIP TO PERSON FIRST NAMED	AGE	SEX	BLOOD	TRIBAL ENROLLMENT		
						YEAR	COUNTY	PAGE
1	Guess, Sabet		46	M	3/4	1897	Panola	2
2	" Joe Jr.	Son	12	"	3/8	1897	"	2
3	" Jimmie	"	1	"	3/8	1897	"	85
4	" Kizzie	Wife	38	F	I.W.			

TRIBAL ENROLLMENT OF PARENTS

	NAME OF FATHER	YEAR	COUNTY	NAME OF MOTHER	YEAR	COUNTY
1	John Guess	Dead	Panola	Angeline Guess	Dead	Panola
2	No. 1			Kizzie Guess		Non citizen
3	No. 1			" "		" "
4	Jas. M. Brooks		Non citz	*(Illegible)* Brookw		" "

(NOTES)

No. 1 Died Jan. 1, 1900; Proof of death filed Aug. 15th 1902

No. 3 On Chickasaw Roll as Jim Guess   *(No. 3 Dawes' Roll No. 4204)*

No. 3 Proof of birth received and filed Decr. 8, 1902

No. 4 Died Aug. 1900; Proof of death filed Nov. 1, 1902.

Oct. 13/98.

RESIDENCE: Choctaw Nation   ~~COUNTY~~   CARD NO.

POST OFFICE: Bengal, Ind. Ter.   FIELD NO.

	NAME	RELATIONSHIP TO PERSON FIRST NAMED	AGE	SEX	BLOOD	TRIBAL ENROLLMENT		
						YEAR	COUNTY	PAGE
1	Welch, Charles A.	NAMED	27	M	1/8			
2	" Adelia	Wife	28	F	I.W.			
3	" Maney	Son	8	M	1/16			
4	" Earl	"	6	"	1/16			
5	" Paul	"	3	"	1/16			
6	" Fitzhugh Lee	"	5mo	"	1/16			
7	" Lucile Matilda	Dau	2mo	F	1/16			

TRIBAL ENROLLMENT OF PARENTS

	NAME OF FATHER	YEAR	COUNTY	NAME OF MOTHER	YEAR	COUNTY
1	Wm A. Welch (I.W.)		Chick residing in Choctaw N. 3rd Dist.	Alice Welch	Dead	Chick residing in Choctaw N. 3rd Dist.
2	C.F. Morton	Dead	Non Citizen	Mary G. Morton		non citizen
3	No. 1			No. 2		
4	No. 1			No. 2		
5	No. 1			No. 2		
6	No. 1			No. 2		
7	No. 1			No. 2		

(NOTES)

All except Nos. 2 & 6 on Choctaw Census Record No. 2, Page 460; transferred by Dawes Com to Chick Roll

No. 2   "   "   Intermarried Roll -   "   112   "   "   "   "   "   "   "

No. 1 On Choctaw Roll as Charles Welch

No. 1 On Chickasaw Roll 1896, Sugarloaf County, No. 12881, as Charley Welch

No. 2 "   "   " 1896   "   "   " 15755 " Adeliah Welch

No. 3 "   "   "   1896   "   "   " 12882
No. 4 "   "   "   1896   "   "   " 12883
No. 5 "   "   "   1896   "   "   " 12884
No. 7 Enrolled May 16ᵗʰ 1900

Oct. 13/98.

CANCELLED Stamped across card

RESIDENCE: Choctaw Nation	COUNTY				CARD NO.			
POST OFFICE: Red Oak, Ind. Ter.					FIELD NO.			
NAME	RELATION-SHIP TO PERSON FIRST NAMED	AGE	SEX	BLOOD	TRIBAL ENROLLMENT			
					YEAR	COUNTY	PAGE	
1 Welch, Robert C.		31	M	1/8				
2 " Minnie L.	Wife	30	F	I.W.				
3 " Alice	Dau	9	"	1/16				
4 " Joe	Son	7	M	1/16				
5 " Frank	"	5	"	1/16				
6 " John H	"	2	"	1/16				
7 " Mildred B.	Dau	6mo	F	1/16				

TRIBAL ENROLLMENT OF PARENTS

	NAME OF FATHER	YEAR	COUNTY	NAME OF MOTHER	YEAR	COUNTY
1	Wm A. Welch (I.W.)		Chick residing in Choctaw N. 3ʳᵈ Dist.	Alice Welch	Dead	Chick residing in Choctaw N. 3ʳᵈ Dist.
2	James Carter	Dead	Non-citizen	Rebecca Carter		Non Citizen
3	No. 1			No. 2		
4	No. 1			No. 2		
5	No. 1			No. 2		
6	No. 1			No. 2		
7	No. 1			No. 2		

(NOTES)

All except No. 2 on Choctaw Census Record No. 2, Page 461; transferred by Dawes Com
        No. 2 "   "   Intermarried Roll   " 112;   "   "   "   "
No. 1 On Choctaw Roll 1896 Sugar Loaf County, No. 12881
No. 2 "   "   "   1896   "   "   "   "   15156 as Minnie L. Welch
No. 3 "   "   "   1896   "   "   "   "   12887
No. 4 "   "   "   1896   "   "   "   "   12888
No. 5 "   "   "   1896   "   "   "   "   12889
No. 6 "   "   "   1896   "   "   "   "   12890
No. 7 Enrolled Nov. 4, 1899
No. 2 Died Sept. 11, 1901; Proof of Death filed June 9, 1902

Oct. 13/98.

CANCELLED Stamped across card

Chickasaw Enrollment Cards 1898-1914
Chickasaw by Blood   Volume III

RESIDENCE: Choctaw Nation 3rd Dist.   COUNTY   CARD NO.

POST OFFICE: Durant, Ind. Ter.   FIELD NO.

NAME	RELATION-SHIP TO PERSON FIRST NAMED	AGE	SEX	BLOOD	TRIBAL ENROLLMENT		
					YEAR	COUNTY	PAGE
1 Busby, Smith Jefferson	NAMED	37	M	I.W.			
2 " Biddie Caroline	Wife	20	F	1/8			

TRIBAL ENROLLMENT OF PARENTS

	NAME OF FATHER	YEAR	COUNTY	NAME OF MOTHER	YEAR	COUNTY
1	John Busby	Dead	Non citizen	Eliza Busby	Dead	Non citizen
2	Henry Thompson	"	" "	Caroline (Illegible)	1897	Chick residing in Choctaw N 3rd Dist.

(NOTES)
No. 1 On Choctaw Intermarried Roll Page 10; transferred to Chickasaw Card by Dawes Com
No. 2 "   "   Census Record No. 1 " 38   "   "   "   "   "   "   "
No. 1 On Choctaw Roll as J.S. Buzbey 1896, Blue County No. 14340
No. 2 "   "   "   " Biddie Busby 1896 "   "   " 1539

Oct. 13/98.

CANCELLED Stamped across card

RESIDENCE: Choctaw Nation   COUNTY   CARD NO.

POST OFFICE: Tuskahoma, Ind. Ter.   FIELD NO.

NAME	RELATION-SHIP TO PERSON FIRST NAMED	AGE	SEX	BLOOD	TRIBAL ENROLLMENT		
					YEAR	COUNTY	PAGE
1 Bohanon, Liney	NAMED	22	F	3/4			
2 " Sam	Son	1	M	5/8			
3 " Vina	Dau	5mo	F	5/8			
4 " Elsie	"	5mo	"	5/8			

TRIBAL ENROLLMENT OF PARENTS

	NAME OF FATHER	YEAR	COUNTY	NAME OF MOTHER	YEAR	COUNTY
1	Solomon Anderson	Dead	Chickasaw Roll	Lena Anderson	Dead	Chickasaw Roll
2	Robert Bohanon	1896	Jacks Fork Co. Choctaw Roll	No. 1		
3	" "	1896	" "	No. 1		
4	" "	1896	" "	No. 1		

(NOTES)
    Both on Choctaw Census Record No. 2, Jacks Fork Co, Page 79, transferred to Chickasaw Roll by Dawes Com
No. 1 Wife of Robern Bohanon, Choctaw Roll Card No. 333
No. 1 On Choctaw Roll 1896 Jacks Fork County, No. 1969
No. 2 "   "   " 1896 "   "   "   " 1970

91

Chickasaw Enrollment Cards 1898-1914
Chickasaw by Blood   Volume III

No. 3 Enrolled March 27/99
No. 4 Born Janu 23, 1902; Enrolled May 14, 1902

Oct. 13/98.

CANCELLED Stamped across card

RESIDENCE: Choctaw Nation COUNTY					CARD NO.			
POST OFFICE: Tuskahoma, Ind. Ter.					FIELD NO.			
NAME	RELATION-SHIP TO PERSON FIRST NAMED	AGE	SEX	BLOOD	TRIBAL ENROLLMENT			
					YEAR	COUNTY	PAGE	
1 Colbert, Billie	FIRST NAMED	69	M	Full	1897	Chick residing in Choctaw N. 3rd Dist.	73	

TRIBAL ENROLLMENT OF PARENTS

NAME OF FATHER	YEAR	COUNTY	NAME OF MOTHER	YEAR	COUNTY
1 Hi-ko-che	Dead	Chickasaw Roll	(Name Illegible)	Dead	Chickasaw Roll

(NOTES)
Husband of Martha Colbert, Choctaw Roll Card No. 392

Oct. 13/98.

RESIDENCE: Choctaw Nation COUNTY					CARD NO.			
POST OFFICE: Tie, Ind. Ter.					FIELD NO.			
NAME	RELATION-SHIP TO PERSON FIRST NAMED	AGE	SEX	BLOOD	TRIBAL ENROLLMENT			
					YEAR	COUNTY	PAGE	
1 Reed, Simon	FIRST NAMED	20	M	1/2	1897	Chick residing in Choctaw N. 1st Dist.	71	

TRIBAL ENROLLMENT OF PARENTS

NAME OF FATHER	YEAR	COUNTY	NAME OF MOTHER	YEAR	COUNTY
1 Timby Reed		Chick Freedman	Pakey	Dead	Chick residing in Choctaw N. 1st Dist.

(NOTES)

Oct. 13/98.

RESIDENCE: Choctaw Nation COUNTY					CARD NO.			
POST OFFICE: Atoka, Ind. Ter.					FIELD NO.			
NAME	RELATION-SHIP TO PERSON FIRST NAMED	AGE	SEX	BLOOD	TRIBAL ENROLLMENT			
					YEAR	COUNTY	PAGE	
1 Sexton, Annie	NAMED	32	F	Full				
2 " Mandy	Dau	3	"	"				

TRIBAL ENROLLMENT OF PARENTS						
NAME OF FATHER	YEAR	COUNTY	NAME OF MOTHER	YEAR	COUNTY
1	Newt Pierson	Dead	Panola	Lucinda Pierson	Dead	Pickens
2	Emmerson Sexton		Atoka Co Choctaw Roll	No. 1		

(NOTES)

Both on Choctaw Census Record No. 2, Atoka Co, Page, 431 transferred to Chickasaw Roll by Dawes Com
No. 1 Wife of Emmerson Sexton, Choctaw Roll Card No. 391
No. 1 On Choctaw Roll, 1896, Atoka County, No. 11645
No. 2 "   "   " 1896   "   "   " 11647

Oct. 13/98.

CANCELLED Stamped across card

RESISTANCE: Choctaw Nation ~~COUNTY~~   CARD NO.

POST OFFICE: Alderson, Ind. Ter.   FIELD NO.

NAME	RELATION-SHIP TO PERSON FIRST NAMED	AGE	SEX	BLOOD	TRIBAL ENROLLMENT		
					YEAR	COUNTY	PAGE
1 Reed, Kissen		35	M	1/2	1897	Chick residing in Choctaw N. 1st Dist.	69
2 " Rhoda	Wife	30	F	Full	1897	" " " "	69
3 " Jimmy	Son	7	M	3/4	1897	" " " "	69
4 " Hagen	"	4	"	3/4	1897	" " " "	69
5 " Ed	"	1	"	3/4			
6 Anderson, Dickson	St.Son	17	"	1/2	1897	Chick residing in Choctaw N. 1st Dist.	69
7 Reed, Robinson	Son	7wks	"	3/4			

TRIBAL ENROLLMENT OF PARENTS						
NAME OF FATHER	YEAR	COUNTY	NAME OF MOTHER	YEAR	COUNTY
1	To-ah-len-stubby	Dead	Choctaw Roll	Milsey	Dead	Chickasaw Roll
2	Carmen Wesley	"	Chickasaw Roll	Ellen Wesley	1897	Chick residing in Choctaw N 1st Dist.
3	No. 1			No. 2		
4	No. 1			No. 2		
5	No. 1			No. 2		
6	Joe Anderson		Tobucksy Co Choctaw Roll	No. 2		
7	No. 1			No. 2		

(NOTES)

No. 7 Born Aug. 31, 1902. Enrolled Oct. 11, 1902.   *(No. 7 Dawes' Roll No. 4293)*

93

P.O. Savanna, I.T. 10/11/02   Oct. 13/98.

	RESIDENCE: Choctaw Nation ~~County~~					CARD No.			
	POST OFFICE: Sans Bois, Ind. Ter.					FIELD No.			

	NAME	RELATION-SHIP TO PERSON FIRST NAMED	AGE	SEX	BLOOD	TRIBAL ENROLLMENT		
						YEAR	COUNTY	PAGE
1	Burris, Sydney	NAMED	40	M	Full			
2	Carnes, Lewis	Nephew	13	"	1/2			

TRIBAL ENROLLMENT OF PARENTS

	NAME OF FATHER	YEAR	COUNTY	NAME OF MOTHER	YEAR	COUNTY
1	Jim Hamer	Dead	Chickasaw Roll	Stim-ma-hi-ya	Dead	Chickasaw Roll
2	Lewis Carnes	"	Choctaw Roll	Wincey Carnes	"	Chick residing in Choctaw N. 1st Dist.

(NOTES)

No. 1 On Choctaw Census Record *(illegible)* Page 23; transferred to Chickasaw Roll by Dawes Com
No. 2 "   "   "   "   "   " 87   "   "   "   "   "   "   "
No. 1 On Choctaw Roll 1896, Sans Bois Co, No. 685, as Sidney Burris
No. 2 "   "   " 1896   "   "   "   " 2160

Oct. 13/98.

CANCELLED Stamped across card

	RESIDENCE: Choctaw Nation ~~County~~					CARD No.			
	POST OFFICE: Atoka, Ind. Ter.					FIELD No.			

	NAME	RELATION-SHIP TO PERSON FIRST NAMED	AGE	SEX	BLOOD	TRIBAL ENROLLMENT		
						YEAR	COUNTY	PAGE
1	Walton, Powell	NAMED	40	M	Full	1897	Chick residing in Choctaw N. 3rd Dist.	74

TRIBAL ENROLLMENT OF PARENTS

	NAME OF FATHER	YEAR	COUNTY	NAME OF MOTHER	YEAR	COUNTY
1	Ah-wan-tan-tubby	Dead	Chickasaw Roll	*(Name Illegible)*	Dead	Chickasaw Roll

(NOTES)

Oct. 13/98

Chickasaw Enrollment Cards 1898-1914
Chickasaw by Blood   Volume III

RESIDENCE: Choctaw Nation ~~COUNTY~~					CARD NO.		
POST OFFICE: Hartshorne, Ind. Ter.					FIELD NO.		

NAME	RELATION-SHIP TO PERSON FIRST NAMED	AGE	SEX	BLOOD	TRIBAL ENROLLMENT		
					YEAR	COUNTY	PAGE
1 James. Wilson H		52	M	Full	Oct. 29 1896	Chick residing in Choctaw N. 1st Dist.	8
2 " Mary J.	Wife	33	F	I.W.	"	" " " "	8
3 " Jacob	Son	17	M	1/2	"	" " " "	8
4 " Gilbert	"	16	"	1/2	"	" " " "	8
5 " Moses	"	13	"	1/2	"	" " " "	8
6 " Joseph	"	11	"	1/2	"	" " " "	8
7 " Cephus	"	9	"	1/2	"	" " " "	8
8 " Ruthielane	Dau	5	F	1/2	"	" " " "	8
9 " Miriem	"	1	"	1/2			

TRIBAL ENROLLMENT OF PARENTS

	NAME OF FATHER	YEAR	COUNTY	NAME OF MOTHER	YEAR	COUNTY
1	Jim-ma-na-cha	Dead	Chickasaw Roll	Shim-na-ho-mey	Dead	Chickasaw Roll
2	Murray	"	Non Citizen	Martha Murray	"	Non citizen
3	No. 1			No. 2		
4	No. 1			No. 2		
5	No. 1			No. 2		
6	No. 1			No. 2		
7	No. 1			No. 2		
8	No. 1			No. 2		
9	No. 1			No. 2		

(NOTES)

Nos. 1 to 8 admitted by Com. 1896 Case #137 Chickasaw
Nos. 1 to 8 inclusive were denied by United States Court in Ind. Ter. Southern Dist. March 9 1898 Court #52
3/22/99 Born, raised and lived all his life in Choctaw Nation, and married in Choctaw Nation, No license being
   required
No. 2 Marriage license and certificate to be supplied. Certificate received Oct. 31/98. *(No. 2 Dawes' Roll No. 351)*
No. 2 Dec. 9/99; Also on 1897 Roll Page 84
No. 2 Dec. 9/99; See Dawes Com. Record 1896 Case 137
No. 9 Born July 20th 1901. Enrolled July 14th 1892
Nos. 1-3-4-5-6-7 & 8 incl. admitted as citizens by blood of the Chickasaw Nation, *(remainder illegible)*

Oct. 13/98.

95

Chickasaw Enrollment Cards 1898-1914
Chickasaw by Blood   Volume III

RESIDENCE: Choctaw Nation   ~~COUNTY~~   CARD NO.

POST OFFICE: Hartshorne, Ind. Ter.   FIELD NO.

NAME	RELATION-SHIP TO PERSON FIRST NAMED	AGE	SEX	BLOOD	TRIBAL ENROLLMENT		
					YEAR	COUNTY	PAGE
1 James, Wesley	FIRST NAMED	44	M	Full	1897	Chick residing in Choctaw N. 3rd Dist.	73

TRIBAL ENROLLMENT OF PARENTS

	NAME OF FATHER	YEAR	COUNTY	NAME OF MOTHER	YEAR	COUNTY
1	Ston-non-tub-by	Dead	Chickasaw Roll	I-ah-ho-che	Dead	Chickasaw Roll

(NOTES)

Husband of Ellen James, Choctaw Roll Card No. 390.

Oct. 13/98.

RESIDENCE: Pickens   COUNTY   CARD NO.

POST OFFICE: Elmore, Ind. Ter.   FIELD NO.

	NAME	RELATION-SHIP TO PERSON FIRST NAMED	AGE	SEX	BLOOD	TRIBAL ENROLLMENT		
						YEAR	COUNTY	PAGE
1	Raines, Stephen M	NAMED	37	M	I.W.	1897	Pickens	78
2	" Nancy	Dau	9	F	1/2	1897	"	13
3	" ~~Mary~~	"	8	"	~~1/2~~	~~1897~~	"	~~13~~
4	" John	Son	6	M	1/2	1897	"	13
5	" Lillie	Dau	4	F	1/2	1897	"	13
6	" Rosa	"	2	"	1/2	1897	"	22

TRIBAL ENROLLMENT OF PARENTS

	NAME OF FATHER	YEAR	COUNTY	NAME OF MOTHER	YEAR	COUNTY
1	Stephen G. Raines	Dead	Non Citizen	Nancy Raines	Dead	Non citizen
2	No. 1			Siney Raines	"	Pickens
3	~~No. 1~~			" "	"	"
4	No. 1			" "	"	"
5	No. 1			" "	"	"
6	No. 1			" "	"	"

(NOTES)

No. 1 On Chickasaw Roll as Stephen N. Reines   *(No. 1 Dawes' Roll No. 550)*

No. 3 Died Aug. 5, 1899, Proof of Death filed Oct. 28th 1902   *(No. 3 Dawes' Roll No. 257)*

No. 1 formerly husband of Sine (or Siney) Raines 1893 Pay Roll, No. 2, page 191 (as Siney Raines) and who died in 1897.

Oct. 13/98.

96

Chickasaw Enrollment Cards 1898-1914
Chickasaw by Blood   Volume III

RESIDENCE: Panola COUNTY   CARD NO.

POST OFFICE: Mead, Ind. Ter.   FIELD NO.

	NAME	RELATION-SHIP TO PERSON FIRST NAMED	AGE	SEX	BLOOD	TRIBAL ENROLLMENT		
						YEAR	COUNTY	PAGE
1	Jeflow, Joe	NAMED	34	M	Full	1897	Panola	5
2	" Maulsie	Wife	18	F	"			
3	" Rena	Dau	9mo	"	"			
4	" Sallie	"	13	"	"	1897	Panola	5
5	" Jane	"	1mo	"	"			

TRIBAL ENROLLMENT OF PARENTS

	NAME OF FATHER	YEAR	COUNTY	NAME OF MOTHER	YEAR	COUNTY
1	Joseph Jeflow	Dead	Chickasaw Roll	Siley Jeflow	Dead	Panola
2	Stephen Chester	"	" "	Silvey Chester	"	"
3	No. 1			No. 2		
4	No. 1			Serena Jeflow	Dead	Panola
5	No. 1			No. 2		

(NOTES)

No. 2 On Choctaw Census Record No. 2 Blue Co, Page 118. Transferred to Chickasaw Roll by Dawes Com
   On Choctaw Roll as Maulsie Chester
No. 2 On Choctaw Roll 1896 Blue County No. 2899 as Molsey Chester
No. 5 Enrolled June 25th 1900
No. 2 *(illegible)*

                                                              Oct. 13/98.

RESIDENCE: Panola COUNTY   CARD NO.

POST OFFICE: Mead, Ind. Ter.   FIELD NO.

	NAME	RELATION-SHIP TO PERSON FIRST NAMED	AGE	SEX	BLOOD	TRIBAL ENROLLMENT		
						YEAR	COUNTY	PAGE
1	James, Emmerson	NAMED	25	M	Full	1897	Panola	5
2	" Frank	Son	14mo	"	1/2			
3	" Albert Levi	"	1mo	"	1/2			

TRIBAL ENROLLMENT OF PARENTS

	NAME OF FATHER	YEAR	COUNTY	NAME OF MOTHER	YEAR	COUNTY
1	Bob James	Dead	Panola	Phoebe James	Dead	Panola
2	No. 1			Annie James		Non citizen
3	No. 1			" "		" "

(NOTES)

No. 1 is now the Husband of Annie James, a non-citizen. Evidence of marriage filed March 26th 1902
No. 2 Born Jany 25th 1901; Enrolled March 26, 1902

No. 3 Born June 4th 1902; Enrolled July 2nd 1902

Oct. 13/98.

	NAME	RELATION-SHIP TO PERSON FIRST NAMED	AGE	SEX	BLOOD	TRIBAL ENROLLMENT		
						YEAR	COUNTY	PAGE
1	Duckworth, Berry		47	M	I.W.	1897	Panola	76
2	" Lou	Wife	43	F	Full	1897	"	3
3	" Benjamin Allen	Son	20	M	1/2	1897	"	3
4	Massey, Nancy Elizabeth	Dau	17	F	1/2	1897	"	3
5	Duckworth, Maude	"	15	"	1/2	1897	"	3
6	" Claude Gay	Son	13	M	1/2	1897	"	3
7	" Sallie	Dau	11	F	1/2	1897	"	3
8	" Berry A. Jr.	Son	8	M	1/2	1897	"	3
9	" Wiley J	"	6	"	1/2	1897	"	3
10	" Perry Polaski	"	4	"	1/2	1897	"	3
11	Massey, Berry Esther	Gr.Dau	4mo	F	1/4			

TRIBAL ENROLLMENT OF PARENTS

	NAME OF FATHER	YEAR	COUNTY	NAME OF MOTHER	YEAR	COUNTY
1	W.J. Duckworth	Dead	Non Citizen	Nancy E. Duckworth	Dead	Non Citizen
2	Allen Greenwood	"	Panola	Nancy Greenwood	"	Panola
3	No. 1			No. 2		
4	No. 1			No. 2		
5	No. 1			No. 2		
6	No. 1			No. 2		
7	No. 1			No. 2		
8	No. 1			No. 2		
9	No. 1			No. 2		
10	No. 1			No. 2		
11	Guss R. Massey		Non Citizen	No. 4		

(NOTES)

No. 1 On Chickasaw Roll as D.A. Duckworth,
No. 2 "   "   " " Lou   "
No. 3 "   "   " " Ben   "
No. 4 "   "   " " Nannie   "
No. 6 "   "   " " Cloud   "
No. 8 "   "   " " Berry   " , Jr.
No. 9 "   "   " " J.W.   "
No. 10 "   "   " " Perry   "

No. 11 Born April 13, 1902; Enrolled Aug. 13th 1902
No. 1 Died Jan 29th 1902 Proof of Death filed Aug. 12th 1902
No. 4 is now the wife of Guss R. Massey, non citizen. Evidence of marriage requested Aug. 13, 1902.   Oct. 13/98.

RESIDENCE: Panola COUNTY					CARD NO.			
POST OFFICE: Albany, Ind. Ter.					FIELD NO.			
NAME	RELATION-SHIP TO PERSON FIRST NAMED	AGE	SEX	BLOOD	**TRIBAL ENROLLMENT**			
					YEAR	COUNTY	PAGE	
1 McDonald, Albert S.	NAMED	23	M	Full	1897	Panola	1	
2 " Eliza J	Wife	20	F	1/2				
3 " Margaret B.	Dau	9mo	"	1/4				

TRIBAL ENROLLMENT OF PARENTS							
NAME OF FATHER	YEAR	COUNTY	NAME OF MOTHER	YEAR	COUNTY		
1 Joseph McDonald	Dead	Panola	Amy McDonald	Dead	Panola		
2 Nelson Lewis		Blue Co Choctaw Roll	Martha Lewis	1897	Chick residing in Choctaw N. 3rd Dist.		
3 No. 1			No. 2				

(NOTES)

No. 1 On Chickasaw Roll as Albert McDonald
No. 2 On Choctaw Census Record No. 2, Blue Co, Page 340, transferred to Chickasaw Roll by Dawes Com
No. 2 On Choctaw Roll, 1896, Blue County, No. 8217 as Eliza Lewis
No. 3 Affidavit of midwife to be supplied. Received Oct. 21/98.
(Notation illegible)

Oct. 13/98.

RESIDENCE: Panola COUNTY					CARD NO.			
POST OFFICE: Yarnaby, Ind. Ter.					FIELD NO.			
NAME	RELATION-SHIP TO PERSON FIRST NAMED	AGE	SEX	BLOOD	**TRIBAL ENROLLMENT**			
					YEAR	COUNTY	PAGE	
1 Stowers, Mary Elizabeth	NAMED	23	F	1/4	1897	Panola	1	
2 " Mamie E.	Dau	4	"	1/8	1897	"	1	
3 " Thomas Cecil	Son	1	M	1/8				
4 " Mattie Lucile	Dau	1mo	F	1/8				
5 " Lottie Esther	"	2mo	"	1/8				

TRIBAL ENROLLMENT OF PARENTS							
NAME OF FATHER	YEAR	COUNTY	NAME OF MOTHER	YEAR	COUNTY		
1 Tom Barker	1897	Panola	Kittie Barker	Dead	Panola		
2 J.D. Stowers		Non citizen	No. 1				

3	" " "		" "	No. 1		
4	" " "		" "	No. 1		
5	" " "		" "	No. 1		

(NOTES)

Surname on Chickasaw Roll as Stamers.

No. 1 Admitted by Dawes Commission 1896 Chickasaw Card #269   *(No. 1 Dawes' Roll No. 1800)*

Note: Chickasaw Case #269 was appealed to U.S. Court, Southern District.   *(No. 2 Dawes' Roll No. 1801)*

     and on March 7, 1898, Appeal was dismissed.   *(No. 3 Dawes' Roll No. 1802)*

     Correct given name of No. 1 is Mary Elizabeth See letter filed herein May 20, 1901

No. 4 Enrolled March 18/99   *(No. 4 Dawes' Roll No. 1803)*

No. 5 Enrolled May 19, 1901   *(No. 5 Dawes' Roll No. 1804)*

     Oct. 13/98.

RESIDENCE: Choctaw Nation   ~~COUNTY~~   **CARD NO.**

POST OFFICE: Hackshorn, Ind. Ter.   **FIELD NO.**

	NAME	RELATION-SHIP TO PERSON FIRST NAMED	AGE	SEX	BLOOD	TRIBAL ENROLLMENT		
						YEAR	COUNTY	PAGE
1	James, Alen	FIRST NAMED	27	M	1/2	1897	Chick residing in Choctaw N. 1st Dist.	67
2	" Elizabeth	Wife	28	F	1/2			
3	Hancock, Smite	St.Son	1	M	1/4			

TRIBAL ENROLLMENT OF PARENTS

	NAME OF FATHER	YEAR	COUNTY	NAME OF MOTHER	YEAR	COUNTY
1	Joseph James		Tobucksy Co Choctaw Roll	Te-yo James	Dead	Chick residing in Choctaw N. 1st Dist.
2	Williston Ward			Patsey Ward	"	" " " "
3	Israel Hancock		Gaines Co. Choctaw Roll	No. 2		

(NOTES)

No. 2 on Choctaw Census Record No. 2 Gaines Co. Page 394 as Elizabeth Pierson; transferred to Chickasaw Roll
     by Dawes Com.

No. 2 On Choctaw Roll 1896 Gaines Co, No. 11203 as Elizabeth Pierson

No. 3 on Colored Card Oct. 31/98.

     Oct. 13/98.

RESIDENCE: Pontotoc   *COUNTY*   *CARD NO.*

POST OFFICE: Stonewall, Ind. Ter.   *FIELD NO.*

	NAME	RELATION-SHIP TO PERSON FIRST NAMED	AGE	SEX	BLOOD	TRIBAL ENROLLMENT		
						YEAR	COUNTY	PAGE
1	Carrell, Mary		32	F	1/2	1897	Pontotoc	42
2	Smith, Zona	Dau	15	"	1/4	1897	"	42
3	" Myrtle	"	13	"	1/4	1897	"	42
4	Middleton, Bessie	"	10	"	1/4	1897	"	42
5	" Nora	"	8	"	1/4	1897	"	42
6	Carrell, Richard	Son	4	M	1/4	1897	"	42
7	" Alice	Dau	15mo	F	1/4			
8	Abbott, Allee May	Gr.Dau	2	F				
9	Abbott, Barnabas	" Son	8mo	M				
10	Carrell, Stella	Dau	2	F	1/4			
11	Carrell, Joe	Son	3mo	M	1/4			
12	Hurley, Bertha	Gr.Dau	3mo	F				

TRIBAL ENROLLMENT OF PARENTS

	NAME OF FATHER	YEAR	COUNTY	NAME OF MOTHER	YEAR	COUNTY
1	*(Illegible)* Maytubby	Dead		Nannie Maytubby		
2	Charley Smith	"	Non citizen	No. 1		
3	" "	"	" "	No. 1		
4	*(Illegible)* Middleton			No. 1		
5	" "			No. 1		
6	*(Illegible)* Carrell			No. 1		
7	" "			No. 1		
8	Jordan Abbott			No. 2		
9	Jordan Abbott			No. 2		
10	*(Illegible)* Carrell			No. 1		
11	" "			No. 1		
12	John Hurley			No. ?		

(NOTES)

No. 1 on Chickasaw roll as M.A. Carrel

No. 2 is now the wife of Jordan Abbott. Evidence of marriage to be supplied.

No. 3 is now the wife of John Hurley, non-citizen.

No. 8 born Aug. 16, 1900; enrolled Nov. 18, 1902   *(No. 8 Dawes' Roll No. 4199)*

No. 9 born Mch 2, 1902; enrolled Nov. 18, 1902   *(No. 9 Dawes' Roll No. 4200)*

No. 10 born Feb. 16, 1900; enrolled Nov. 18, 1902   *(No. 10 Dawes' Roll No. 4201)*

No. 11 born July 28, 1902; enrolled Nov. 18, 1902   *(No. 11 Dawes' Roll No. 4202)*

No. 12 born Sept. 4, 1902; enrolled Dec. 24, 1902   *(No. 12 Dawes' Roll No. 4756)*

Oct. 13/98.

Chickasaw Enrollment Cards 1898-1914
Chickasaw by Blood   Volume III

RESIDENCE: Panola COUNTY   CARD NO.
POST OFFICE: Silo, Ind. Ter.   FIELD NO.

NAME	RELATION-SHIP TO PERSON FIRST NAMED	AGE	SEX	BLOOD	TRIBAL ENROLLMENT		
					YEAR	COUNTY	PAGE
1 Allen, Birdie	FIRST NAMED	23	F	1/8	1897	Chick residing in Choctaw N. 3rd Dist.	72
2 " Hattie	Dau	4mo	"	1/16			

TRIBAL ENROLLMENT OF PARENTS

NAME OF FATHER	YEAR	COUNTY	NAME OF MOTHER	YEAR	COUNTY
1 Hugh M. Cooper		Non citizen	Hattie Cooper	Dead	
2 (Illegible) Allen		" "	(Illegible) Allen		

(NOTES)

On Chickasaw Roll as Gordie Cooper

Oct. 13/98.

RESIDENCE: Panola COUNTY   CARD NO.
POST OFFICE: Colbert, Ind. Ter.   FIELD NO.

NAME	RELATION-SHIP TO PERSON FIRST NAMED	AGE	SEX	BLOOD	TRIBAL ENROLLMENT		
					YEAR	COUNTY	PAGE
1 Potts, John Taylor	NAMED	50	M	1/8	1897	Panola	2
2 " Goldey Abner	Son	15	"	1/16	1897	"	2
3 " John Taylor, Jr.	"	8	"	1/16	1897	"	2
4 " Allie May	Dau	6	F	1/16	1897	"	2
5 " Mary Myrtle	"	3	"	1/16	1897	"	2
6 " Benjamin Alexander	Son	1	M	1/16	~~1897~~	~~"~~	~~2~~
7 " Annie Eliza	Dau	7wks	F	1/16			

TRIBAL ENROLLMENT OF PARENTS

NAME OF FATHER	YEAR	COUNTY	NAME OF MOTHER	YEAR	COUNTY
1 Joe B. Potts	Dead	Non Citizen	Rhoda Potts	Dead	Panola
2 No. 1			Mollie Potts		Non Citizen
3 No. 1			" "		" "
4 No. 1			" "		" "
5 No. 1			" "		" "
6 No. 1			" "		" "
7 No. 1			Mary M. Potts		" "

(NOTES)

No. 1 On Chickasaw Roll as J.T. Potts.
No. 2 "   "   "   " G.A.   "

102

No. 3 "   "   "   " J.T.   " , Jr.
No. 4 "   "   "   " A.M.   "
No. 5 "   "   "   " W.M.   "
No. 6 "   "   "   " Benj. Alex "   *(No. 6 Dawes' Roll No. 4498)*
No. 6 Proof of Birth received and filed Sept. 25th 1902.
No. 7 Enrolled March 29th 1902.

    See letter of John Taylor Potts with reference to mother's name. March 29, 1901.

Oct. 13/98.

RESIDENCE: Choctaw Nation   ~~COUNTY~~   **CARD NO.**

POST OFFICE: Utica, Ind. Ter.   **FIELD NO.**

	NAME	RELATION-SHIP TO PERSON FIRST NAMED	AGE	SEX	BLOOD	TRIBAL ENROLLMENT		
						YEAR	COUNTY	PAGE
1	Pruitt, Willis	FIRST NAMED	38	M	I.W.	1897	Chick residing in Choctaw N. 3rd Dist.	82
2	" Alice	Wife	32	F	1/16	1897	" " " "	75
3	" James Thomas	Son	4	M	1/32	1897	" " " "	75
4	" Cecil Roy	"	2	"	1/32	1897	" " " "	75

TRIBAL ENROLLMENT OF PARENTS

	NAME OF FATHER	YEAR	COUNTY	NAME OF MOTHER	YEAR	COUNTY
1	Charley Pruitt	Dead	Non Citizen	Elizabeth Pruitt	Dead	Non Citizen
2	Jas H. Willis	"	Chickasaw Roll	Catherine Willis	"	Panola
3	No. 1			No. 2		
4	No. 1			No. 2		

(NOTES)

Nos. 3 & 4 On Chickasaw Roll as "Two Children"

Oct. 13/98.

RESIDENCE: Choctaw Nation   ~~COUNTY~~   **CARD NO.**

POST OFFICE: Hartshorne, Ind. Ter.   **FIELD NO.**

	NAME	RELATION-SHIP TO PERSON FIRST NAMED	AGE	SEX	BLOOD	TRIBAL ENROLLMENT		
						YEAR	COUNTY	PAGE
1	Pickens, Gincy	FIRST NAMED	20	F	Full	1897	Chick residing in Choctaw N. 1st Dist.	71
2	" Sampson	Son	11/2	M	1/2			
3	" Frances	Dau	6mo	F	1/2			
4	" Isaiah	Son	2	M	1/2			
5	" Eunice	Dau	10mo	F	1/2			

103

Chickasaw Enrollment Cards 1898-1914
Chickasaw by Blood   Volume III

TRIBAL ENROLLMENT OF PARENTS

	NAME OF FATHER	YEAR	COUNTY	NAME OF MOTHER	YEAR	COUNTY
1	Allen Colbert	Dead	Chickasaw Roll	Louiney Colbert	Dead	Chick residing in Choctaw N. 3rd Dist.
2	Isham Pickens		Gaines Co. Choctaw Roll	No. 1		
3	" "		" "	No. 1		
4	" "		" "	No. 1		
5	" "		" "	No. 1		

(NOTES)

No. 1 wife of Isom Pickens, Choctaw Roll Card No. ?
No. 3 Enrolled April 27/99
No. 4 Born Decr 17, 1899, Enrolled Nov. ?, 1901
No. 5 " Feby 21, 1902, application made Dec. 24, 1902.   *(No. 5 Dawes' Roll No. 4426)*
No. 5 Additional Proof of birth filed Feby. *(illegible)*

P.O. Blanco, I.T.   Oct. 13/98.

RESIDENCE: Choctaw Nation   ~~COUNTY~~   CARD NO.
POST OFFICE: Coalgate, Ind. Ter.   FIELD NO.

	NAME	RELATION-SHIP TO PERSON FIRST NAMED	AGE	SEX	BLOOD	TRIBAL ENROLLMENT		
						YEAR	COUNTY	PAGE
1	Harrison, Benj. F.		23	M	1/4			
2	" Joseph Colbert	Bro	22	"	1/4			
3	" Charles Colbert	"	22	"	1/4			

TRIBAL ENROLLMENT OF PARENTS

	NAME OF FATHER	YEAR	COUNTY	NAME OF MOTHER	YEAR	COUNTY
1	Hilton Harrison		*(Illegible)*Co. Choctaw Roll	Sarah Harrison	Dead	Chick residing in Choctaw N. 3rd Dist.
2	" "		" "	" "	"	" " "
3	" "		" "	" "	"	" " "

(NOTES)

All on Choctaw Census Record No. 2, Tobucksy County, Page 228, transferred to Chickasaw Roll by Dawes Com.
No. 2 On Choctaw Roll as Joseph C. Harrison
No. 3 "   "   " " Charlie C. "
No. 1 On Chickasaw Roll 1896 Tobucksey County, No. 5360, as Ben F. Harrison
No. 2 "   "   " 1896 "   "   " 5361 " Joseph C. "
No. 3 "   "   " 1896 "   "   " 5362 " Charles C. "
No. 3 Also "   "   " 1896 Atoka   "   " 6041 " Charley   "

                                                        Oct. 13/98.

CANCELLED Stamped across card

Chickasaw Enrollment Cards 1898-1914
Chickasaw by Blood   Volume III

RESIDENCE: Choctaw Nation   COUNTY   CARD NO.

POST OFFICE: Bennington, Ind. Ter.   FIELD NO.

	NAME	RELATION-SHIP TO PERSON FIRST NAMED	AGE	SEX	BLOOD	TRIBAL ENROLLMENT		
						YEAR	COUNTY	PAGE
1	Lloyd, John M.		28	M	I.W.			
2	" Ida	Wife	24	F	1/4			
3	" Annetta	Dau	3	"	1/8			
4	" Charley	Son	2	M	1/8			
5	" Willaim Gregg	"	3mo	"	1/8			
6	" Russell	"	12da	F	1/8			

TRIBAL ENROLLMENT OF PARENTS

	NAME OF FATHER	YEAR	COUNTY	NAME OF MOTHER	YEAR	COUNTY
1	D.J.D. Lloyd		non-citizen	Mattie Lloyd		non-citizen
2	Dave Wall	Dead	Choctaw Roll	Manerva Wall	Dead	Chick residing in Choctaw N. 3rd Dist.
3	No. 1			No. 2		
4	No. 1			No. 2		
5	No. 1			No. 2		
6	No. 1			No. 2		

(NOTES)

No. 1   On Choctaw Intermarried Roll, Page 64, transferred to Chickasaw Roll by Dawes Com

No. 2, 3, & 4 "   "   Census Record, No. 2 " 338   "   "   "   " "   "   "

No. 1 On Chickasaw Roll 1896 Jackson County, No. 14772 as John Lloyd

No. 2 "   "   " 1896   "   "   " 8168

No. 3 "   "   " 1896   "   "   " 8169 as Annetta Lloyd

No. 4 "   "   " 1896   "   "   " 8170 " Charlie Lloyd

No. 6 Enrolled Feb. 13th 1901

Oct. 13/98.

CANCELLED Stamped across card

RESIDENCE: Choctaw Nation   COUNTY   CARD NO.

POST OFFICE: Stigler, Ind. Ter.   FIELD NO.

	NAME	RELATION-SHIP TO PERSON FIRST NAMED	AGE	SEX	BLOOD	TRIBAL ENROLLMENT		
						YEAR	COUNTY	PAGE
1	Palmer, Myrtle		12	F	1/4			
2	" Benjamin Cleveland	Bro	9	M	1/4			

Chickasaw Enrollment Cards 1898-1914
Chickasaw by Blood   Volume III

		TRIBAL ENROLLMENT OF PARENTS				
NAME OF FATHER	YEAR	COUNTY	NAME OF MOTHER	YEAR	COUNTY
1 Benj. F. Palmer		white man	Adaline Palmer	Dead	Chick residing in Choctaw N. 1st Dist.
2 " " "		" "	" "	"	" " " "

(NOTES)

Both on Choctaw Census Roll (Sans Bois Co) No. 2 Page 390 transferred Chickasaw Roll by Dawes Com.

No. 2 On Choctaw Roll as Benjamin Palmer

No. 1 On Choctaw Roll 1896, Sans Bois Co, No. 10050

No. 2 "   "   " 1896 "   "   " No. 10051 as Benjamin Palmer

Benjamin F. Palmer father of Nos. 1 & 2 on Chickasaw D.165

Oct. 13/98.

CANCELLED Stamped across card

RESIDENCE: Choctaw Nation   **COUNTY**   **CARD NO.**

POST OFFICE: Kiowa, Ind. Ter.   **FIELD NO.**

	NAME	RELATION-SHIP TO PERSON FIRST NAMED	AGE	SEX	BLOOD	TRIBAL ENROLLMENT		
						YEAR	COUNTY	PAGE
1	~~Hargis, Sallie J.~~		25	F	I.W.	1897	~~Chick residing in Choctaw N. 1st Dist.~~	82
2	Johnson, George A.	Son	7	M	1/4	1897	" " " "	77
3	" Sallie Elizabeth	Dau	4	F	1/4	1897	" " " "	77
4	" Iney	"	2	"	1/4	1897	" " " "	77
5	" Louisa	"	10mo	"	1/4			

		TRIBAL ENROLLMENT OF PARENTS				
NAME OF FATHER	YEAR	COUNTY	NAME OF MOTHER	YEAR	COUNTY
1 ~~Bud Wilson~~	~~Dead~~	~~Non-citizen~~	~~Katie Wilson~~		~~Non-citizen~~
2 Geo. M. Johnson		Chick residing in Choctaw N. 1st Dist.	No. 1		
3 " " "		" " " "	No. 1		
4 " " "		" " " "	No. 1		
5 " " "		" " " "	No. 1		

(NOTES)

For child of No. 1 see N B. (Apr. 26-06) Card # *(illegible)*

(Notation illegible)

No. 1 marriage papers on file in office of Dawes Com, Muskogee

No. 1 Denied by Dawes Commission in 1896, Chickasaw Case # *(illegible)* No appeal

No. 1 is now wife of Douglas Hargis a non-citizen June 16th 1902

No. 2 on Chickasaw Roll as George A Johnson

No. 3 "   "   " " Sallie   "

No. 4 "   "   " " Inecy   "

106

Chickasaw Enrollment Cards 1898-1914
Chickasaw by Blood   Volume III

No. 5 Affidavit of mother to be supplied

No. 5 Evidence of Birth received June 16, 1902; returned for correction *(remainder illegible)*

No. 1 was formerly wife of George W. Johnson, 1896, Chickasaw Census Roll Choctaw District now deceased.

Oct. 13/98.

CANCELLED Stamped across card

RESIDENCE: Panola   **COUNTY**   **CARD NO.**

POST OFFICE: Utica, Ind. Ter.   **FIELD NO.**

NAME	RELATION-SHIP TO PERSON FIRST NAMED	AGE	SEX	BLOOD	TRIBAL ENROLLMENT		
					YEAR	COUNTY	PAGE
1 Jones, Wesley	NAMED	39	M	1/2	1897	Panola	73
2 Houston, Frank	Bro	22	"	1/2	1897	"	73

TRIBAL ENROLLMENT OF PARENTS

	NAME OF FATHER	YEAR	COUNTY	NAME OF MOTHER	YEAR	COUNTY
1	Shum-pah-la-by	Dead	Choctaw Roll	*(Name Illegible)*	Dead	Chickasaw Roll
2	"	"	" "	"	"	" "

(NOTES)

No. 1 is now the husband of Ellen *(Illegible)*, Choctaw Card #289, May 19, 1904.

Oct. 13/98.

RESIDENCE: Choctaw Nation   **COUNTY**   **CARD NO.**

POST OFFICE: Hartshorn, Ind. Ter.   **FIELD NO.**

NAME	RELATION-SHIP TO PERSON FIRST NAMED	AGE	SEX	BLOOD	TRIBAL ENROLLMENT		
					YEAR	COUNTY	PAGE
1 Pulcher, Sarah	NAMED	40	F	Full			
2 " Belle	Dau	10	"	1/2			
3 " Alice	"	9	"	1/2			
4 " Osborn	Son	1	M	1/2			

TRIBAL ENROLLMENT OF PARENTS

	NAME OF FATHER	YEAR	COUNTY	NAME OF MOTHER	YEAR	COUNTY
1	George Johnson	Dead	Chickasaw Roll	Lucy Johnson	Dead	Chickasaw Roll
2	John Pulcher		Gaines Co Choctaw Roll	No. 1		
3	" "		" "	No. 1		
4	" "		" "	No. 1		

(NOTES)

All except No. 4 on Choctaw Census Record, Gaines Co, Page 394, transferred to Chickasaw Roll by Dawes Com.

No. 1 On Choctaw Roll 1896 Gaines County, No. 10213

107

Chickasaw Enrollment Cards 1898-1914
Chickasaw by Blood   Volume III

No. 2 "   "   "   1896   "   "   "   10214
No. 3 "   "   "   1896   "   "   "   10215

Oct. 12/98.

CANCELLED Stamped across card

RESIDENCE: Pontotoc   COUNTY   CARD NO.
POST OFFICE: (Illegible) , Ind. Ter.   FIELD NO.

NAME	RELATION-SHIP TO PERSON FIRST NAMED	AGE	SEX	BLOOD	TRIBAL ENROLLMENT		
					YEAR	COUNTY	PAGE
1 Wright, Sam B.	NAMED	26	M	1/16	1897	(Illegible)	56
2 " Ora R.	Son	3	"	1/32	1897	"	56
3 " Menge P.	"	2	"	1/32	1897	"	56
4 " Gertrude	Dau	1	F	1/32			
5 " Nettie	Wife	23	F	I.W.			

TRIBAL ENROLLMENT OF PARENTS

	NAME OF FATHER	YEAR	COUNTY	NAME OF MOTHER	YEAR	COUNTY
1	Jack Wright		(Illegible) Co. Choctaw Roll	Delilah Wright	1897	Pontotoc
2	No. 1			Nettie Wright		white woman
3	No. 1			" "		" "
4	No. 1			" "		" "
5	Butch Nash		Non Citz	Josie Nash		Non Citz

(NOTES)

No. 1 Also on 1896 Choctaw Roll, Page 369, No. 14101, S.O. Wright, Jacks Fork Co   (No. 1 Dawes' Roll No. 691)
No. 1 is Husband of Nettie Wright, on Chickasaw Card #D.164.   (No. 2 Dawes' Roll No. 4196)
   Certificate of marriage between parents of children (illegible)   (No. 3 Dawes' Roll No. 4197)
No. 3 On Chickasaw Roll as Monz Wright   (No. 4 Dawes' Roll No. 692)
No. 4 Born Feb. 22, 1901; Enrolled May 23, 1902   (No. 5 Dawes' Roll No. 475)
No. 5 Did No. 5 apply for citizenship in 1896? See original petition of Sam Wright filed with original papers in
   Choctaw Court case #42, U.S. Court. Central District, Stephe Krebbs
    No. 5 transferred from Chick Card #D.164. See Decision of Sept. 8, 1904

P.O. Byrne, I.T.   Oct. 12, 1898.

RESIDENCE:	Choctaw Nation	COUNTY				CARD NO.		
POST OFFICE:	Krebs, Ind. Ter.					FIELD NO.		

	NAME	RELATION-SHIP TO PERSON FIRST NAMED	AGE	SEX	BLOOD	TRIBAL ENROLLMENT		
						YEAR	COUNTY	PAGE
1	Pope, Frank	NAMED	26	M	1/2	1897	Chick residing in Choctaw N. 1st Dist.	68
2	James, Lewis	Nephew	6	"	1/4			

TRIBAL ENROLLMENT OF PARENTS

	NAME OF FATHER	YEAR	COUNTY	NAME OF MOTHER	YEAR	COUNTY
1	Sampson Pope	Dead	Choctaw Roll	Liney Pope	Dead	Chickasaw Roll
2	(Illegible) James	"	Chick residing in Choctaw N. 1st Dist.	(Illegible) James	"	Chick residing in Choctaw N. 1st Dist.

(NOTES)

No. 1 Husband of Nancy Pope, Choctaw Roll Card #382
No. 2 On Choctaw Census Record No. 2?, Skullyville Co, (remainder illegible)
No. 2 On Chickasaw Roll 1896 Skullyville, Co. No. 6473, in (remainder illegible)
No. 2 transferred to Chickasaw Roll (illegible)

Oct. 12/98.

RESIDENCE:	Choctaw Nation	COUNTY				CARD NO.		
POST OFFICE:	Waupannuka, Ind. Ter.					FIELD NO.		

	NAME	RELATION-SHIP TO PERSON FIRST NAMED	AGE	SEX	BLOOD	TRIBAL ENROLLMENT		
						YEAR	COUNTY	PAGE
1	Ray, Henry (Illegible)	NAMED	27	M	I.W.	1897	Pontotoc	74
2	" Mollie	Wife	22	F	1/8	1897	"	56
3	" Vivian	Dau	16mo	"	1/16			
4	" Opal	"	1wk	"	1/16			
5	" Robert L.	Soon	6wk	M	1/16			

TRIBAL ENROLLMENT OF PARENTS

	NAME OF FATHER	YEAR	COUNTY	NAME OF MOTHER	YEAR	COUNTY
1	John H. Ray	Dead	Non Citizen	Mary Ray	Dead	Non citizen
2	Edmon Parker	"	Chickasaw Roll	Susan Parker	"	Chickasaw Roll
3	No. 1			No. 2		
4	No. 1			No. 2		
5	No. 1			No. 2		

(NOTES)

No. 1 Admitted by Dawes Com, Case No. 125, No Appeal   (No. 1 Dawes' Roll No. 602)
No. 1 On 1897 Roll as H.L. Ray
Nos. 3 & 4 transferred from white card Oct. 19/98.

No. 5 Enrolled July 31, 1901.

P.O. Byrne, I.T. 2/26/03.   Oct, 14/98.

NAME	RELATION-SHIP TO PERSON FIRST NAMED	AGE	SEX	BLOOD	TRIBAL ENROLLMENT		
RESIDENCE: Choctaw Nation COUNTY					CARD NO.		
POST OFFICE: Tallihaney, Ind. Ter.					FIELD NO.		
					YEAR	COUNTY	PAGE
1 Welch, William A.	NAMED	62	M	I.W.			
2 " Bessie	Dau	20	F	1/8	1897	Chick residing in Choctaw N. 3rd Dist.	72

TRIBAL ENROLLMENT OF PARENTS							
NAME OF FATHER	YEAR	COUNTY	NAME OF MOTHER		YEAR	COUNTY	
1 (Name Illegible)	Dead	Non Citizen	Catherine Welch		Dead	Non Citizen	
2 No. 1			Alice Welch		"	Chick residing in Choctaw N. 3rd Dist.	

(NOTES)

(Three entries illegible)   (No. 1 Dawes' Roll No. 240)
No. 1 is husband of Beatrice R. Welch, Choctaw Card #2176.

P.O. Wister, I.T. 1/7/03
P.O. of No. 2 Davis, I.T. 11/19-03   Oct. 12/98.

NAME	RELATION-SHIP TO PERSON FIRST NAMED	AGE	SEX	BLOOD	TRIBAL ENROLLMENT		
RESIDENCE: Panola COUNTY					CARD NO.		
POST OFFICE: Utica, Ind. Ter.					FIELD NO.		
					YEAR	COUNTY	PAGE
1 Imatobby, Calvin	NAMED	42	M	Full	1897	Panola	3
2 " Susie	Wife	42	F	"	1897	"	3
3 " Hannah	Dau	7	"	"	1897	"	3
4 " Lonnie	"	3	"	"	1897	"	3

TRIBAL ENROLLMENT OF PARENTS							
NAME OF FATHER	YEAR	COUNTY	NAME OF MOTHER		YEAR	COUNTY	
1 Imatobby	Dead	Chickasaw Roll	Whe-ah-na-cha		Dead	Chickasaw Roll	
2 Shum-pah-la	"	Choctaw Roll	Hah-lin-ney		"	" "	
3 No. 1			No. 2				
4 No. 1			No. 2				

(NOTES)

Surname of all on Chickasaw Roll is Colbert

No. 1 On Chickasaw Roll as Calvin Colbert   *(No. 1 Dawes' Roll No. 687)*

No. 3 " " " " Mary "   *(No. 2 Dawes' Roll No. 688)*

No. 1 On 1896 Choctaw Roll, Page 68, #2890, as Calvin Colbert   *(No. 3 Dawes' Roll No. 689)*

No. 2 " 1896 " " " " #2891 " Susan "   *(No. 4 Dawes' Roll No. 690)*

No. 3 " 1896 " " " " #1892 " Hannah "

No. 4 " 1896 " " " " #2893 " Lonnie "

Oct. 12/98.

RESIDENCE: Panola   **COUNTY**   **CARD NO.**

POST OFFICE: Utica, Ind. Ter.   **FIELD NO.**

NAME	RELATION-SHIP TO PERSON FIRST NAMED	AGE	SEX	BLOOD	TRIBAL ENROLLMENT		
					YEAR	COUNTY	PAGE
1 Alberson, John	NAMED	70	M	Full	1897	Panola	3

TRIBAL ENROLLMENT OF PARENTS

	NAME OF FATHER	YEAR	COUNTY	NAME OF MOTHER	YEAR	COUNTY
1	Ta-ko-wah-hi	Dead	Chickasaw Roll	Sho-ke-key	Dead	Chickasaw Roll

(NOTES)

Oct. 12/98.

RESIDENCE: Choctaw Nation   **COUNTY**   **CARD NO.**

POST OFFICE: Boggy Depot, Ind. Ter.   **FIELD NO.**

NAME	RELATION-SHIP TO PERSON FIRST NAMED	AGE	SEX	BLOOD	TRIBAL ENROLLMENT		
					YEAR	COUNTY	PAGE
1 Culberson, James	NAMED	26	M	Full	1896	Pontotoc	51

TRIBAL ENROLLMENT OF PARENTS

	NAME OF FATHER	YEAR	COUNTY	NAME OF MOTHER	YEAR	COUNTY
1	Culberson	Dead	Chickasaw Roll	Lorinia Billos		Chick residing in Choctaw N. 3rd Dist.

(NOTES)

Husband of Eliza Culberson, Choctaw Roll Card #381.

On Chickasaw Roll as James Colbert

Also " " " " J.C. " Page 93, Pontotoc Co.

Oct. 12/98.

RESIDENCE: Choctaw Nation   **COUNTY**   **CARD NO.**

POST OFFICE: Featherston, Ind. Ter.   **FIELD NO.**

	NAME	RELATION-SHIP TO PERSON FIRST	AGE	SEX	BLOOD	TRIBAL ENROLLMENT		
						YEAR	COUNTY	PAGE
1	Colbert, Lily	NAMED	28	F	Full			
2	Choate, Jimmie	Son	12	M	1/2			
3	" Mary	Dau	9	F	1/2			
4	Colbert, Willie	Son	6	M	Full			

TRIBAL ENROLLMENT OF PARENTS

	NAME OF FATHER	YEAR	COUNTY	NAME OF MOTHER	YEAR	COUNTY
1	Charles Wright	Dead	Chickasaw Roll	Tom-mah-ho-ye	Dead	Chickasaw Roll
2	Albert Choate	"	Choctaw Roll	No. 1		
3	" "	"	" "	No. 1		
4	Elias Colbert	"	Chick residing in Choctaw N. 1st Dist.	No. 1		

(NOTES)

All on Choctaw Census Record, Sans Bois Co, Page 25, Transferred to Chickasaw Roll by Dawes Com
No. 1 On Choctaw Roll; 1896, Sans Bois Co., No. 2104
No. 2 "   "   " 1896 "   "   "   " 2105
No. 3 "   "   " 1896 "   "   "   " 2106
No. 4 "   "   " 1896 "   "   "   " 2107

Oct. 12/98.

CANCELLED Stamped across card

RESIDENCE: Choctaw Nation   **COUNTY**   **CARD NO.**

POST OFFICE: Featherston, Ind. Ter.   **FIELD NO.**

	NAME	RELATION-SHIP TO PERSON FIRST	AGE	SEX	BLOOD	TRIBAL ENROLLMENT		
						YEAR	COUNTY	PAG
1	Byington, Nancy	NAMED	23	F	Full			
2	Lewis, Emily	Dau	2	"	"			
3	Riddle, Luanda	"	3m	"	"			

TRIBAL ENROLLMENT OF PARENTS

	NAME OF FATHER	YEAR	COUNTY	NAME OF MOTHER	YEAR	COUNTY
1	Wallace Byington	Dead	Chickasaw Roll	Phoebe Byington	Dead	Chickasaw Roll
2	Tom Lewis	1897	Chick residing in Choctawe N. 1st Dist.	No. 1		
3	Coleman Riddle			No. 1		Illegitimate

(NOTES)

Both on Choctaw Census Record No. 2, Sans Bois Co. transferred to Chickasaw Roll by Dawes Com.

No. 1 On Choctaw Roll as Nancy Lewis

No. 1 On   "   " 1896 Sans Bois Co, No. 7696 as Nancy Lewis

No. 2 "   "   "   "   "   '"   "   " 7697

9/6/99

Oct. 12/98.

CANCELLED Stamped across card

NAME	RELATION-SHIP TO PERSON FIRST NAMED	AGE	SEX	BLOOD	TRIBAL ENROLLMENT		
					YEAR	COUNTY	PAGE
1 Moore, Joseph	NAMED	34	M	Full			

RESIDENCE: Choctaw Nation ~~COUNTY~~   **CARD NO.**

POST OFFICE: Featherston, Ind. Ter.   **FIELD NO.**

TRIBAL ENROLLMENT OF PARENTS

NAME OF FATHER	YEAR	COUNTY	NAME OF MOTHER	YEAR	COUNTY
1 No-ubby Moore	Dead	Chickasaw Roll	Emeline Moore	Dead	Chickasaw Roll

(NOTES)

Husband of Mary Moore, Choctaw Roll Card No. 380

On Choctaw Census Record No. 2 Sans Bois Co, Page 345, transferred to Chickasaw Roll by Dawes Com

On Choctaw Roll 1896 Sans Bois Co, No. 8417

Oct. 12/98.

CANCELLED Stamped across card

RESIDENCE: Panola **COUNTY**   **CARD NO.**

POST OFFICE: Colbert, Ind. Ter.   **FIELD NO.**

NAME	RELATION-SHIP TO PERSON FIRST NAMED	AGE	SEX	BLOOD	TRIBAL ENROLLMENT		
					YEAR	COUNTY	PAGE
1 Eastman, Lorena	NAMED	8	F	3/8	1897	Panola	2

TRIBAL ENROLLMENT OF PARENTS

NAME OF FATHER	YEAR	COUNTY	NAME OF MOTHER	YEAR	COUNTY
1 Charles E. Eastman	Dead	Panola	Retta Hollingsworth		White woman

(NOTES)

On Chickasaw Roll as Larena Eastman

No. 1 is daughter of Retta Hollingsworth on Chickasaw Card #D.162

Oct. 12/98.

Chickasaw Enrollment Cards 1898-1914
Chickasaw by Blood   Volume III

RESIDENCE: Choctaw Nation   ~~COUNTY~~   CARD NO.

POST OFFICE: Kosoma, Ind. Ter.   FIELD NO.

NAME	RELATION-SHIP TO PERSON FIRST	AGE	SEX	BLOOD	TRIBAL ENROLLMENT		
					YEAR	COUNTY	PAGE
1 Cheadle, Ben F.	NAMED	28	M	1/8	1897	Tishomingo	92
2 " Annie	Wife	26	F	I.W.			
3 " Lillian Hortense	Dau	8mo	"	1/16			
4 " Cara E.	"	4mo	"	1/16			

TRIBAL ENROLLMENT OF PARENTS

NAME OF FATHER	YEAR	COUNTY	NAME OF MOTHER	YEAR	COUNTY
1 Thomas Cheadle	Dead	Tishomingo	Margaret Cheadle		Non-Citizen
2 Jesse Boyd	"	Non-citizen	Elizabeth Brown		"
3 No. 1			No. 2		
4 No. 1			No. 2		

(NOTES)

No. 1 On Chickasaw Roll as B.F. Cheadle
No. 1 On 1893 Chickasaw Pay Roll No. 1 Page 112 as B.F. Cheadle
No. 1 Died July 8th 1900; Evidence of Death filed April 11th 1901
No. 4 Enrolled April 18th 1901
No. 4 Died Jany 17, 1902; Proof of Death filed Oct. 23, 1902

P.O. De Queen, Ark. 2/26/03   Oct. 12/98.

RESIDENCE: Panola   COUNTY   CARD NO.

POST OFFICE: Albany, Ind. Ter.   FIELD NO.

NAME	RELATION-SHIP TO PERSON FIRST	AGE	SEX	BLOOD	TRIBAL ENROLLMENT		
					YEAR	COUNTY	PAGE
1 Hampton, Mary	NAMED	20	F	Full	1897	Panola	1
2 " Alice I.	Dau	5mo	"	1/2			
3 " Lethe J.	"	2mo	"	1/2			

TRIBAL ENROLLMENT OF PARENTS

NAME OF FATHER	YEAR	COUNTY	NAME OF MOTHER	YEAR	COUNTY
1 Sloan Hawkins	Dead	Panola	Sallie Corley	1897	Panola
2 (Name Illegible)			No. 1		
3 Jesse W. Hampton		Non-Citizen	No. 1		

(NOTES)

On Chickasaw Roll as Mary Hawkins

114

Chickasaw Enrollment Cards 1898-1914
Chickasaw by Blood   Volume III

No. 2 Enrolled April 29/99
No. 3 Born Nov. 19, 1901; Enrolled Jany 16, 1902

Oct. 12/98.

	NAME	RELATION-SHIP TO PERSON FIRST NAMED	AGE	SEX	BLOOD	TRIBAL ENROLLMENT		
						YEAR	COUNTY	PAGE
1	Corley, Charley	NAMED	37	M	Full	1897	Panola	1
2	" Sallie	Wife	47	F	"	1897	"	1

RESIDENCE: Panola COUNTY   CARD NO.
POST OFFICE: Albany, Ind. Ter.   FIELD NO.

TRIBAL ENROLLMENT OF PARENTS

	NAME OF FATHER	YEAR	COUNTY	NAME OF MOTHER	YEAR	COUNTY
1	San Corley	Dead	Panola	Harriet Corley	Dead	Panola
2	Jim Factor	"	"	Nancy Factor	"	"

(NOTES)

No. 1 On Chickasaw Roll as Charley Colbey
No. 2 "   "   " " Sallie   "

Oct. 12/98.

RESIDENCE: Panola COUNTY   CARD NO.
POST OFFICE: Colbert, Ind. Ter.   FIELD NO.

	NAME	RELATION-SHIP TO PERSON FIRST NAMED	AGE	SEX	BLOOD	TRIBAL ENROLLMENT		
						YEAR	COUNTY	PAGE
1	Hampton, Bessie	NAMED	24	F	1/2	1897	Panola	5
2	" Lela	Dau	4	F	1/4	1897	"	5
3	" Hollis	Son	2	M	1/4	1897	"	5
4	" Retta Lenora	Dau	2mo	F	1/4			
5	" Theta	"	5mo	"	1/4	DIED PRIOR TO SEPTEMBER 25, 1902		
6	" Herbert R.	Son	6mo	M	1/4			

TRIBAL ENROLLMENT OF PARENTS

	NAME OF FATHER	YEAR	COUNTY	NAME OF MOTHER	YEAR	COUNTY
1	J.J. Cravens (I.W.)	1897	Panola	Mary Cravebs	1897	Panola
2	A.L. Hampton		Non-Citizen	No. 1		
3	" " "		" "	No. 1		
4	" " "		" "	No. 1		
5	" " "		" "	No. 1		
6	" " "		" "	No. 1		

115

(NOTES)

No. 1 Enrolled Mar. 6th 1899
No. 4 Died Feb. 5, 1899. See testimony of Bessie Hampton taken at Colbert, I.T. *(remainder illegible)*
No. 5 Enrolled June 15, 1900
No. 6 Born April 13th 1902; Enrolled Oct. 23. 1902 *(No. 6 Dawes' Roll No. 4195)*
No. 5 Died Sept. 15, 1901. *(remainder illegible)* Oct. 12/98.

RESIDENCE: Panola ***COUNTY*** ***CARD NO.***
POST OFFICE: Kemp, Ind. Ter. ***FIELD NO.***

	NAME	RELATION-SHIP TO PERSON FIRST NAMED	AGE	SEX	BLOOD	TRIBAL ENROLLMENT		
						YEAR	COUNTY	PAGE
1	Willis, Hamilton		26	M	1/2	1897	Panola	3
2	" Anna	Wife	26	F	I.W.	1897	"	76
3	" Lemmie	Son	7	M	1/4	1897	"	3
4	" Agnes	Dau	4	F	1/4	1897	"	3
5	" Robert B.	Son	8mo	M	1/4			
6	~~" Anne C.~~	~~Dau~~	~~3mo~~	~~F~~	~~1/4~~	DIED PRIOR TO SEPTEMBER 25, 1902		

TRIBAL ENROLLMENT OF PARENTS

	NAME OF FATHER	YEAR	COUNTY	NAME OF MOTHER	YEAR	COUNTY
1	J.H. Willis	Dead	Chickasaw Roll	Catherine Willis	Dead	Chickasaw Roll
2	John Duncan		Non Citizen	Ellen Duncan	"	Non-Citizen
3	No. 1			No. 2		
4	No. 1			No. 2		
5	No. 1			No. 2		
6	~~No. 1~~			~~No. 2~~		

(NOTES)

No. 1 On Chickasaw Roll as Hamp Willis
No. 2 " " " " Mrs. Annie S. " *(No. 2 Dawes' Roll No. 164)*
No. 5 Enrolled Nov. 4/99
No. 6 Born Nov. 1st 1901. Enrolled Jan. 28th 1902
No. 6 Died March 31st 1902; Proof of Death filed Nov. 22, 1902.

Oct. 12/98.

RESIDENCE: Choctaw Nation ~~***COUNTY***~~ ***CARD NO.***
POST OFFICE: Sans Bois, Ind. Ter. ***FIELD NO.***

	NAME	RELATION-SHIP TO PERSON FIRST NAMED	AGE	SEX	BLOOD	TRIBAL ENROLLMENT		
						YEAR	COUNTY	PAGE
1	Noel, Ben		23	M	1/4			

2	" Edward		Son	6wk	"	1/8				

TRIBAL ENROLLMENT OF PARENTS

	NAME OF FATHER	YEAR	COUNTY	NAME OF MOTHER	YEAR	COUNTY
1	Peter Noel	Dead	Sans Bois Co Choctaw Roll	Lorinda Noel	Dead	Chick residing in Choct. N. 1st Dist.
2	No. 1			Chaney Noel		

(NOTES)

On Choctaw Census Record (Sans Bois Co) No. 2, Page 376; transferred to Chickasaw Roll by Dawes Com.
On Choctaw Roll, 1896. Sans Bois Co, No. 9544
Father, Peter Noel, full blood Choctaw, Mother Lorinda Noel, half Choctaw and half Chickasaw
Maternal grandmother, full-blood Chickasaw
Wife of No. 1 Chaney Noel, on Chickasaw Card #D.159
No. 2 Enrolled March 15th 1901

Oct. 12/98.

CANCELLED Stamped across card

RESIDENCE: Choctaw Nation	COUNTY		CARD NO.	
POST OFFICE: McAlester, Ind. Ter.			FIELD NO.	

	NAME	RELATION-SHIP TO PERSON FIRST NAMED	AGE	SEX	BLOOD	TRIBAL ENROLLMENT		
						YEAR	COUNTY	PAGE
1	Folsom, Alfred W.	NAMED	45	M	1/2			
2	" Jensy N.	Wife	40	F	I.W.			

TRIBAL ENROLLMENT OF PARENTS

	NAME OF FATHER	YEAR	COUNTY	NAME OF MOTHER	YEAR	COUNTY
1	Alen Folsom	Dead	Choctaw Roll	(Name Illegible)	Dead	Chickasaw Roll
2	Reynolds	"	Non-Citizen	(Name Illegible)	"	Non Citizen

(NOTES)

No. 1 On Choctaw Census Record No. 2, Page 110, transferred to Chickasaw Roll by Dawes Com
No. 2 "   "   Intermarried Roll   "   30   "   "   "   "   "   "   "
No. 1 On Choctaw Roll 1896 Tobacksy Co, No. 4009 as Alford W. Fulsom
No. 2 "   "   "   1896   "   "   " 14523 " Jensy N. Folsom
    Marriage Certificate to be supplied. Received Oct. 31, 1898.

Oct. 12/98.

CANCELLED Stamped across card

RESIDENCE: Choctaw Nation   COUNTY   CARD NO.

POST OFFICE: Cale, Ind. Ter.   FIELD NO.

	NAME	RELATION-SHIP TO PERSON	AGE	SEX	BLOOD	TRIBAL ENROLLMENT		
						YEAR	COUNTY	PAGE
1	Moore, Lemuel Capel	FIRST NAMED	51	M	1/16	1897	Chick residing in Choctaw N. 3rd Dist.	74
2	" Charles Edward	Son	19	"	1/32	1897	" " " "	74
3	" Ella Minerva	Dau	16	F	1/32	1897	" " " "	74
4	" Nettie May	"	12	"	1/32	1897	" " " "	74
5	" Ludie Grace	"	8	"	1/32	1897	" " " "	74
6	" Daisy	"	5	"	1/32	1897	" " " "	74
7	" Ruby	"	3	"	1/32	1897	" " " "	74
8	" Lemuel Paul	Son	1	M	1/32			
9	" Eugene Chapell	"	2mo	"	1/32			
10	" Walter	"	1mo	"	1/32			

TRIBAL ENROLLMENT OF PARENTS

	NAME OF FATHER	YEAR	COUNTY	NAME OF MOTHER	YEAR	COUNTY
1	Christopher Moore	Dead	Non-Citizen	Catherine Moore	Dead	Chickasaw Roll
2	No. 1			Octavia Moore	"	Non Citizen
3	No. 1			" "	"	" "
4	No. 1			" "	"	" "
5	No. 1			Nora Moore		" "
6	No. 1			" "		" "
7	No. 1			" "		" "
8	No. 1			" "		" "
9	No. 1			" "		" "
10	No. 1			" "		" "

(NOTES)

No. 1 On Chickasaw Roll as L.C. Moore
No. 2 "   "   "   " C.E   "
No. 3 "   "   "   " E.M. "
No. 4 "   "   "   " N.M. "
No. 5 "   "   "   " L.G. "
No. 7 "   "   "   " Rubie "
No. 9 Born Sept 9, 1902 and Enrolled Nov. 1?, 1901
No. 10 Born Nov. 27, 1899. Transferred to this card February 1st 1902
Dec. 16/99 A Son born Nov. 27/99 on Card D.298.

Oct. 12/98.

RESIDENCE: Panola COUNTY					CARD NO.		
POST OFFICE: Kemp, Ind. Ter.					FIELD NO.		

NAME	RELATION-SHIP TO PERSON FIRST NAMED	AGE	SEX	BLOOD	TRIBAL ENROLLMENT		
					YEAR	COUNTY	PAGE
1 Kemp, Rhoda	NAMED	7	F	1/4	1897	Panola	4

TRIBAL ENROLLMENT OF PARENTS							
NAME OF FATHER	YEAR	COUNTY		NAME OF MOTHER	YEAR	COUNTY	
1 Lem Kemp	Dead	Panola		Mary Ellis		White woman	

(NOTES)

Mother Mary Ellis On Choctaw Card D.70
    "   "   "   " Chickasaw C.218
Evidence of marriage of Lem Kemp and Mary Ellis filed with Choctaw Card #.19, June 30, 1900
11/7/02 No. 1 now the ward of Benjamin Franklin Kemp,
    Chickasaw Card *(remainder illegible)*

Oct. 12/98.

RESIDENCE: Choctaw Nation COUNTY					CARD NO.		
POST OFFICE: South Canadian, Ind. Ter.					FIELD NO.		

NAME	RELATION-SHIP TO PERSON FIRST NAMED	AGE	SEX	BLOOD	TRIBAL ENROLLMENT		
					YEAR	COUNTY	PAGE
1 McLish, John E.	NAMED	27	M	1/8			

TRIBAL ENROLLMENT OF PARENTS							
NAME OF FATHER	YEAR	COUNTY		NAME OF MOTHER	YEAR	COUNTY	
1 Ben McLish	Dead	Chickasaw Roll		Julia McLish	Dead	Pontotoc	

(NOTES)

On Choctaw Census Record, No. 2, Tobucksy Co, Page 361, transferred to Chickasaw Roll by Dawes Com
On Choctaw Roll, 1896, Tobucksy County,No. 9218 as Jno. W. McClish

Oct. 12/98.

CANCELLED Stamped across card

RESIDENCE: Panola COUNTY					CARD NO.		
POST OFFICE: Yarnaby, Ind. Ter.					FIELD NO.		

NAME	RELATION-SHIP TO PERSON FIRST NAMED	AGE	SEX	BLOOD	TRIBAL ENROLLMENT		
					YEAR	COUNTY	PAGE
1 Barker, Charles C.	NAMED	25	M	1/4	1897	Panola	1
2 " Stella A.	Dau	3	F	1/8	1897	"	1

119

Chickasaw Enrollment Cards 1898-1914
Chickasaw by Blood   Volume III

TRIBAL ENROLLMENT OF PARENTS

	NAME OF FATHER	YEAR	COUNTY	NAME OF MOTHER	YEAR	COUNTY
1	Thomas S. Barker I.W.	1897	Panola	Catherine Barker	Dead	Panola
2	No. 1			Sarah C. Barker		Non citizen

(NOTES)

No. 1 Admitted by Dawes Commission in 1896, Chickasaw Case #569   *(No. 1 Dawes' Roll No. 4798)*
    Evidence of marriage of No. 1 to Sarah C. Barker, filed April 10, 1902
No. 1 On Chickasaw Roll as C.C. Barker
No. 2 "   "   "   " Stella O. "   *(No. 2 Dawes' Roll No. 4799)*
                                                        Oct. 12/98.

RESIDENCE: Panola   COUNTY   CARD NO.
POST OFFICE: Yarnaby, Ind. Ter.   FIELD NO.

	NAME	RELATION-SHIP TO PERSON FIRST NAMED	AGE	SEX	BLOOD	TRIBAL ENROLLMENT		
						YEAR	COUNTY	PAGE
1	Carter, Colbert	NAMED	32	M	1/4	1897	Panola	3
2	" Henry E.	Son	2	"	1/8	1897	"	3
3	" Alberta	Dau	6mo	F	1/8			
4	" Stella E.	"	2	"	1/8			

TRIBAL ENROLLMENT OF PARENTS

	NAME OF FATHER	YEAR	COUNTY	NAME OF MOTHER	YEAR	COUNTY
1	Colbert Carter	Dead	Panola	Lizzie Carter	Dead	Non Citizen
2	No. 1			Minnie Carter		" "
3	No. 1			" "		" "
4	No. 1			" "		" "

(NOTES)

No. 4 Born Oct. 30, 1900. Enrolled Oct. 22, 1902   *(No. 4 Dawes' Roll No. 4494)*
                                                        Oct. 12/98.

RESIDENCE: Choctaw Nation   ~~COUNTY~~   CARD NO.
POST OFFICE: Krebbs, Ind. Ter.   FIELD NO.

	NAME	RELATION-SHIP TO PERSON FIRST NAMED	AGE	SEX	BLOOD	TRIBAL ENROLLMENT		
						YEAR	COUNTY	PAGE
1	Godfrey, Joseph H.	NAMED	48	M	I.W.	1897	Pickens	78
2	" Mary C.	Wife	38	F	1/16	1897	"	15
3	Hayward, Mona E.	Dau	19	"	1/32	1897	"	15
4	Godfrey, Frank E.	Son	17	M	1/32	1897	"	16

120

Chickasaw Enrollment Cards 1898-1914
Chickasaw by Blood   Volume III

5	"	Charles B.	"	12	"	1/32	1897	"	16
6	"	Harriet Edna	Dau	7	F	1/32	1897	"	16
7	"	Earl Jay	Son	5	M	1/32	1897	"	16

TRIBAL ENROLLMENT OF PARENTS

	NAME OF FATHER	YEAR	COUNTY	NAME OF MOTHER	YEAR	COUNTY
1	Joseph Godfrey	Dead	non citizen	Eliza Godfrey		Non citizen
2	Charles E. Gooding	"	" "	Mourning Gooding	1897	Panola
3	No. 1			No. 2		
4	No. 1			No. 2		
5	No. 1			No. 2		
6	No. 1			No. 2		
7	No. 1			No. 2		

(NOTES)

No. 1 .On Chickasaw Roll as J.H. Godfrey   *(No. 1 Dawes' Roll No. 756)*
No. 2 "   "   " " Mary   "
No. 3 "   "   " " Monna "   ; Is now the wife of James L. Hayward on Chickasaw Card D.351. Oct. 24, 1901
No. 4 "   "   " " Frank "
No. 5 "   "   " " Charley "
No. 6 "   "   " " Edna   "
No. 7 "   "   " " Earl   "

P.O. Edwards, I.T. 12/4-03   Oct. 12/98.

RESIDENCE: Panola COUNTY   CARD NO.
POST OFFICE: Yarnaby, Ind. Ter.   FIELD NO.

	NAME	RELATION-SHIP TO PERSON FIRST NAMED	AGE	SEX	BLOOD	TRIBAL ENROLLMENT		
						YEAR	COUNTY	PAGE
1	Beshirs, Aaron	NAMED	39	M	1/8	1897	Panola	1
2	" Laura Belle	Wife	29	F	1/8	1897	"	1
3	" William	Son	10	M	1/8	1897	"	1
4	" James Alexander	"	8	"	1/8	1897	"	1
5	" Joel Wendgel	"	6	"	1/8	1897	"	1
6	" Elbert	"	4	"	1/8	1897	"	1
7	" Aaron, Jr.	"	1	"	1/8			
8	Thompson, Green Wood	1/2 Bro	17	"	1/8	1897	Panola	1
9	Beshirs, Ada	Dau	1	F	1/8			
10	" Francis	"	2	"	1/8			

121

Chickasaw Enrollment Cards 1898-1914
Chickasaw by Blood   Volume III

	TRIBAL ENROLLMENT OF PARENTS						
	NAME OF FATHER	YEAR	COUNTY	NAME OF MOTHER	YEAR	COUNTY	
1	Tobias Beshirs	Dead	Choctaw Roll	Susan Beshirs	Dead	Chickasaw Roll	
2	Thos. Thompson		non citizen	Maria Thompson	"	" "	
3	No. 1			No. 2			
4	No. 1			No. 2			
5	No. 1			No. 2			
6	No. 1			No. 2			
7	No. 1			No. 2			
8	G.W. Thompson	Dead	Choctaw Roll	Susan Beshirs	Dead	Chickasaw Roll	
9	No. 1			No. 2			
10	No. 1			No. 2			

(NOTES)

No. 2 On Chickasaw Roll as Laura Beshirs
No. 3 "   "   "   " Will   "
No. 4 "   "   "   " James   "   ' On Chickasaw Roll as John A. Beshirs, Page 6 Panola Co.
No. 5 "   "   "   " Joel   "
No. 8 "   "   "   " Greenwood "
No. 9 Enrolled Dec. 5/99. Proof of Birth filed Dec. 1, 1902
No. 10 Born Jany 27, 1901; Enrolled Dec. 1, 1902   *(No. 10 Dawes' Roll No. 4193)*

P.O. Yuba, IT 11/29/02   Oct. 12/98.

RESIDENCE: Panola **COUNTY**						CARD NO.		
POST OFFICE: Colbert, Ind. Ter.						FIELD NO.		

	NAME	RELATIONSHIP TO PERSON FIRST NAMED	AGE	SEX	BLOOD	TRIBAL ENROLLMENT		
						YEAR	COUNTY	PAGE
1	Roark, Alphonso Bailey	NAMED	31	M	1/2	1897	Panola	4
2	" Dora	Wife	20	F	I.W.	1897	"	16
3	" Annie L.	Dau	4	"	1/4	1897	"	4
4	" William Edgar	Son	3	M	1/4	1897	"	4
5	" Ruthie Pearl	Dau	7mo	F	1/4			
6	" Charlie Zierser	Son	1wk	M	1/4			

	TRIBAL ENROLLMENT OF PARENTS						
	NAME OF FATHER	YEAR	COUNTY	NAME OF MOTHER	YEAR	COUNTY	
1	Ben Roark	Dead	Panola	Frances E. Mead	1897	Panola	
2	Tom Smith	"	non citizen	Zornida Con		non-citizen	
3	No. 1			No. 2			
4	No. 1			No. 2			

Chickasaw Enrollment Cards 1898-1914
Chickasaw by Blood   Volume III

5	No. 1			No. 2		
6	No. 1			No. 2		

(NOTES)

No. 1 On Chickasaw Roll as A.B. Roark   *(No. 2 Dawes' Roll No. 549)*
No. 4 "   "   "   " Billie E. "
No. 6 Born Nov. 25, 1901. Enrolled Nov. 30. 1901

P.O. Reagan, I.T. 9/8-04
Paucaunla[sic]
P.O. Pauchunla, I.T. 2/26/03   Oct. 12/98.

RESISTANCE: *RESIDENCE:* Choctaw Nation ~~COUNTY~~   CARD NO.

POST OFFICE: Durant, Ind. Ter.   FIELD NO.

NAME	RELATION-SHIP TO PERSON FIRST NAMED	AGE	SEX	BLOOD	TRIBAL ENROLLMENT		
					YEAR	COUNTY	PAGE
1 Bates, William Lafayette		47	M	I.W.	1897	Chick residing in Choctaw N. 3rd Dist.	82
2 " Emma	Wife	36	F	3/8	1897	" " " "	73
3 " William A.	Son	16	M	3/16	1897	" " " "	73
4 " Thomas B.	"	14	"	3/16	1897	" " " "	73
5 " Nora E.	Dau	12	F	3/16	1897	" " " "	73
6 " Ned	Son	10	M	3/16	1897	" " " "	73
7 " Charles M	"	8	M	3/16	1897	" " " "	73
8 " Emma M.	Dau	6	F	3/16	1897	" " " "	73

TRIBAL ENROLLMENT OF PARENTS

	NAME OF FATHER	YEAR	COUNTY	NAME OF MOTHER	YEAR	COUNTY
1	William Bates	Dead	Non-citizen	Lucinda Bates	Dead	Non citizen
2	Art Chase (I.W.)	1897	Perkins	Nancy Chase	1897	Pickens
3	No. 1			No. 2		
4	No. 1			No. 2		
5	No. 1			No. 2		
6	No. 1			No. 2		
7	No. 1			No. 2		
8	No. 1			No. 2		

(NOTES)

No. 1 On Chickasaw Roll as W.L. Bates   *(No. 1 Dawes' Roll No. 163)*
No. 2 "   "   " " Ema   "   *(No. 2 Dawes' Roll No. 262)*
No. 7 "   "   " " Chas. W. "   *(No. 3 Dawes' Roll No. 263)*
No. 3 is now the husband of Mary Pearl Godfrey on Chickasaw Card #1173, Nov. 19, 1902

(No. 4 Dawes' Roll No. 264)   *(No. 5 Dawes' Roll No. 265)*   *(No. 6 Dawes' Roll No. 266)*
(No. 7 Dawes' Roll No. 267)   *(No. 8 Dawes' Roll No. 268)*

P.O. Robbers Roost, I.T. 11/17/02.   Oct. 12/98.

RESIDENCE: Choctaw Nation   ~~COUNTY~~   **CARD NO.**
POST OFFICE: Silo, Ind. Ter.   **FIELD NO.**

	NAME	RELATION-SHIP TO PERSON FIRST NAMED	AGE	SEX	BLOOD	TRIBAL ENROLLMENT		
						YEAR	COUNTY	PAGE
1	Godfrey, Mary Pearl	FIRST NAMED	16	F	1/2	1897	Chick residing in Choctaw N. 3rd Dist.	74
2	" Peter	Father	41	M	I.W.	1897	"	84

TRIBAL ENROLLMENT OF PARENTS

	NAME OF FATHER	YEAR	COUNTY	NAME OF MOTHER	YEAR	COUNTY
1	Peter Godfrey		White man	Eliza Godfrey	Dead	Panola
2	Joseph Godfrey	Dead	Non Citz.	Eliza Godfrey		Non citizen

(NOTES)

On Chickasaw Roll as Pearl Godfrey
No. 1 is daughter of Peter Godfrey, on Chickasaw Card D. #157   *(No. 1 Dawes' Roll No. 181)*
No. 1 is not the wife of William A. Bates on Chickasaw Card #1174. Evidence of marriage filed Nov. 1902
No. 2 married Eliza Gaylord a Chickasaw woman July 29, 1882 who died in 1899,   *(No. 2 Dawes' Roll No. 139)*
No. 2 married Addie Magison, a white woman in 1890
No. 2 transferred from Chickasaw Card #D,157. See decision of Aug. 16, 1904, Sept. 1, 1904.

                                                                          Oct. 12/98.

RESIDENCE: Choctaw Nation   ~~COUNTY~~   **CARD NO.**
POST OFFICE: Atoka, Ind. Ter.   **FIELD NO.**

	NAME	RELATION-SHIP TO PERSON FIRST NAMED	AGE	SEX	BLOOD	TRIBAL ENROLLMENT		
						YEAR	COUNTY	PAGE
1	Adams, John Quincy	FIRST NAMED	40	M	I.W.			
2	" Arabella F.	Wife	26	F	1/2			
3	" Manava M.	Dau	2mo	"	1/4			

TRIBAL ENROLLMENT OF PARENTS

	NAME OF FATHER	YEAR	COUNTY	NAME OF MOTHER	YEAR	COUNTY
1	Heber W. Adams		non citizen	Elizabeth Adams		non citizen
2	Alford W. Folsom		Blue Co Choctaw Roll	Leima Folsom	1897	Chick residing in Choctaw N. 3rd Dist.
3	No. 1			No. 2		

124

Chickasaw Enrollment Cards 1898-1914
Chickasaw by Blood   Volume III

(NOTES)

No. 1 Admitted by Dawes Com, but by judgement U.S. Court at Ardmore of 3/9/98 he was denied citizenship.

No. 2 On Choctaw Census Record No. 2 (Blue Co) Page 186, transferred to Chickasaw Roll by Dawes Com.
   On Choctaw Roll as Arabekka B. Folsom

No. 2 On Choctaw Roll 1896 Blue Co, No. 4359 as Arabelle B. Folsom

No. 3 Affidavit of attending physician to be supplies. Received Oct. 31/98.

No. 1 Admitted by Dawes Com but reversed by U.S. Court Nov. 14, 1899,

Note: The action of the Commission and US. Court as to his application was as to his marriage to Mary Parker at the time of his marriage to No. 2 Mar. 25, 1897, he was in possession of a Dawes Commission Judgement and Judgement of Court was not until Nov. 14, 1897.

Oct. 12/98.

CANCELLED Stamped across card

RESIDENCE: Pickens	COUNTY					CARD NO.		
POST OFFICE: Woodville, Ind. Ter.						FIELD NO.		
NAME	RELATION-SHIP TO PERSON FIRST NAMED	AGE	SEX	BLOOD		TRIBAL ENROLLMENT		
						YEAR	COUNTY	PAGE
1 Strite, Arminta	NAMED	24	F	I.W.				
2 Christian, Mattie E.	Dau	2	"	1/16		1897	Pickens	13

	NAME OF FATHER	YEAR	COUNTY	NAME OF MOTHER	YEAR	COUNTY
1	I.R. McCuan		Non citizen	Lucy McCuan	Dead	Non citizen
2	Ed. Christian	1897	Pickens	No. 1		

(NOTES)

Both admitted by Dawes Com Case No. 267 and No appeal taken.

No. 1   "   "   "   "   as Mintie Christian   *(No. 1 Dawes' Roll No. 474)*

No. 2 On Chickasaw Roll as Mattie Christian
   Husband of No. 1 Enrolled on Chickasaw Card #154.

No. 2 is the ward of I.R. McCuan, Woodville, I.T. 11/13/02.

RESIDENCE: Choctaw Nation	~~COUNTY~~					CARD NO.		
POST OFFICE: Kiowa, Ind. Ter.						FIELD NO.		
NAME	RELATION-SHIP TO PERSON FIRST NAMED	AGE	SEX	BLOOD		TRIBAL ENROLLMENT		
						YEAR	COUNTY	PAGE
1 Pound, George W.	NAMED	48	M	I.W.		1897	Chick residing in Choctaw N. 1st Dist.	82
2 " Carrie	Wife	40	F	1/8		1897	" " " "	70
3 McMorries, Alice	Dau	17	"	1/16		1897	" " " "	70
4 Pollock, Georgia	"	15	"	1/16		1897	" " " "	70
5 Pound, Nina	"	13	"	1/16		1897	" " " "	70

125

Chickasaw Enrollment Cards 1898-1914
Chickasaw by Blood   Volume III

6	"	Willie	"	11	"	1/16	1897	"	" " "	70
7	"	Florence	"	8	"	1/16	1897	"	" " "	70
8	"	Lizzie	"	6	"	1/16	1897	"	" " "	70
9	"	Madge	"	4	"	1/16	1897	"	" " "	70
10	"	Annie May	"	2	"	1/16				
11	McMorries, Lee, Jr.		Gr Son	1mo	M	1/32				
12	" " Lee W.		Husband of No. 3	35	M	I.W.				
13	Pollock, Lee		Husband of No. 4	23	M	I.W.				

TRIBAL ENROLLMENT OF PARENTS

	NAME OF FATHER	YEAR	COUNTY	NAME OF MOTHER	YEAR	COUNTY
1	David W. Pound	Dead	Non Citizen	Margaret Pound	Dead	Non citizen
2	Charles Missex		" "	Sophia Messen[sic]	"	Chick residing in Choctaw N. 1st Dist.
3	No. 1			No. 2		
4	No. 1			No. 2		
5	No. 1			No. 2		
6	No. 1			No. 2		
7	No. 1			No. 2		
8	No. 1			No. 2		
9	No. 1			No. 2		
10	No. 1			No. 2		
11	Lee W. McMorries		white man	No. 3		
12	A.B. McMorries		non citz	Helen McMorries		non citz
13	A.D. Pollock I.W.	1896	Tobucksy	Hannah Pollock		non-citizen

(NOTES)

No. 1 On Chickasaw Roll as George W. Pounds   *(No. 1 Dawes' Roll No. 341)*

No. 3 is now the wife of Lee W. McMorries on Chickasaw Card D.333   *(No. 13 Dawes' Roll No. 227)*

No. 4 is now the wife of Lee Pollock on Chickasaw Card #D.344 March 20, 1902

No. 10 Affidavit of attending physician to be supplied. Received Oct. 17/98.

No. 10 Died Sept 1900. Proof of Death filed Nov. 16, 1902. Enrollment cancelled by Dept. July 2, 190?.

No. 11 Enrolled May 29, 1902.

No. 12 transferred from Chickasaw Card #D222 March 29, 1903

(Two other entries illegible)

Oct. 12/98.

RESIDENCE: Choctaw Nation   COUNTY   CARD NO.

POST OFFICE: Steward, Ind. Ter.   FIELD NO.

NAME	RELATION-SHIP TO PERSON FIRST NAMED	AGE	SEX	BLOOD	TRIBAL ENROLLMENT		
					YEAR	COUNTY	PAGE
1 Wesley, Elias		24	M	1/2			

TRIBAL ENROLLMENT OF PARENTS

NAME OF FATHER	YEAR	COUNTY	NAME OF MOTHER	YEAR	COUNTY
1 Te-i-nin-tub-by	Dead	Choctaw Roll	Joy Wade	1897	Chick residing in Choctaw N. 1st Dist.

(NOTES)

(All Notations Illegible)

Oct. 12/98.

CANCELLED Stamped across card

RESIDENCE: Choctaw Nation   ~~COUNTY~~   CARD NO.

POST OFFICE: Nelson, Ind. Ter.   FIELD NO.

NAME	RELATION-SHIP TO PERSON FIRST NAMED	AGE	SEX	BLOOD	TRIBAL ENROLLMENT		
					YEAR	COUNTY	PAGE
1 Pierce, Ed	NAMED	28	M	1/4			
2 " Belle	Wife	28	F	1/4			
3 " Hattie	Dau	6	"	1/4			
4 " Alice	"	5	"	1/4			
5 " Siney	"	2	"	1/4			
6 " Susan D.	Mother	55	"	1/2			
7 " Robert L.	Bro	23	M	1/4			
8 " Henry C.	Son	5mo	"	1/4			
9 " Ella May	Dau	3mo	F	1/4			

TRIBAL ENROLLMENT OF PARENTS

NAME OF FATHER	YEAR	COUNTY	NAME OF MOTHER	YEAR	COUNTY
1 Robert Pierce	Dead	Non Citizen	Susan *(Illegible)*	1897	Chick residing in Choctaw N. 3rd Dist.
2 Robert Thompson		Gaines Co. Choctaw Roll	Siney Thompson	1897	" " " "
3 No. 1			No. 2		
4 No. 1			No. 2		
5 No. 1			No. 2		
6 *(Illegible)*/Stewart	Dead	Chickasaw Roll	Matilda Stewart	Dead	Chickasaw Roll
7 Robert Pierce	"	Non Citizen	No. I[sic]		

Chickasaw Enrollment Cards 1898-1914
Chickasaw by Blood   Volume III

| 8 | No. 1 | | | No. 2 | | |
| 9 | No. 1 | | | No. 2 | | |

(NOTES)

All except No. 5 on Chickasaw Record No. 2, Page 400, transferred to Chickasaw Roll by Dawes Com.

No. 5 Affidavit of Attending Physician to be supplied. Received Nov. 7/98.

No. 1 is now husband of Maudie May Pierce on Chickasaw Card #D.369, Sept. 22, 1902

No. 7 Now at San Antonio, Texas, Member 4th Texas Volunteer

No. 9 Born May 23rd 1904. Enrolled Sept. 4, 1902

No. 8 Enrolled May 17th/99

No. 1 On Choctaw Roll 1896, Kiamitia Co, No. 10440

No. 2 "   "   " 1896 "   "   " 10441

No. 3 "   "   " 1896 "   "   " 10442

No. 4 "   "   " 1896 "   "   " 10443

No. 6 "   "   " 1896 "   "   " 10444

No. 7 "   "   " 1896 "   "   " 10445

Oct. 12/98.

CANCELLED Stamped across card

| RESIDENCE: Choctaw Nation | COUNTY | | | CARD NO. | | |
| POST OFFICE: Nelson, Ind. Ter. | | | | FIELD NO. | | |

NAME	RELATION-SHIP TO PERSON FIRST NAMED	AGE	SEX	BLOOD	TRIBAL ENROLLMENT		
					YEAR	COUNTY	PAGE
1	Woods, Robert A.	NAMED	36	M	I.W.			
2	" Mary A.	Wife	26	F	1/4			
3	" Lillie May	Dau	6	"	1/8			
4	" Arthur	Son	2	M	1/8			
5	" Ida Belle	Dau	4mo	F	1/8			

TRIBAL ENROLLMENT OF PARENTS

	NAME OF FATHER	YEAR	COUNTY	NAME OF MOTHER	YEAR	COUNTY
1	Robert A. Woods	Dead	Non Citizen	(Illegible)Woods	Dead	Non Citizen
2	Robert Thompson		Gaines Co. Choctaw Roll	Lucy Thompson	1897	Chick residing in Choctaw N. 1st Dist.
3	No. 1			No. 2		
4	No. 1			No. 2		
5	No. 1			No. 2		

(NOTES)

No. 1 On Choctaw Intermarried Roll Page 116, transferred to Chickasaw Roll by Dawes Com.

No. 2 & 3 "   " Census Record,   " 482,   "   "   "   "   "   "   "

No. 3 "   "   "   " as Lila M. Woods

No. 4 Affidavit of attending physician to be supplied. Received Nov. 21/98.

No. 5 Enrolled May 12/99.

No. 1 On Choctaw Roll, 1896, Kiamitia County, No. 15184
No. 2 "   "   " 1896   "   "   " 13770
No. 3 "   "   " 1896   "   "   " 13771 as Lila M. Woods.

Oct. 12/98.

CANCELLED Stamped across card

NAME	RELATION-SHIP TO PERSON FIRST NAMED	AGE	SEX	BLOOD	TRIBAL ENROLLMENT		
					YEAR	COUNTY	PAGE
1 Harris, Lila	FIRST NAMED	22	F	1/2	1897	Chick residing in Choctaw N. 1st Dist.	11
2 " Frank	Son	2	M	1/4			
3 " Wes	"	6mo	"	1/4			
4 " Emma	Dau	6mo	F	1/4			
5 " Mamie	"	4mo	"	1/4			

RESIDENCE: Choctaw Nation   ~~COUNTY~~   CARD NO.
POST OFFICE: Sans Bois, Ind. Ter.   FIELD NO.

TRIBAL ENROLLMENT OF PARENTS

	NAME OF FATHER	YEAR	COUNTY	NAME OF MOTHER	YEAR	COUNTY
1	Jonas Brown		Chick Freedman	Tennessee Brown	Dead	Chick residing in Choctaw N. 1st Dist.
2	Isaac Harris		Col. Non-citizen	No. 1		
3	" "		" " "	No. 1		
4	" "		Choc. Freedman	No. 1		
5	" "		" "	No. 1		

(NOTES)

No. 1 On Chickasaw Roll as Lillie Harris
No. 1 is the daughter of Jonas Brown, a Choctaw freedman on Card #87
No. 1 is now the wife of Isaac Harris a Choctaw freedman Card #1140
No. 2 Affidavit of mid wife to be supplied. Received Oct. 31/98
No. 3 "   " " "   "   " " "   " Oct. 31/98.
No. 4 Enrolled Feby 19th 1901
No. 5 Born July 16th 1902; Enrolled Nov. 13, 1902   (No. 5 Dawes' Roll No. 192)
No. 2 Born July 6, 1898; Proof of birth filed March 9, 1903.
Additional affidavit as to birth (remainder illegible)

Oct. 12/98.

Chickasaw Enrollment Cards 1898-1914
Chickasaw by Blood   Volume III

RESIDENCE: Choctaw Nation   ~~COUNTY~~   CARD NO.

POST OFFICE: Sans Bois, Ind. Ter.   FIELD NO.

NAME	RELATION-SHIP TO PERSON	AGE	SEX	BLOOD	TRIBAL ENROLLMENT		
					YEAR	COUNTY	PAGE
1 Brown, Sampson	FIRST NAMED	19	M	1/2	1897	Chick residing in Choctaw N. 1st Dist.	71

	TRIBAL ENROLLMENT OF PARENTS						
NAME OF FATHER	YEAR	COUNTY	NAME OF MOTHER	YEAR	COUNTY		
1 Jonas Brown		Chick Freedman	Tennessee Brown	Dead	Chick residing in Choctaw N. 1st Dist.		

(NOTES)

Oct. 12/98.

RESIDENCE: Choctaw Nation   ~~COUNTY~~   CARD NO.

POST OFFICE: So. McAlester, Ind. Ter.   FIELD NO.

NAME	RELATION-SHIP TO PERSON	AGE	SEX	BLOOD	TRIBAL ENROLLMENT		
					YEAR	COUNTY	PAGE
1 Johnson, Emma	FIRST NAMED	27	F	1/2	1897	Chick residing in Choctaw N. 1st Dist.	69

	TRIBAL ENROLLMENT OF PARENTS						
NAME OF FATHER	YEAR	COUNTY	NAME OF MOTHER	YEAR	COUNTY		
1 Jonas Brown		Chick Freednab	Tennessee Brown	Dead	Chick residing in Choctaw N. 1st Dist.		

(NOTES)

On Chickasaw Roll as Ema Johnson   *(No. I Dawes' Roll No. 1797)*
Wife of Randall Johnson, U.S. Citz.
Alleged that she has not *(remainder illegible)*
Proof again requested Dec. 12, 1899
See testimony Dec. 30, 1899.

P.O. Sherman, Tex 5/2-04   Oct. 12/98.

RESIDENCE: Choctaw Nation   COUNTY   CARD NO.

POST OFFICE: Bennington, Ind. Ter.   FIELD NO.

NAME	RELATION-SHIP TO PERSON	AGE	SEX	BLOOD	TRIBAL ENROLLMENT		
					YEAR	COUNTY	PAGE
1 Folsom, Levina C.	FIRST NAMED	52	F	3/4			
2 " Lewis L.	Son	28	M				

3	"	Robert E.	"	21	"			
4	"	Nannie A.	Dau	14	F			
5	"	Maud H.	"	11	"			
6	"	Ava V.	"	6	"			
7	"	Roy E.	Gr.Son	3mo	M			

TRIBAL ENROLLMENT OF PARENTS

	NAME OF FATHER	YEAR	COUNTY	NAME OF MOTHER	YEAR	COUNTY
1	Robert Colbert	Dead	Chickasaw Roll	Mah-lo-ta-ka	Dead	Chickasaw Roll
2	Alfred W. Folsom		Blue County Choctaw Roll	No. 1		
3	" " "		" "	No. 1		
4	" " "		" "	No. 1		
5	" " "		" "	No. 1		
6	" " "		" "	No. 1		
7	No. 3			Laura Folsom		Non Citizen

(NOTES)

No. 1 The husband of No. 1 and father of chilcren on *(illegible)* card as Alfred Wright Folsom on Choctaw Card #374
No. 3 is now the husband of Laura Folsom, a non-citizen. Evidence of marriage filed April 25, 1902.
No. 7 Born Jany 29th 1902. Enrolled April 25th 1902.
Nos. 1 & 2 On Choctaw Census Record No. 2 Page 186, transferred to Chickasaw Roll by Dawes Com.
Nos. 3,4.5.& 6   "   "   "   "   "   "   " 187   "   "   "   " "   "   "
No. 1 On Choctaw Roll as Piney C. Folsom
No. 5 "   "   "   " Maude A.   "
No. 6 "   "   "   " Ava N.   "
No. 1 On Choctaw Roll 1896 Blue County, No. 4357 as Piney C. Folsom
No. 2 "   "   " 1896   "   "   " 4358
No. 3 "   "   " 1896   "   "   " 4360 as Robt. L. Folsom
No. 4 "   "   " 1896   "   "   " 4361
No. 5 "   "   " 1896   "   "   " 4362 as Maud A. Folsom
No. 6 "   "   " 1896   "   "   " 4363 " Ava N.   "

Oct. 12/98,

CANCELLED Stamped across card

RESIDENCE: Choctaw Nation ~~COUNTY~~					CARD NO.			
POST OFFICE: Durant, Ind, Ter,					FIELD NO.			

	NAME	RELATION-SHIP TO PERSON FIRST NAMED	AGE	SEX	BLOOD	TRIBAL ENROLLMENT		
						YEAR	COUNTY	PAGE
1	Spears. David Freeman		46	M	I.W.			
2	" Caroline	Wife	48	F	3/8			
3	" Julia Ann	Dau	6	"	3/16			

131

4	Thompson, Dora Ellen	St.Dau	11	"	3/16			

TRIBAL ENROLLMENT OF PARENTS

	NAME OF FATHER	YEAR	COUNTY	NAME OF MOTHER	YEAR	COUNTY
1	Clayton Spears	Dead	Non Citizen	Ann Spears	Dead	Non Citizen
2	Sam Colbert	"	Chickasaw Roll	Lousanna Colbert	"	Chickasaw Roll
3	No. 1			No. 2		
4	Henry Thompson	Dead	Non Citizen	No. 2		

(NOTES)

No. 1 Admitted by Dawes Com, Case No. *(illegible)* and No Appeal taken.
Marriage License & Certificate on file in office of Dawes Com at Muskogee
No. 1 On Choctaw Intermarried Roll, Page 101, transferred to Chickasaw Roll by Dawes Com.
No. 2 & 3 " " Census Record, " 429 " " " " " " "
No. 4 " " " " " 449 " " " " " " "
No. 1 On Choctaw Roll as C.F. Spearce, 1896, Blue County, No. 15060
No. 2 " " " " Carolins Spears 1896 " " " 11585
No. 3 " " " " Julia A " 1896 " " " 12402
No. 4 " " " " Dora Thompson 1896 " " " 11584

Oct. 12/98.

CANCELLED Stamped across card

RESIDENCE: Panola COUNTY					CARD NO.			
POST OFFICE: Kemp, Ind. Ter.					FIELD NO.			
	NAME	RELATION-SHIP TO PERSON FIRST NAMED	AGE	SEX	BLOOD	TRIBAL ENROLLMENT		
						YEAR	COUNTY	PAGE
1	McLaughlin, Corrilla		39	F	I.W.	1897	Panola	76
2	" James B.	Son	5	M	3/8	1897	"	5

TRIBAL ENROLLMENT OF PARENTS

	NAME OF FATHER	YEAR	COUNTY	NAME OF MOTHER	YEAR	COUNTY
1	R.W. Malone	Dead	Non Citizen	*(Illegible)* Malone	Dead	Non Citizen
2	Jas. McLaughlin	Dead	Panola	No. 1		

(NOTES)

No. 1 On Chickasaw Roll as C.R. McLaughlin *(No. 1 Dawes' Roll No. 226)*
No. 1 widow of James McLaughlin
Certified copy of divorce proceedings between C.R. and J.B. Dollahite filed March 11, 1903.

Oct. 12/98

RESIDENCE: Panola   COUNTY   CARD NO.

POST OFFICE: Kemp, Ind. Ter.   FIELD NO.

	NAME	RELATION-SHIP TO PERSON FIRST NAMED	AGE	SEX	BLOOD	TRIBAL ENROLLMENT		
						YEAR	COUNTY	PAGE
1	Kemp, Alexander Commoder	NAMED	48	M	3/8	1897	Panola	2
2	" David	Son	12	"	3/16	1897	"	2
3	" Charley	"	10	"	3/16	1897	"	2
4	" Martha Myrtle	Dau	5	F	3/16	1897	"	2
5	" Patsey	Mother	80	"	1/2	1897	"	3

TRIBAL ENROLLMENT OF PARENTS

	NAME OF FATHER	YEAR	COUNTY	NAME OF MOTHER	YEAR	COUNTY
1	Jackson Kemp	Dead	Panola	Patsey Kemp	1897	Panola
2	No. 1			Emma Kemp		Non Citizen
3	No. 1			" "		" "
4	No. 1			" "		" "
5	Levi Colbert	Dead	Chickasaw Roll	Dollie Colbert	Dead	Chickasaw Roll

(NOTES)

Evidence of marriage between No. 1 and Emma Kemp filed March 26, 1902.

No. 4 On Chickasaw Roll as Martha M. Kemp

No. 1 "   "   "   "   A.C.   "

No. 5 Died Aug. 5th 1900. Proof of Death filed Aug. 15th 1902.

Oct. 12/98

RESIDENCE: Panola   COUNTY   CARD NO.

POST OFFICE: Kemp, Ind. Ter.   FIELD NO.

	NAME	RELATION-SHIP TO PERSON FIRST NAMED	AGE	SEX	BLOOD	TRIBAL ENROLLMENT		
						YEAR	COUNTY	PAGE
1	Harper, Joseph Lea	NAMED	29	M	1/2	1897	Panola	3
2	" Helen Josephine	Dau	5	F	1/4	1897	"	3
3	" Joshua Robert	Son	3	M	1/4	1897	"	3
4	" Bettie Leona	Dau	2mo	F	1/4			
5	" Viola	Wife	27	"	I.W.			

TRIBAL ENROLLMENT OF PARENTS

	NAME OF FATHER	YEAR	COUNTY	NAME OF MOTHER	YEAR	COUNTY
1	J.K. Harper	Dead	Non Citizen	Serena Short	1897	Panola
2	No. 1			Viola Harper		White woman
3	No. 1			" "		" "
4	No. 1			" "		" "
5	George Shockey	Dead	Non Citizen	Lou Shockey		non citizen

(NOTES)

Viola Harper wife of No. 1 on Chickasaw D.155
No. 1 On Chickasaw Roll as J.L. Harper
No. 2 "   "   " " Helen "
Nol 3 "   "   " " J.R. "
No. 4 Born Feb. 21, 1902; Enrolled April 28th 1892
No. 5 transferred from Chickasaw Card #D-155 July 2 1904.
See decision of June 16, 1904.   *(No. 5 Dawes' Roll No. 406)*

P.O. Cumberland, I.T.   Oct. 12/98

RESIDENCE: Panola COUNTY					CARD NO.			
POST OFFICE: Kemp, Ind. Ter.					FIELD NO.			
NAME	RELATION-SHIP TO PERSON FIRST NAMED	AGE	SEX	BLOOD	TRIBAL ENROLLMENT			
					YEAR	COUNTY		PAGE
1 Kemp, Joe	NAMED	29	M	3/4	1897	Panola		5
2 " Marilous E.	Wife	23	F	I.W.	1897	"		76
3 " Henry	Son	5	M	3/8	1897	"		5
4 " Lenora	Dau	2	F	3/8	1897	"		5
5 " Robert Lemuel	Son	9mo	M	3/8				
6 " Joseph Franklin	"	4mo	"	3/8				

TRIBAL ENROLLMENT OF PARENTS

	NAME OF FATHER	YEAR	COUNTY	NAME OF MOTHER	YEAR	COUNTY
1	B.J. Kemp	1897	Tishomingo	Rhoda Kemp	Dead	Panola
2	*(Name Illegible)*		non citizen	Mary Walton		non citizen
3	No. 1			No. 2		
4	No. 1			No. 2		
5	No. 1			No. 2		
6	No. 1			No. 2		

(NOTES)

No. 2 On Chickasaw Roll as Mary Louise E. Kemp.   *(No. 1 Dawes' Roll No. 433)*
No. 6 Enrolled Aug. 5, 1901.   *(No. 2 Dawes' Roll No. 54)*
(No. 3 Dawes' Roll No. 434) (No. 4 Dawes' Roll No. 435) (No. 5 Dawes' Roll No. 436) (No. 6 Dawes' Roll No. 437)
                                                                    Oct. 12/98

Chickasaw Enrollment Cards 1898-1914
Chickasaw by Blood   Volume III

| RESIDENCE: | Choctaw Nation | COUNTY | | | CARD NO. | | | |

RESIDENCE: Choctaw Nation *COUNTY*   *CARD NO.*

POST OFFICE: McAlester, Ind. Ter.   *FIELD NO.*

	NAME	RELATION- SHIP TO PERSON FIRST NAMED	AGE	SEX	BLOOD	TRIBAL ENROLLMENT		
						YEAR	COUNTY	PAGE
1	Ott, Kitsie		38	F	Full			
2	" Joe	Son	6	M	1/2			
3	" Simeon	"	5	"	1/2			
4	" Sallie	Dau	1	F	1/2			
5	" Sam	Step Son	15	M	1/2			
6	Eddy, Ida O.	Dau	12	F				
7	" Elsie O.	"	9	"				

TRIBAL ENROLLMENT OF PARENTS

	NAME OF FATHER	YEAR	COUNTY	NAME OF MOTHER	YEAR	COUNTY
1	Johnson Perry	Dead	Chickasaw Roll	Lizzie Perry	Dead	Pontotoc
2	Willie Ott		Tobucksy Co. Choctaw Roll	No. 1		
3	" "		" "	No. 1		
4	" "		" "	No. 1		
5	" "		" "	Liza Ott	Dead	Chick residing in Choctaw N. 1st Dist.
6	Sam Eddy	Dead	Chick residing in Choctaw N. 1st Dist.	No. 1		
7	" "	"	" " " "	No. 1		

(NOTES)

No. 1 Wife of Willie Ott, Choctaw Roll Card No. 311.

Nos. 1,2,3 & 5 On Choctaw Census Record, No. 2, Page 386 Transferred to Chickasaw Roll by Dawes Com.

No. 6 & 7   "   "   "   "   "   " 154   "   "   "   "   "   "   "

No. 1 On Choctaw Roll, 1896, Tobucksy Co. No. 9922

No. 2 "   "   " 1896   "   " " 9924

No. 3 "   "   " 1896   "   " " 9925

No. 5 "   "   " 1896   "   " " 9923

No. 6 "   "   " 1896   "   " " 3702

No. 7 "   "   " 1896   "   " " 3701 as Elsie Eddy

Oct. 12/98

CANCELLED Stamped across card

135

Chickasaw Enrollment Cards 1898-1914
Chickasaw by Blood   Volume III

RESIDENCE: Choctaw Nation   COUNTY   CARD NO.

POST OFFICE: Scipio, Ind. Ter.   FIELD NO.

NAME	RELATION-SHIP TO PERSON FIRST NAMED	AGE	SEX	BLOOD	TRIBAL ENROLLMENT		
					YEAR	COUNTY	PAGE
1 Anderson, Rhonda	NAMED	24	F	1/2			
2 " Dora	Dau	6	"	1/4			

TRIBAL ENROLLMENT OF PARENTS

	NAME OF FATHER	YEAR	COUNTY	NAME OF MOTHER	YEAR	COUNTY
1	Thomas Folsom	Dead	Choctaw Roll	Jennie Folsom	Dead	Chick residing in Choctaw N. 1st Dist.
2	Andie Anderson		Tobucksy Co. Choctaw Roll	No. 1		

(NOTES)

Both on Choctaw Census Record No. 2 Tobucksy Co, Page 5. Transferred to Chickasaw Roll by Dawes Com.
No. 1 Wife of Andie Anderson, Choctaw Roll Card No. 370.
No. 1 On Choctaw Roll, 1896, Tobucksy Co, No. 119.
No. 2 "   "   "   1896   "   "   "   110.

Oct. 12/98.

CANCELLED Stamped across card

RESIDENCE: Choctaw Nation   COUNTY   CARD NO.

POST OFFICE: Scipio, Ind. Ter.   FIELD NO.

NAME	RELATION-SHIP TO PERSON FIRST NAMED	AGE	SEX	BLOOD	TRIBAL ENROLLMENT		
					YEAR	COUNTY	PAGE
1 Folsom, Silas D.	NAMED	26	M	1/2			
2 " Morgany	Wife	25	F	Full	1897	Chick residing in Choctaw N. 1st Dist.	69
3 " Joseph P.	Son	4	M	3/4	1897	" " " "	69
4 " ~~Edwin E.~~	~~"~~	~~10mo~~	~~"~~	~~3/4~~			
5 " Levina	Sister	19	F	1/2			
6 " Tandy	Son	3mo	M	3/4			
7 " Alice Julia	Dau	3mo	F	3/4			

TRIBAL ENROLLMENT OF PARENTS

	NAME OF FATHER	YEAR	COUNTY	NAME OF MOTHER	YEAR	COUNTY
1	Thomas Folsom	Dead	Choctaw Roll	Jennie Folsom	Dead	Chick residing in Choctaw N. 1st. Dist.
2	Fillmore Perry	"	Chick residing in Choctaw N. 1st Dist.	Cha-lo-way	"	" " " " "
3	No. 1			No. 2		

4	~~No. 1~~			~~No. 2~~		
5	Thomas Folsom	Dead	Choctaw Roll	Jennie Folsom	Dead	Chick residing in Choctaw N. 1st Dist.
6	No. 1			No. 2		
7	No. 1			No. 2		

(NOTES)

No. 1 On Choctaw Census Record No. 2, Page 1711, Tobucksy Co, transferred to Chickasaw Roll by Dawes Com.

No. 1 On Choctaw Roll 1896 Tobucksy Co, No. 4040

No. 5 "   "   " 1896   "   " " 3902

No. 5 "   " Census Record No. 2 Page 165 (San Bois Co.); Transferred to Chickasaw Roll by Dawes Com.

No. 2 Pm Cjoclasaw Rp" as Mprgam Fi;sp,e

Nos. 6 & 7 Twins Born Sept. 5, 1901; Enrolled Dec 26th 1902

Nos 1 & 5 Transferred to Choctaw Card No. 5496, Oct. 21, 1902

No. 4 Died Oct. 24, 1899: Proof of death filed Dec. 24, 1902.

No. 4 Died Oct. 24, 1899. Enrollment cancelled by Dept. July 2, 1904.

Oct. 12/98.

RESIDENCE: Panola **COUNTY**					CARD NO.		
POST OFFICE: Kemp, Ind. Ter.					FIELD NO.		

	NAME	RELATION-SHIP TO PERSON FIRST NAMED	AGE	SEX	BLOOD	TRIBAL ENROLLMENT		
						YEAR	COUNTY	PAGE
1	Reynolds, Frank	NAMED	22	M	1/2	1897	Panola	4
2	" James Allen	Son	6mo	"	1/4			
3	" Lillie Francis	Dau	8mo	F	1/4			

TRIBAL ENROLLMENT OF PARENTS

	NAME OF FATHER	YEAR	COUNTY	NAME OF MOTHER	YEAR	COUNTY
1	Jim Reynolds	Dead	Panola	Amanda Reynolds	1897	Panola
2	No. 1			Laura Reynolds		non citizen
3	No. 1			Vivia Reynolds		" "

(NOTES)

Evidence of marriage between No. 1 and Laura Reynolds received and filed Sept. 10, 1902. The mother of No. 2 died Nov. 19, 1899

No. 1 is now the husband of Vivia Reynolds a non-citizen. Evidence of marriage filed Sept. 23, 1901.

No. 3 Died Oct. 12, 1901. Proof of Death filed Aug. 12, 1902.

No. 3 Enrolled Sept. 23rd 1901.

Oct. 12/98.

Chickasaw Enrollment Cards 1898-1914
Chickasaw by Blood   Volume III

RESIDENCE: Choctaw Nation COUNTY

CARD NO.

POST OFFICE: Kiowa, Ind. Ter,

FIELD NO.

NAME	RELATION-SHIP TO PERSON FIRST NAMED	AGE	SEX	BLOOD	TRIBAL ENROLLMENT		
					YEAR	COUNTY	PAGE
1 Duke, Sam	NAMED	50	M	Full	1897	Pontotoc	59

TRIBAL ENROLLMENT OF PARENTS

NAME OF FATHER	YEAR	COUNTY	NAME OF MOTHER	YEAR	COUNTY
1 Ben Duke	Dead	Chickasaw Roll	Ste-mon-hoh-na	Dead	Chickasaw Roll

(NOTES)

No. 1 is husband of Epsey Duke on Chickasaw Card #D.228
No. 1 said to have died about March 1, 1902.

Oct. 11/98.

RESIDENCE: Choctaw Nation COUNTY

CARD NO.

POST OFFICE: Hartshorn, Ind. Ter.

FIELD NO.

NAME	RELATION-SHIP TO PERSON FIRST NAMED	AGE	SEX	BLOOD	TRIBAL ENROLLMENT		
					YEAR	COUNTY	PAGE
1 Thompson, Culberson	NAMED	20	M	Full	1897	Chick residing in Choctaw N. 1st Dist.	71

TRIBAL ENROLLMENT OF PARENTS

NAME OF FATHER	YEAR	COUNTY	NAME OF MOTHER	YEAR	COUNTY
1 Alum Thompson	Dead	Chickasaw Roll	Rhoda Thompson	Dead	Chickasaw Roll

(NOTES)

Husband of Lucy Thompson, Choctaw Roll Card No. 369.

P.O. Gawen, I.T.

Oct. 11/98.

RESIDENCE: Panola COUNTY

CARD NO.

POST OFFICE: Colbert, Ind. Ter,

FIELD NO.

NAME	RELATION-SHIP TO PERSON FIRST NAMED	AGE	SEX	BLOOD	TRIBAL ENROLLMENT		
					YEAR	COUNTY	PAGE
1 Hamblin, Henry C.	NAMED	55	M	I.W.	1897	Panola	76
2 " Jessie F.	Wife	44	F	I.W.	1897	"	76

TRIBAL ENROLLMENT OF PARENTS

NAME OF FATHER	YEAR	COUNTY	NAME OF MOTHER	YEAR	COUNTY
1 Char. B. Hamblin	Dead	Non-Citizen	Cynthia J. Hamblin	Dead	Non-Citizen
2 Jim Webb	"	" "	Mary Webb		" "

(NOTES)

No. 1 on 1818 Annuity Roll, Panola County, No. 2?   *(No. 1 Dawes' Roll No. 437)*
No. 2 "   "   "   "   "   "   " 39 as Jessie Greenwood   *(No. 2 Dawes' Roll No. 438)*
No. 1 on 1893 Pay Roll No. 2 Page 9
No. 2 "   "   "   "   "   "   "

P.O. of No. 1 Durant, I.T.
P.O. of No. 2 Sterrett, I.T.   Oct. 11/98.

	NAME	RELATION-SHIP TO PERSON FIRST NAMED	AGE	SEX	BLOOD	TRIBAL ENROLLMENT		
						YEAR	COUNTY	PAGE
1	Guess, Robert	NAMED	37	M	3/4	1897	Panola	2
2	" Edward	Son	16	"	3/8	1897	"	2
3	" Robert, Jr.	"	10	"	3/8	1897	"	2
4	" Emmet	"	8	"	3/8	1897	"	2
5	" Jeff	"	8	"	3/8	1897	"	2
6	" Elizabeth	Dau	3	F	3/8	1897	"	2
7	" ~~Jesse Clarence~~	~~Son~~	~~20da~~	~~M~~	~~3/8~~			

RESIDENCE: Panola   COUNTY   CARD No.
POST OFFICE: Colbert, Ind. Ter.   FIELD No.

TRIBAL ENROLLMENT OF PARENTS

	NAME OF FATHER	YEAR	COUNTY	NAME OF MOTHER	YEAR	COUNTY
1	John Guess	Dead	Panola	Angeline Guess	Dead	Panola
2	No. 1			Fannie Guess	"	Non-Citizen
3	No. 1			" "	"	" "
4	No. 1			" "	"	" "
5	No. 1			" "	"	" "
6	No. 1			Martha Guess		" "
7	~~(Name Illegible)~~			~~(Name Illegible)~~		

(NOTES)

No. 1 was married to Martha Guess Nov. 28th 1899; Evidence of marriage filed Oct. 10, 1900.
No. 2 On Chickasaw Roll as Ed. Guess
No. 4 "   "   "   " Emet "
No. 6 "   "   "   " Bettie "
No. 7 Enrolled Oct. 10th 1900' Died Oct. 31, 1901, Proof of Death Filed Oct. 11/1902.
No. 7 Died Oct. 31, 1901. Enrollment cancelled by Dept. *(illegible)*

Oct. 11/98

CANCELLED Stamped across card

Chickasaw Enrollment Cards 1898-1914
Chickasaw by Blood   Volume III

RESIDENCE: Panola COUNTY   CARD NO.
POST OFFICE: Colbert, Ind. Ter.   FIELD NO.

NAME	RELATION-SHIP TO PERSON FIRST NAMED	AGE	SEX	BLOOD	TRIBAL ENROLLMENT		
					YEAR	COUNTY	PAGE
1 Guess, Joe	NAMED	38	M	3/4	1897	Panola	2

TRIBAL ENROLLMENT OF PARENTS

NAME OF FATHER	YEAR	COUNTY	NAME OF MOTHER	YEAR	COUNTY
1 John Guess	Dead	Panola	Angeline Guess	Dead	Panola

(NOTES)

Oct. 11/98.

RESIDENCE: Panola COUNTY   CARD NO.
POST OFFICE: Colbert, Ind. Ter.   FIELD NO.

NAME	RELATION-SHIP TO PERSON FIRST NAMED	AGE	SEX	BLOOD	TRIBAL ENROLLMENT		
					YEAR	COUNTY	PAGE
1 Leecraft, Arthur N.	NAMED	31	M	I.W.	1897	Panola	83
2 " Lelah N.C.	Wife	24	F	1/8	1897	"	4
3 " Bertram M.	Son	5	M	1/16	1897	"	4
4 " Mildred	Dau	3	F	1/16	1897	"	4
5 Maupin, Helen E.	Mother in Law	48	"	1/4	1897	"	4
6 Leecraft, Frances	Dau	6wks	"	1/16			

TRIBAL ENROLLMENT OF PARENTS

NAME OF FATHER	YEAR	COUNTY	NAME OF MOTHER	YEAR	COUNTY
1 Benj. Leecraft	Dead	Non-Citizen	Susan E. Leecraft		Non-citizen
2 John Maupin	"	" "	Helen E. Maupin	1897	Panola
3 No. 1			No. 2		
4 No. 1			No. 2		
5 Perry Eastman I.W.	Dead	Chickasaw Roll	Harriet Eastman	Dead	Panola
6 No. 1			No. 2		

(NOTES)

No. 1 See decision of June 13 '04
No. 1 On Chickasaw Roll as Arthur N. Leecraft
No. 2 "   "   "   " Lela M. Lecroft
No. 3 "   "   "   " Bertram M. "
No. 6 Enrolled Dec. 13/98.

Oct. 11/98

Chickasaw Enrollment Cards 1898-1914
Chickasaw by Blood   Volume III

RESIDENCE: Choctaw Nation *COUNTY*   CARD NO.
POST OFFICE: Stringtown, Ind. Ter.   FIELD NO.

	NAME	RELATION-SHIP TO PERSON FIRST NAMED	AGE	SEX	BLOOD	TRIBAL ENROLLMENT		
						YEAR	COUNTY	PAGE
1	Carnes, Dora	NAMED	18	F	3/4			
2	Calvin, Ella M.	Dau	1 1/2	"	3/8			
3	Carnes, Melvin B.	Son	3mo	M				

TRIBAL ENROLLMENT OF PARENTS

	NAME OF FATHER	YEAR	COUNTY	NAME OF MOTHER	YEAR	COUNTY
1	Wm B. Anderson	1897	Chick residing in Choctaw N. 3rd Dist.	Lizzie Anderson	Dead	Chick residing in Choctaw N. 3rd Dist.
2	Morris Calvin	Dead	Choctaw Roll	No. 1		
3	Ellis H. Carnes	1897	" "	No. 1		

(NOTES)
No. 1 On Choctaw Census Record No. 2 Jacks Fork Co, Page 124 as Dora Calvin,

transferred to Chickasaw Roll by Dawes Com.

No. 1 "   "   Roll 1896, Jacks Fork County, No. 3052 as Dora Calvin
No. 1 wife of Ellis Harris Carnes, Choctaw Roll Card No. 368.
No. 3 Enrolled May 16th 1899.

Oct. 11/98.

CANCELLED Stamped across card

RESIDENCE: Choctaw Nation *COUNTY*   CARD NO.
POST OFFICE: Hartshorn, Ind. Ter.   FIELD NO.

	NAME	RELATION-SHIP TO PERSON FIRST NAMED	AGE	SEX	BLOOD	TRIBAL ENROLLMENT		
						YEAR	COUNTY	PAGE
1	Anderson, Tom	NAMED	25	M	3/4	~~1897~~	~~Pontotoc~~	~~45~~
2	" Alice	Wife	18	F	I.W.			
3	" Lena	Dau	3mo	"	3/8			
4	" Mary Jane	"	3mo	"	3/8			
5	" Graham	Son	7wks	"	3/8			

TRIBAL ENROLLMENT OF PARENTS

	NAME OF FATHER	YEAR	COUNTY	NAME OF MOTHER	YEAR	COUNTY
1	Wm Anderson	1897	Chick residing in Choctaw N. 3rd Dist.	Lizzie Anderson	Dead	Chickasaw Roll
2	Wm Ridge	Dead	Non citizen	Mary Ridge		Non citizen
3	No. 1			No. 2		
4	No. 1			No. 2		
5	No. 1			No. 2		

(NOTES)

No. 1 On Choctaw Census Record No. 2 Jacks Fork Co, Page 20; Transferred to Chickasaw Roll by Dawes Com

No. 1 On Choctaw Roll, 1896, Jacks Fork Co, No. 497 as Thomas Anderson

~~No. 1 On 1897 Roll as Thomas Anderson~~ *(remainder illegible)*

No. 2 Marriage certificate to be supplied. Received Nov. 1, 1898.

No. 4 Enrolled June 23rd 1900

No. 5 Born Aug. 5, 1902; Enrolled Sept. 30, 1902.

Oct. 11/98

CANCELLED Stamped across card

Transferred to Choctaw Card #5626 Jan. 16, 1903

NAME	RELATIONSHIP TO PERSON FIRST NAMED	AGE	SEX	BLOOD	TRIBAL ENROLLMENT		
					YEAR	COUNTY	PAGE
1 Moore, Austin	NAMED	30	M	Full			

RESIDENCE: Choctaw Nation   COUNTY   CARD NO.
POST OFFICE: Featherston, Ind. Ter.   FIELD NO.

TRIBAL ENROLLMENT OF PARENTS

NAME OF FATHER	YEAR	COUNTY	NAME OF MOTHER	YEAR	COUNTY
1 No-ub-by	Dead	Chickasaw Roll	Emeline	Dead	Chickasaw Roll

(NOTES)

On Choctaw Census Record No. 2 Page 345; Transferred to Chickasaw Roll by Dawes Com

Husband of Lily Moore, Choctaw Roll Card No. 367

On Choctaw Roll 1896 Sans Bois County, No. 8421.

Oct. 11/98.

CANCELLED Stamped across card

RESIDENCE: Choctaw Nation   COUNTY   CARD NO.
POST OFFICE: Featherston, Ind. Ter.   FIELD NO.

NAME	RELATIONSHIP TO PERSON FIRST NAMED	AGE	SEX	BLOOD	TRIBAL ENROLLMENT		
					YEAR	COUNTY	PAGE
1 Perry, Coleman	NAMED	41	M	3/4			
2 " Hattie	Wife	30	F	1/2			
3 " Isaac	Son	7	M	5/8			
4 " Jefferson	"	5	"	5/8			
5 " Beckey	Dau	6mo	F	5/8			

TRIBAL ENROLLMENT OF PARENTS

NAME OF FATHER	YEAR	COUNTY	NAME OF MOTHER	YEAR	COUNTY
1 Jackson Perry	Dead	Chickasaw Roll	Salima Perry	Dead	Chickasaw Roll

2	Wallace Carney		Sans Bois Cp Choctaw Roll	Susie Carney	"	"	"
3	No. 1			No. 2			
4	No. 1			No. 2			
5	No. 1			No. 2			

(NOTES)

All on Choctaw Census Record No. 2, Page 390; Transferred to Chickasaw Roll by Dawes Com.

No. 1 On Choctaw Roll 1896 Sans Bois Co, No. 10064
No. 2 "   "   " 1896 "   " " " 10065
No. 3 "   "   " 1896 "   " " " 10067
No. 4 "   "   " 1896 "   " " " 10068
No. 5 Enrolled Aug. 1/99.

Oct. 11/98

CANCELLED Stamped across card

RESIDENCE: Panola   COUNTY   CARD NO.
POST OFFICE: Silo, Ind. Ter.   FIELD NO.

NAME		RELATION-SHIP TO PERSON FIRST NAMED	AGE	SEX	BLOOD	TRIBAL ENROLLMENT		
						YEAR	COUNTY	PAGE
1	Gardner, Susie		19	F	1/8	1897	Chick residing in Choctaw N. 3rd Dist.	73
2	" Sudie	Dau	2	"	1/16	1897	" " " "	74
3	" Dollie	"	1	"	1/16			
4	" Fitzhugh L.	Son	2mo	M	1/16			

TRIBAL ENROLLMENT OF PARENTS

	NAME OF FATHER	YEAR	COUNTY	NAME OF MOTHER	YEAR	COUNTY
1	U.M. Cooper (I.W.)	1897	Chick residing in Choctaw N. 3rd Dist.	Deuk Cooper	Dead	Pickens
2	Robert Gardner		Blue County Choctaw Roll	No. 1		
3	" "		" "	No. 1		
4	" "		" "	No. 1		

(NOTES)

No. 1 Wife of Robert Gardner, Choctaw Roll card No. 366
No. 2 On Chickasaw Roll as Sadie Gardner
No. 4 Enrolled Aug. 18th 1900

Oct. 11/98.

Chickasaw Enrollment Cards 1898-1914
Chickasaw by Blood   Volume III

RESIDENCE: Choctaw Nation   *COUNTY*   CARD NO.
POST OFFICE: Featherston, Ind. Ter.   FIELD NO.

NAME	RELATION-SHIP TO PERSON FIRST NAMED	AGE	SEX	BLOOD	TRIBAL ENROLLMENT		
					YEAR	COUNTY	PAGE
1 Carney, Allen	NAMED	25	M	1/2			

TRIBAL ENROLLMENT OF PARENTS

| NAME OF FATHER | YEAR | COUNTY | NAME OF MOTHER | YEAR | COUNTY |
| 1 Wallace Carney | | Sans Bois Co Choctaw Roll | Susie Carney | Dead | Chickasaw Roll |

(NOTES)
On Choctaw Census Record, Sans Bois Co, Page 86, Transferred to Chickasaw Roll by Dawes Com.
On Choctaw Roll 1896, Sans Bois County, No. 2101
Husband of Susan Carney, Choctaw Roll, Card No. 365.

Oct. 11/98.

CANCELLED Stamped across card

RESIDENCE: Panola   *COUNTY*   CARD NO.
POST OFFICE: Mead, Ind. Ter.   FIELD NO.

NAME	RELATION-SHIP TO PERSON FIRST NAMED	AGE	SEX	BLOOD	TRIBAL ENROLLMENT		
					YEAR	COUNTY	PAGE
1 O'Brien, Joe Frank	NAMED	45	M	I.W.	1897	Pickens	77
2 " Katie	Wife	45	F	1/16	1897	"	11
3 Orndorff, Calivn[sic] P.	StepSon	8	M	1/32	1897	"	11

TRIBAL ENROLLMENT OF PARENTS

NAME OF FATHER	YEAR	COUNTY	NAME OF MOTHER	YEAR	COUNTY
1 Thomas O'Brien	Dead	Non-citizen	Sophia O'Brien	Dead	Non-citizen
2 Joel Sturdivant	"	" "	Osabella Sturdivant	1897	Pickens
3 Ed Orndorff	"	" "	No. 2		

(NOTES)
No. 1 On Chickasaw Roll as J.F. O'Brien
No. 3 "   "   " " E.P. Orndof

P.O. Oakland, I.T. 11/10/02   Oct.
11/98.

CANCELLED Stamped across card

144

Chickasaw Enrollment Cards 1898-1914
Chickasaw by Blood   Volume III

RESIDENCE: Panola COUNTY   CARD NO.

POST OFFICE: Colbert, Ind. Ter.   FIELD NO.

	NAME	RELATION-SHIP TO PERSON FIRST NAMED	AGE	SEX	BLOOD	TRIBAL ENROLLMENT		
						YEAR	COUNTY	PAGE
1	Mashburn, John Horton	NAMED	53	M	I.W.	1897	Panola	76
2	" Laura A.	Wife	38	F	1/4	1897	"	4
3	Easky. Ruth	Step-Dau	11	"	1/8	1897	"	4
4	" Tandy	Ward	19	M	1/8	1897	"	4

TRIBAL ENROLLMENT OF PARENTS

	NAME OF FATHER	YEAR	COUNTY	NAME OF MOTHER	YEAR	COUNTY
1	Geo. W. Mashburn	Dead	Non citizen	Martha A. Mashburn	Dead	Non citizen
2	Joel Kemp	"	Choctaw Roll	Frances Kemp	"	Panola
3	Janeska Easkey	"	Cherokee Roll	No. 2		
4	Buck "	"	" "	Lucy Kemp	Dead	Panola

(NOTES)

No. 1 See decision of June 13 '04

No. 1 Certified copy of marriage certificate to first Chickasaw wife to be supplied. Received Oct. 11/98.

No. 1 On Chickasaw Roll as J.H. Mashburn

No. 2 "   "   "   " LA. Easky.

Oct. 11/98.

CANCELLED Stamped across card

RESIDENCE: Panola COUNTY   CARD NO.

POST OFFICE: Cale, Ind. Ter.   FIELD NO.

	NAME	RELATION-SHIP TO PERSON FIRST NAMED	AGE	SEX	BLOOD	TRIBAL ENROLLMENT		
						YEAR	COUNTY	PAGE
1	Perkins, Walter William	NAMED	27	M	I.W.	1897	Panola	85
2	" Laura B.	Wife	20	F	1/4	1897	"	6
3	" Hearl M	Son	1mo	M	1/8			
4	" Julia Frances	Dau	3mo	F	1/8			

TRIBAL ENROLLMENT OF PARENTS

	NAME OF FATHER	YEAR	COUNTY	NAME OF MOTHER	YEAR	COUNTY
1	William Perkins	Dead	Non-citizen	Julia Perkins		Non-citizen
2	Albert H. Moberly	"	" "	Fannie Mead	1897	Panola
3	No. 1			No. 2		
4	No. 1			No. 2		

(NOTES)

No. 1 On Chickasaw Roll as William Walter Perkins   *(No. 1 Dawes' Roll No. 162)*

Chickasaw Enrollment Cards 1898-1914
Chickasaw by Blood   Volume III

No. 2 "   "   "   " Laura B. Moberly
No. 3 Enrolled Nov. 4, 1899
No. 4 Enrolled June 5, 1901

P.O. Sterrett, I.T.   Oct. 11/98.

RESIDENCE: Panola COUNTY					CARD NO.			
POST OFFICE: Colbert, Ind. Ter.					FIELD NO.			
	NAME	RELATION- SHIP TO PERSON FIRST NAMED	AGE	SEX	BLOOD	TRIBAL ENROLLMENT		
						YEAR	COUNTY	PAGE
1	Grinslade, Henry		37	M	I.W.	1897	Panola	76
2	" Sallie	Wife	29	F	1/2	1897	"	3
3	" Benjamin Jackson	Son	12	M	1/4	1897	"	3
4	" William Edward	"	11	"	1/4	1897	"	3
5	" Martha Elizabeth	Dau	9	F	1/4	1897	"	3
6	" John Wilson	Son	7	M	1/4	1897	"	3
7	" Albert Milton	"	5	"	1/4	1897	"	3
8	" Henry Martin	"	3	"	1/4	1897	"	3
9	" Walter Lee	"	1	"	1/4			
10	" Hattie May	Dau	2mo	F	1/4			

TRIBAL ENROLLMENT OF PARENTS

	NAME OF FATHER	YEAR	COUNTY	NAME OF MOTHER	YEAR	COUNTY
1	Benj. Grinslade		non citizen	Mary C. Grinslade	Dead	non citizen
2	Jackson Kemp	1897	Panola	Ziley Kemp	1897	Panola
3	No. 1			No. 2		
4	No. 1			No. 2		
5	No. 1			No. 2		
6	No. 1			No. 2		
7	No. 1			No. 2		
8	No. 1			No. 2		
9	No. 1			No. 2		
10	No. 1			No. 2		

(NOTES)

No. 3 On Chickasaw Roll as B.J. Grinsdale   *(No. 1 Dawes' Roll No. 840)*
No. 4 "   "   "   " W.E.   "
No. 5 "   "   "   " M.E.   "
No. 6 "   "   "   " J.W.   "
No. 7 "   "   "   " A.M.   "
No. 8 "   "   "   " H.M.   "
    Sir name of All on Chickasaw Roll "

No. 10 Born May 6th 1902; Enrolled July 1st 1902.

P.O. Paucannda, I.T. 11/6/02 Oct. 11/98.

CANCELLED Stamped across card

RESIDENCE: Panola **COUNTY**				**CARD NO.**				
POST OFFICE: Mead, Ind. Ter.				**FIELD NO.**				

	NAME	RELATION-SHIP TO PERSON FIRST NAMED	AGE	SEX	BLOOD	TRIBAL ENROLLMENT		
						YEAR	COUNTY	PAGE
1	Frankln, Edward Q,		39	M	I.W.	1897	Panola	76
~~2~~	~~" Louisa~~	~~Wife~~	~~30~~	~~F~~	~~Full~~	~~1897~~	~~"~~	~~1~~
3	" Jesse James	Son	13	M	1/2	1897	"	1
4	" Johnson	"	11	"	1/2	1897	"	1
5	" Joe	"	9	"	1/2	1897	"	1
6	" Edna Lou Sophia	Dau	7	F	1/2	1897	"	1
7	" Samuel Wesley	Son	5	M	1/2	1897	"	1
8	" Dollie Ulid	Dau	2	F	1/2	1897	"	1
~~9~~	~~" Oliver Vest~~	~~Son~~	~~6wks~~	~~M~~	~~1/2~~			

TRIBAL ENROLLMENT OF PARENTS

	NAME OF FATHER	YEAR	COUNTY	NAME OF MOTHER	YEAR	COUNTY
1	J.H. Franklin	Dead	Non citizen	Martha Franklin	Dead	Non citizenb
~~2~~	~~John Calhoun~~	~~"~~	~~Panola~~	~~Emily Calhoun~~	~~"~~	~~Panola~~
3	No. 1			No. 2		
4	No. 1			No. 2		
5	No. 1			No. 2		
6	No. 1			No. 2		
7	No. 1			No. 2		
8	No. 1			No. 2		
~~9~~	~~No. 1~~			~~No. 2~~		

(NOTES)

No. 1 See decision of June 13 '04, *(No. 1 Dawes' Roll No. 403)*
No. 1 On Chickasaw Roll as Ed. Franklin
No. 3 " " " " Jessie "
No. 6 " " " " Sophia "
No. 7 " " " " Sam W. "
No. 8 " " " " Dollie "
No. 9 Enrolled Nov. 23/98. *(No. 9 Dawes' Roll No. 3389)*
No. 9 Died Sept 22, 1899; Proof of Death filed Nov. 8, 1902.
No. 2 Died Nov. 5, 1900; Proof of Death filed Nov. 8th 1902
(Other notations illegible)

Oct. 11/98.

Chickasaw Enrollment Cards 1898-1914
Chickasaw by Blood   Volume III

RESIDENCE: Choctaw Nation   ~~COUNTY~~   CARD NO.

POST OFFICE: Cale, Ind. Ter.   FIELD NO.

NAME	RELATION-SHIP TO PERSON FIRST NAMED	AGE	SEX	BLOOD	TRIBAL ENROLLMENT		
					YEAR	COUNTY	PAGE
1 Moore, Luke Pr?or	FIRST NAMED	68	M	1/2	1897	Chick residing in Choctaw N. 3rd Dist.	74
2 Feland, John R.	Ward	18	"	1/8	1897	Pickens	18
3 " James C.	"	15	"	1/8	1897	"	18

TRIBAL ENROLLMENT OF PARENTS

NAME OF FATHER	YEAR	COUNTY	NAME OF MOTHER	YEAR	COUNTY
1 Christopher Moore	Dead	Non citizen	Catherine Moore	Dead	Chickasaw Roll
2 George Feland	"	" "	Mollie Feland	"	Panola
3 " "	"	" "	" "	"	"

(NOTES)

No. 1 On Chickasaw Roll as L.P. Moore
No. 3 " " " " James Feland
No. 2 Also on 1897 Roll Panola Co, Page 92 as J.J. Fielding
No. 3 " " 1897 " " " " 92 " J.C. "

Nos. 2 and 3 P.O. Chickasha, I.T.   Oct. 11/98.

RESIDENCE: Panola   COUNTY   CARD NO.

POST OFFICE: Colbert   FIELD NO.

NAME	RELATION-SHIP TO PERSON FIRST NAMED	AGE	SEX	BLOOD	TRIBAL ENROLLMENT		
					YEAR	COUNTY	PAGE
1 Love, Wyatt	FIRST NAMED	65	M	1/4	1897	Panola	2

TRIBAL ENROLLMENT OF PARENTS

NAME OF FATHER	YEAR	COUNTY	NAME OF MOTHER	YEAR	COUNTY
1 Isaac Love	Dead	Chickasaw Roll	Eliza Love	Dead	Chickasaw Roll

(NOTES)

No. 1 Died June 21, 1899. Evidence of Death filed April 2, 1902.

                                                  Oct. 11/98.

CANCELLED Stamped across card

	RESIDENCE: Panola COUNTY				CARD NO.			
	POST OFFICE: Colbert, Ind. Ter.				FIELD NO.			

	NAME	RELATION-SHIP TO PERSON FIRST NAMED	AGE	SEX	BLOOD	TRIBAL ENROLLMENT		
						YEAR	COUNTY	PAGE
1	Graham, Edward	NAMED	47	M	I.W.	1897	Panola	76
2	" Minerva	Wife	52	F	1/2	1897	"	4
3	" Fred J.	Son	14	M	1/4	1897	"	4

TRIBAL ENROLLMENT OF PARENTS							
	NAME OF FATHER	YEAR	COUNTY	NAME OF MOTHER	YEAR	COUNTY
1	Thos. M. Graham		Non citizen	Ann Graham		Non citizen
2	James *(Illegible)*	Dead	Choctaw Roll	*(Name Illegible)*	Dead	Chickasaw Roll
3	No. 1			No. 2		

(NOTES)

No. 1 On Chickasaw Roll as Ed. Graham   *(No. 1 Dawes' Roll No. 161)*
No. 2 "   "   "   " Minerva "

Oct. 11/98.

	RESIDENCE: Panola COUNTY				CARD NO.			
	POST OFFICE: Kemp, Ind. Ter.				FIELD NO.			

	NAME	RELATION-SHIP TO PERSON FIRST NAMED	AGE	SEX	BLOOD	TRIBAL ENROLLMENT		
						YEAR	COUNTY	PAGE
1	Reynolds, Darius	NAMED	33	M	1/2	1897	Panola	4
2	" Elizabeth	Wife	28	F	1/2	1897	"	5
3	" Elsie D.	Dau	9	"	1/2	1897	"	5
4	" James	Son	5	M	1/2	1897	"	5
5	" Mamie	Dau	3	F	1/2	1897	"	5
6	" Manilla	"	7mo	"	1/2			
7	~~Powell, Bettie~~	~~Sister~~	~~46~~	~~"~~	~~1/2~~	~~1897~~	~~Panola~~	~~5~~
8	Reynolds, Colbert U.H.	Son	4mo	M	1/2			

TRIBAL ENROLLMENT OF PARENTS							
	NAME OF FATHER	YEAR	COUNTY	NAME OF MOTHER	YEAR	COUNTY
1	Tom Reynolds	Dead	Panola	Liley Reynolds	Dead	Panola
2	Wall Kemp	"	"	Elsie Kemp	"	"
3	No. 1			No. 2		
4	No. 1			No. 2		
5	No. 1			No. 2		
6	No. 1			No. 2		
7	Tom Reynolds	Dead	Panola	Liley Reynolds	Dead	Panola

8	No. 1			No. 2		

(NOTES)

No. 1 On Chickasaw Roll as Davius Reynolds
No. 2 "   "   "   " Lizzie   "
No. 4 "   "   "   " Jim   "
No. 7 Died about Feb. 1899. Proof of Death filed Nov. 8, 1902
No. 8 Enrolled Oct. 8, 1900.

Oct. 11/98.

RESIDENCE: Panola   *COUNTY*   *CARD NO.*

POST OFFICE: Colbert, Ind. Ter.   *FIELD NO.*

	NAME	RELATION-SHIP TO PERSON FIRST NAMED	AGE	SEX	BLOOD	TRIBAL ENROLLMENT		
						YEAR	COUNTY	PAGE
1	Love, Mart	NAMED	22	M	1/8	1897	Panola	3
2	" Minnie	Wife	18	F	I.W.			
3	" Pierre Sparlin	Son	1mo	M	1/16			

	TRIBAL ENROLLMENT OF PARENTS						
	NAME OF FATHER	YEAR	COUNTY	NAME OF MOTHER	YEAR	COUNTY
1	Wyatt Love	1897	Panola	Sarah Love	Dead	Non Citizen
2	J.T. Sheldon		non citz	Alice Sheldon		" "
3	No. 1			No. 2		

(NOTES)

No. 2 Enrolled Aug. 16/99.   *(No. 2 Dawes' Roll No. 160)*
No. 3 Born Aug. 13th 1902. Enrolled Sept. 17, 1902.

Oct. 11/98.

RESIDENCE: Panola   *COUNTY*   *CARD NO.*

POST OFFICE: Colbert, Ind. Ter.   *FIELD NO.*

	NAME	RELATION-SHIP TO PERSON FIRST NAMED	AGE	SEX	BLOOD	TRIBAL ENROLLMENT		
						YEAR	COUNTY	PAGE
1	Potts, Joseph B.	NAMED	42	M	1/4	1897	Panola	6
2	" Pearl	Dau	16	F	1/8	1897	"	6
3	" Jewel	"	14	"	1/8	1897	"	6
4	" Frank	Son	11	M	1/8	1897	"	6
5	" Joseph B, Jr.	"	9	"	1/8	1897	"	6
6	" Ruby	Dau	2	F	1/8	1897	"	6
7	" Nannie V.	Wife	36	"	I.W.	1897	"	76
8	" Douglas Howard	Son	5mo	M	1/8			

TRIBAL ENROLLMENT OF PARENTS

	NAME OF FATHER	YEAR	COUNTY	NAME OF MOTHER	YEAR	COUNTY
1	Joe Potts	Dead	Non Citizen	Rhoda Potts	Dead	Panola
2	No. 1			Nannie V. Potts		White woman
3	No. 1			" " "		" "
4	No. 1			" " "		" "
5	No. 1			" " "		" "
6	No. 1			" " "		" "
7	J.P. Davis	Dead	Non Citizen	Minnie Davis		Non citizen
8	No. 1			" " "		" "

(NOTES)

No. 1 On Chickasaw Roll as J.B. Potts
No. 5 "   "   "   " Joe " Jr.
No. 6 "   "   " Page 85
No. 7 "   "   " as N.V. Potts
No. 7 Enrolled Oct. 12/98
No. 8 Enrolled December 3, 1900
No. 2 is now wife of Harley Colbert Chickasaw Roll Card No. 1258
     Evidence of marriage filed Dec. 24, 1902.   Oct. 11/98.

RESIDENCE: Panola COUNTY   CARD NO.
POST OFFICE: Cale, Ind. Ter.   FIELD NO.

	NAME	RELATION-SHIP TO PERSON FIRST NAMED	AGE	SEX	BLOOD	TRIBAL ENROLLMENT		
						YEAR	COUNTY	PAGE
1	Lemon, Robert Breckinridge	NAMED	30	M	I.W.	1897	Panola	76
2	" Maria	Wife	29	F	3/8	1897	"	6
3	" Bennie	Son	8	M	3/16	1897	"	6
4	" Fannie	Dau	7	F	3/16	1897	"	6
5	" Willie	Son	4	M	3/16	1897	"	6
6	" Maggie	Dau	3	F	3/16	1897	"	6
7	" Robert Emory	Son	7mo	M	3/16			
8	" Mary R.	Dau	1mo	F	3/16			

TRIBAL ENROLLMENT OF PARENTS

	NAME OF FATHER	YEAR	COUNTY	NAME OF MOTHER	YEAR	COUNTY
1	Preston Lemon		Non Citizen	Malissa Lemon		Non citizen
2	Ben Roark	Dead	Chickasaw Roll	Frances E. Mead	1897	Panola
3	No. 1			No. 2		
4	No. 1			No. 2		
5	No. 1			No. 2		

6	No. 1			No. 2		
7	No. 1			No. 2		
8	No. 1			No. 2		

(NOTES)

No. 1 On Chickasaw Roll as R.B. Lemons   *(No. 1 Dawes' Roll No. 159)*
    All others on Chickasaw Roll as Lemmons
No. 8 Enrolled Nov. 4/99.

P.O. Sterrett, I.T.   Oct. 11/98.

RESIDENCE: Panola *COUNTY*   **CARD NO.**
POST OFFICE: Cale, Ind. Ter.   **FIELD NO.**

	NAME	RELATION-SHIP TO PERSON FIRST NAMED	AGE	SEX	BLOOD	TRIBAL ENROLLMENT		
						YEAR	COUNTY	PAGE
1	Mead, Santford Minor		50	M	I.W.	1897	Panola	76
2	" Frances Elizabeth	Wife	50	F	3/4	1897	"	6
3	" Walter Bradford	Son	18	M	1/4	1897	"	6
4	" Martha Frances	Dau	17	F	3/8	1897	"	6
5	" Leve Landers	Son	13	M	3/8	1897	"	6
6	" Simon Minor	"	11	"	3/8	1897	"	6
7	" Abigale	Dau	8	F	3/8	1897	"	6

TRIBAL ENROLLMENT OF PARENTS

	NAME OF FATHER	YEAR	COUNTY	NAME OF MOTHER	YEAR	COUNTY
1	F.A. Mead	Dead	Non Citizen	Chanty B. Mead	Dead	Non Citizen
2	Jack Kemp	"	Chickasaw Roll	Maria Kemp	"	Panola
3	No. 1			Rosanna Mead	"	"
4	No. 1			No. 2		
5	No. 1			No. 2		
6	No. 1			No. 2		
7	No. 1			No. 2		

(NOTES)

No. 1 See decision of June 13 '04.   *(No. 1 Dawes' Roll No. 402)*
No. 1 On Chickasaw Roll as S.M. Mead
No. 2 "   "   "   " Mrs. F.E. "
No. 3 "   "   "   " W.B. "
No. 4 "   "   "   " Martha F "
No. 5 "   "   "   " L.L. "
No. 6 "   "   "   " S.M. " Jr.

11/1/02 P.O. Sterrett I.T.   Oct. 11/98.

Chickasaw Enrollment Cards 1898-1914
Chickasaw by Blood   Volume III

RESIDENCE: Panola   COUNTY

CARD NO.

POST OFFICE: Colbert, Ind. Ter.

FIELD NO.

NAME	RELATION-SHIP TO PERSON FIRST NAMED	AGE	SEX	BLOOD	TRIBAL ENROLLMENT		
					YEAR	COUNTY	PAGE
1 Love, Isaac Newton	NAMED	29	M	1/8	1897	Panola	2

TRIBAL ENROLLMENT OF PARENTS

NAME OF FATHER	YEAR	COUNTY	NAME OF MOTHER	YEAR	COUNTY
1 Wyatt Love	1897	Panola	Sarah Love	Dead	Non-Citizen

(NOTES)

On Chickasaw Roll as Newt Love.

Oct. 11/98.

RESIDENCE: Choctaw Nation 3rd Dist.   COUNTY

CARD NO.

POST OFFICE: Tuckahoma, Ind. Ter.

FIELD NO.

NAME	RELATION-SHIP TO PERSON FIRST NAMED	AGE	SEX	BLOOD	TRIBAL ENROLLMENT		
					YEAR	COUNTY	PAGE
1 McGee, Ellis Void	NAMED	48	M	1/2			
2 " Susan	Wife	37	F	Full	1897	Chick residing in Choctaw N. 3rd Dist.	13
3 " Sol Void	Son	14	M	3/4			
4 " Esau Void	"	11	"	3/4			
5 " Isom Void	"	9	"	3/4			
6 " Mary M. Void	Dau	7	F	3/4			

TRIBAL ENROLLMENT OF PARENTS

NAME OF FATHER	YEAR	COUNTY	NAME OF MOTHER	YEAR	COUNTY
1 Isaac McGee	Dead	Chickasaw Roll	Angeline McGee	Dead	Chickasaw Roll
2 James Polk	"	" "	Margaret Polk	"	" "
3 No. 1			No. 2		
4 No. 1			No. 2		
5 No. 1			No. 2		
6 No. 1			No. 2		

(NOTES)

All except No. 2 on Choctaw Census Record No. 2, Page ???; transferred to Chickasaw Roll by Dawes Com.
No. 1 On Choctaw Roll as Ellis Magee
No. 4 "   "   "   " Ason   "
No. 1 On Choctaw Roll, 1896, Jacks Fork County, No. 8887 as Ellis Magee
No. 3 "   "   " 1896   "   "   "   " 8888 " Sal   "
No. 4 "   "   " 1896   "   "   "   " 8889 " Asin "
No. 5 "   "   " 1896   "   "   "   " 8890 " Ison "

153

No. 6 "   "   " 1896 "   "   "   " 8891 " Mary M "
Nos. 1, 3,4,5 & 6 transferred to Choctaw Card No. 5422 Oct. 17th 1902

Oct. 11/98.

RESIDENCE: Panola COUNTY					CARD NO.			
POST OFFICE: Mead, Ind. Ter.					FIELD NO.			
NAME	RELATION-SHIP TO PERSON FIRST NAMED	AGE	SEX	BLOOD	TRIBAL ENROLLMENT			
					YEAR	COUNTY	PAGE	
1 Yarborough, William Henry	NAMED	20	M	1/8	1897	Panola	5	
2 Morrison, Ella Gertrude	Sister	17	F	1/8	1897	"	5	
3 Yarborough, Minnie May	"	14	"	1/8	1897	"	5	
4 " George Augustus	Bro	12	M	1/8	1897	"	5	
5 " James Martin	"	9	"	1/8	1897	"	5	
6 Morrison, Elva	Dau of No. 2	1mo	F	1/16				

TRIBAL ENROLLMENT OF PARENTS

	NAME OF FATHER	YEAR	COUNTY	NAME OF MOTHER	YEAR	COUNTY
1	G"o" A. Yarborough		Non Citizen	Sally Yarborough	Dead	Panola
2	" " "		" "	" "	"	"
3	" " "		" "	" "	"	"
4	" " "		" "	" "	"	"
5	" " "		" "	" "	"	"
6	E.W. Morrison		" "	No. 2		

(NOTES)

No. 1 On Chickasaw Roll as W.H. Yarborough
No. 2 "   "   " " Ella   "   Is now wife of E.W. Morrison a non citizen.
No. 3 "   "   " " Minnie   "
No. 4 "   "   " " G.A.   "
No. 5 "   "   " " J.M.   "
No. 6 Enrolled Oct. 19th 1900.

Oct. 11/98.

RESIDENCE: Choctaw Nation COUNTY					CARD NO.			
POST OFFICE: McAlester, Ind. Ter.					FIELD NO.			
NAME	RELATION-SHIP TO PERSON FIRST NAMED	AGE	SEX	BLOOD	TRIBAL ENROLLMENT			
					YEAR	COUNTY	PAGE	
1 McAlester, James Jackson	NAMED	56	M	I.W.	1897	Chick residing in Choctaw N. 1st Dist.	82	

2	" Rebecca	Wife	56	F	3/4	1897	" " " "		68
3	" Sudie	Dau	24	"	3/8	1897	" " " "		68
4	" James Burney	Son	22	M	3/8	1897	" " " "		68
5	" William Berry	"	18	"	3/8	1897	" " " "		68
6	" Rebecca Leo	Gr.Dau	1mo	F	3/16				
7	" James J.J.	Son of No. 4	1mo	M	3/16				
8	" Asa	Wife of No. 4	23	F	I.W.				

TRIBAL ENROLLMENT OF PARENTS

	NAME OF FATHER	YEAR	COUNTY	NAME OF MOTHER	YEAR	COUNTY
1	Wm McAlester	Dead	Non citizen	Elizabeth McAlester	Dead	Non citizen
2	David Burney	"	Chickasaw Roll	Lucy Burney	"	Chickasaw Roll
3	No. 1			No. 2		
4	No. 1			No. 2		
5	No. 1			No. 2		
6	No. 4			Asa McAlester		white woman
7	No. 4			" "		" "
8	Edw. Jewett		non citz	Jeanne Jewett		non citz

(NOTES)

No. 1 Admitted by Dawes Commission in 1896 as an intermarried citizen   *(No. 1 Dawes' Roll No. 401)*
    Choctaw Case No. 1293. No Appeal.
No. 1 On Chickasaw Roll as J.J. McAlester   *(No. 8 Dawes' Roll No. 53)*
No. 3 "   "   " " Sadie   "
No. 4 "   "   " " James B   "
No. 5 "   "   " " William B.   "
No. 6 Enrolled Oct. 13th 1900
No. 7 Born June 7th 1902. Enrolled July 14th 1902
    See Chickasaw Card #D287 for Asa McAlester the wife of No. 4
No. 1 See decision of June 13 '04.
No. 8 transferred from Chickasaw Card #D287 March 24, 1903. See decision of March 13, 1903.

Oct. 11/98.

RESIDENCE: Pickens COUNTY						CARD NO.		
POST OFFICE: Woodville, Ind. Ter.						FIELD NO.		
NAME	RELATIONSHIP TO PERSON FIRST NAMED	AGE	SEX	BLOOD	TRIBAL ENROLLMENT			
					YEAR	COUNTY	PAGE	
1 Thompson, James P.		48	M	I.W.	1897	Pickens	78	

155

Chickasaw Enrollment Cards 1898-1914
Chickasaw by Blood   Volume III

TRIBAL ENROLLMENT OF PARENTS						
NAME OF FATHER	YEAR	COUNTY	NAME OF MOTHER	YEAR	COUNTY	
1 J.G. Thompson	Dead	Non Citizen	Martha Thompson	Dead	non citizen	

(NOTES)

No. I was husband of Lucy Thompson on 1897 Roll of the Chickasaw Nation, Pickens Co., Page 13.

    She died April 2, 1898. *(No. I Dawes' Roll No. 339)*

    Affidavit of J.E. Vonson, a minister of the Gospel, that he performed the marriage ceremony between No. I and his Chickasaw wife Lucy Thompson nee Juzan, near Woodville, I.T. July 1, 1886 filed July 28th 1902.

    Affidavits of Amelia Stelle, Rebecca McDuffis & Robt. S. Bell relative to the marriage between No. I and Lucy Watkins in July 1886, filED Jany. 2, 190?.

Oct. 11, 1898

RESIDENCE: Panola COUNTY					CARD NO.			
POST OFFICE: Colbert, Ind. Ter.					FIELD NO.			

NAME	RELATION-SHIP TO PERSON FIRST NAMED	AGE	SEX	BLOOD	TRIBAL ENROLLMENT		
					YEAR	COUNTY	PAGE
1 ~~Ramsey, Amanda~~	NAMED	~~25~~	F	~~1/4~~	~~1897~~	~~Panola~~	4
2 Ramsey, Mabel	Dau	2mo	"	1/8			
3 " ~~Gustavus A.~~	~~Husband~~	~~45~~	~~M~~	~~I.W.~~			

TRIBAL ENROLLMENT OF PARENTS						
NAME OF FATHER	YEAR	COUNTY	NAME OF MOTHER	YEAR	COUNTY	
1 ~~J.F. Potts~~	~~1897~~	~~Panola~~	~~Emily Potts~~	~~Dead~~	~~Panola~~	
2 G.A. Ramsey		non citizen	No. I			
3 ~~J.Z. Ramsey~~		" "	~~Judith E. Ramsey~~		~~non citizen~~	

(NOTES)

No. I wife of G.A. Ramsey, non citizen

No. I Died April 18th 1902. See testimony of husband of May 9th 1902

    Gustav A. Ramsey husband of No. I on Chickasaw D#253 A.

No. 2 Enrolled Mar. 18/99

No. 3 admitted by Dawes Commission Case #123 and rejected by U.S. Court at Ardmore, I.T.

No. 3 transferred from Chickasaw Card #D253A Oct. 31, 1904. See decision of Oct. 15, 1904.

Enrollment of No. 3 cancelled by order of Dept. *(remainder illegible)*

Oct. 11/98.

RESIDENCE: Panola COUNTY					CARD NO.			
POST OFFICE: Colbert, Ind. Ter.					FIELD NO.			

NAME	RELATION-SHIP TO PERSON FIRST NAMED	AGE	SEX	BLOOD	TRIBAL ENROLLMENT		
					YEAR	COUNTY	PAGE
1 Collins, Dan	NAMED	59	N	I.W.	1897	Panola	76

2	"	Sarah A.	Wife	54	F	1/4	1897	"	2
3	"	Maude	Dau	20	"	1/8	1897	"	2
4	"	Dannie	Son	17	M	1/8	1897	"	2
5	"	Charley	"	13	"	1/8	1897	"	3

TRIBAL ENROLLMENT OF PARENTS

	NAME OF FATHER	YEAR	COUNTY	NAME OF MOTHER	YEAR	COUNTY
1	George Collins	Dead	Non citizen	Mildred Collins	Dead	Non citizen
2	Joe Potts	"	" "	Rhoda Potts	"	Chickasaw Roll
3	No. 1			No. 2		
4	No. 1			No. 2		
5	No. 1			No. 2		

(NOTES)

No. 1 married in 1866 no license and no certificate issued.   (No. 1 Dawes' Roll No. 158)
   (No. 2 Dawes' Roll No. 3328)   (No. 3 Dawes' Roll No. 3329)
No. 4 is husband of Nancy Colbert Chickasaw roll card No. 1635   (No. 4 Dawes' Roll No. 3330)
   Evidence of marriage filed Dec. 24, 1902.   (No. 5 Dawes' Roll No. 3331)
   Oct. 11/98.

| RESIDENCE: Panola   COUNTY | | | | | | CARD NO. | | |
| POST OFFICE: Kemp, Ind. Ter. | | | | | | FIELD NO. | | |

	NAME	RELATION-SHIP TO PERSON FIRST NAMED	AGE	SEX	BLOOD	TRIBAL ENROLLMENT		
						YEAR	COUNTY	PAGE
1	Good, Albert		32	M	I.W.	1897	Panola	76
2	" Minnie E.	Dau	7	F	1/2	1897	"	4
3	" Rutha E.	"	5	"	1/2	1897	"	4

TRIBAL ENROLLMENT OF PARENTS

	NAME OF FATHER	YEAR	COUNTY	NAME OF MOTHER	YEAR	COUNTY
1	Magnus Good		non citizen	Ella Good		non citizen
2	No. 1			Mannie Kemp Good	Dead	Panola
3	No. 1			" " "	"	"

(NOTES)

No. 1 On Chickasaw Roll as Albert Goode.   (No. 1 Dawes' Roll No. 157)
   (No. 2 Dawes' Roll No. 3326)   (No. 3 Dawes' Roll No. 3327)

P.O. Mill Creek, I.T.   Oct. 11/98.

Chickasaw Enrollment Cards 1898-1914
Chickasaw by Blood   Volume III

RESIDENCE: Panola   COUNTY   CARD NO.
POST OFFICE: Colbert, Ind. Ter.   FIELD NO.

	NAME	RELATION-SHIP TO PERSON FIRST NAMED	AGE	SEX	BLOOD	TRIBAL ENROLLMENT		
						YEAR	COUNTY	PAGE
1	Boles, Mary E.	NAMED	24	F	1/8	1897	Panola	6
2	" Maude E.	Dau	9	"	1/16	1897	"	6
3	" Sylvia	"	5	"	1/16	1897	"	6
4	" William Walter	Son	2	M	1/16	1897	"	6
5	" William S.	Husband	34	M	I.W.			

TRIBAL ENROLLMENT OF PARENTS

	NAME OF FATHER	YEAR	COUNTY	NAME OF MOTHER	YEAR	COUNTY
1	A.P. Farmer	Dead	non citizen	Menta Farmer	Dead	Panola
2	W.S. Boles		" "	No. 1		
3	" " "		" "	No. 1		
4	" " "		" "	No. 1		
5	William S. Boles	Dead	non citz	Emily D. Boles		non citz

(NOTES)

Sir name of first name on Chickasaw Roll is Baulds.   (No. 1 Dawes' Roll No. 3322)
William S. Boles Husband of No. 1 on Chickasaw Card D.256.   (No. 2 Dawes' Roll No. 3323)
No. 4 On Chickasaw Roll as William Walker Bowles   (No. 3 Dawes' Roll No. 3324)
No. 4 transferred from Chickasaw Card #D.256 March 29, 1902. (No. 4 Dawes' Roll No. 3325)
    See decision of March 13, 1902.   (No. 5 Dawes' Roll No. 52)

                                                              Oct. 11/98.

RESIDENCE: Panola   COUNTY   CARD NO.
POST OFFICE: Mead. Ind. Ter.   FIELD NO.

	NAME	RELATION-SHIP TO PERSON FIRST NAMED	AGE	SEX	BLOOD	TRIBAL ENROLLMENT		
						YEAR	COUNTY	PAGE
1	Adcock, Ida Virginia	NAMED	22	F	1/4	1897	Panola	5
2	" Onon Thomas	Son	10mo	M	1/8			
3	" James Augustus	"	2mo	"	1/8			
4	" Anna May Gertrude	Dau	2wks	F	1/8			
5	" Thomas Albert	Husb	28	M	I.W.			

TRIBAL ENROLLMENT OF PARENTS

	NAME OF FATHER	YEAR	COUNTY	NAME OF MOTHER	YEAR	COUNTY
1	G.A. Yarborough[sic]		Non-citizen	Sally S. Yarbrough	Dead	Panola
2	Thomas A. Adcock		white man	No. 1		
3	" " "		" "	No. 1		

4	" " "		" "	No. 1		
5	J.P. Adcock		non-citizen	Sarah E. Adcock		non citizen

(NOTES)

No. 1 is wife of Thomas A. Adcock, Chickasaw D.151   *(No. 1 Dawes' Roll No. 3318)*
No. 1 On Chickasaw Roll as Irad Cock   *(No. 2 Dawes' Roll No. 3319)*
No. 2 Enrolled May 24th 1901   *(No. 3 Dawes' Roll No. 3320)*
No. 4 Born April 24th 1902; Enrolled May 3, 1902   *(No. 4 Dawes' Roll No. 3321)*
No. 5 transferred from Chickasaw card #D.151   *(No. 5 Dawes' Roll No. 291)*
See decision of March 5, 1904, Mar. 23, 1904

P.O. Whitebead, I.T. 5/3/02
P.O. Mead, I.T.   Oct. 11/98.

RESIDENCE: Panola COUNTY   CARD NO.
POST OFFICE: Colbert, Ind. Ter.   FIELD NO.

	NAME	RELATION-SHIP TO PERSON FIRST NAMED	AGE	SEX	BLOOD	TRIBAL ENROLLMENT		
						YEAR	COUNTY	PAGE
1	Murray, George G.	NAMED	30	M	3/8	1897	Panola	5
2	" Laura	Wife	28	F	I.W.	1897	"	76
3	" Helen	Dau	3mo	F	3/16			
4	" George Gordon	Son	2mo	M	3/16			

TRIBAL ENROLLMENT OF PARENTS

	NAME OF FATHER	YEAR	COUNTY	NAME OF MOTHER	YEAR	COUNTY
1	Henry F. Murray I.W.	1897	Panola	Margaret Murray	Dead	Panola
2	J.H. Hopper		non citizen	Annie Hopper		non citizen
3	No. 1			No. 2		
4	No. 1			No. 2		

(NOTES)

No. 1 On Chickasaw Roll as George Murray   *(No. 1 Dawes' Roll No. 3316)*
No. 3 Enrolled 6/14/1901   *(No. 2 Dawes' Roll No. 156)*
No. 4 Born July 4th 1902; Enrolled Sept 19, 1902.   *(No. 3 Dawes' Roll No. 3317)*
     (No. 4 Dawes' Roll No. 4491)

Oct. 11/98.

RESIDENCE: Panola COUNTY   CARD NO.
POST OFFICE: Yarnaby, Ind. Ter.   FIELD NO.

	NAME	RELATION-SHIP TO PERSON FIRST NAMED	AGE	SEX	BLOOD	TRIBAL ENROLLMENT		
						YEAR	COUNTY	PAGE
1	Hamilton, Tommie	NAMED	11	M	1/2	1897	Panola	1

TRIBAL ENROLLMENT OF PARENTS						
NAME OF FATHER	YEAR	COUNTY	NAME OF MOTHER	YEAR	COUNTY	
1 John Hamilton	Dead	Non citizen	Amanda Hamilton	Dead	Panola	

(NOTES)

(No. I Dawes' Roll No. 3315)

Oct. 11/98.

RESIDENCE: Panola   COUNTY   CARD NO.

POST OFFICE: Yarnaby, Ind. Ter.   FIELD NO.

NAME	RELATION-SHIP TO PERSON FIRST NAMED	AGE	SEX	BLOOD	TRIBAL ENROLLMENT		
					YEAR	COUNTY	PAGE
1 Cravens, John James	NAMED	57	M	I.W.	1897	Panola	76
2 " Mary	Wife	48	F	7/8	1897	"	1
3 " Charles Thomas	Son	17	M	7/16	1897	"	1
4 Thaxton, Roda	Dau	15	F	7/16	1897	"	1
5 Cravens, John James, Jr.	Son	10	M	7/16	1897	"	1
6 ~~Rose, Lela~~	~~Niece in law~~	18	F	7/16	1897	"	1
7 Dodson, Mattie	Dau	19	F	7/16	1897	"	1
8 Thaxton, Lois Ethel	Gr.Dau	1mo	"	7/32			
9 Patton, Camellia Inez	"	2	"	7/32			
10 Cravens, Lullas Russell	Gr.Son	1	M	7/32			
11 Thaxton, Lullas	husband of No. 4	27	M	I.W.			

TRIBAL ENROLLMENT OF PARENTS						
NAME OF FATHER	YEAR	COUNTY	NAME OF MOTHER	YEAR	COUNTY	
1 John Cravens	Dead	Non-citizen	America Cravens	Dead	Non-citizen	
2 Charley Shico	"	Chickasaw Roll	Pi-c-cha	"	Chickasaw Roll	
3 No. 1			No. 2			
4 No. 1			No. 2			
5 No. 1			No. 2			
6 ~~C.B. Camden~~	~~Dead~~	~~Non-citizen~~	~~Sarah Camden~~	~~Dead~~	~~Panola~~	
7 No. 1			*(Illegible)*			
8 Lullas Thaxton		Non-citizen	No. 4			
9 W.T. Patton		" "	No. 8			
10 No. 3			Willie Cravens		Non-citizen	
11 Ewing Thaxton		non citizen	Eliza Thaxton		non citizen	

(NOTES)

No. 1 On Chickasaw Roll as J.J. Cravens   *(No. I Dawes' Roll No. 338)*

No. 3 " " " " Tommie "	*(No. 2 Dawes' Roll No. 3308)*
No. 5 " " " " J.J. " Jr.	*(No. 3 Dawes' Roll No. 3309)*
No. 6 is now the wife of Wm M. Rose, non citz	*(No. 4 Dawes' Roll No. 3310)*
No. 7 was married to W.T. Patton See testimony of June 21, 1900 June 21 1900	*(No. 5 Dawes' Roll No. 3311)*
No. 8 Enrolled May 20ᵗʰ 1901	*(No. 6 Dawes' Roll No. 3312)*
No. 9 Born Nov. 20ᵗʰ 1899; Enrolled Dec. 7, 1901	*(No. 8 Dawes' Roll No. 3313)*
No. 10 Proof of Birth filed Dec. 4, 1902	*(No. 9 Dawes' Roll No. 3314)*

No. 3 is now the Husband of Willie Cravens a non-citizen. Evidence of marriage filed Dec. 4, 1902.

No. 4 is now the wife of Lullas Thaxton on Chickasaw Card D,327   *(No. 10 Dawes' Roll No. 190)*

No. 9 died in year 1899 or 1900; enrollment cancelled by Dept. June 9-1906.   *(No. 11 Dawes' Roll No. 197)*

No. 9 died in April 1900; Proof of death forwarded by Muskogee 11-3-05.

No. 6 " Sept. 27, 1901; " " "   "   "   "   "

No. 9 died in 1899; Proof of death filed Dec. 23/02.

No. 6 " Oct. 1900; " " "   " Dec. 23/02.

No. 7 " Oct. 1899; " " "   " Dec. 23/02.

No. 11 transferred from Chickasaw Card #D.327. See decision of May 1, 1902.

P.O. Yarnaby I.T. 12/23/02

P.O. seems to be Yuba I.T. (mistake)   Oct. 11/98.

RESIDENCE: Pickens   **COUNTY**   **CARD NO.**

POST OFFICE: Cumberland, Ind. Ter.   **FIELD NO.**

	NAME	RELATION-SHIP TO PERSON FIRST NAMED	AGE	SEX	BLOOD	TRIBAL ENROLLMENT		
						YEAR	COUNTY	PAGE
1	Whitthorne, Angie		26	F	Full	1897	Tishomingo	33
2	" Martin	Son	5	M	1/2	1897	"	33
3	" Hardin Coleman	"	11/2	"	1/2	~~1897~~	"	~~87~~
4	" Thomas K.	Husband	45	"	I.W.			
5	~~" Ellen E.~~	~~Dau~~	~~1mo~~	F	~~1/2~~	~~DIED PRIOR TO SEPT. 25, 1902~~		
6	" Matthew Thomas	Son	2mo	M	1/2			

TRIBAL ENROLLMENT OF PARENTS

	NAME OF FATHER	YEAR	COUNTY	NAME OF MOTHER	YEAR	COUNTY
1	Alberson	Dead	Panola	Eliza Robinson	1897	Tishomingo
2	J.R. Whitthorne			No. 1		
3	" " "			No. 1		
4	Martin "	Dead	Non-citizen	Ellen Whitthorne	Dead	Non-citizen
5	~~J.R. Whitthorne~~			~~No. 1~~		
6	" " "			No. 1		

(NOTES)

No. 1 On Chickasaw Roll as Angie Whitmore	*(No. 1 Dawes' Roll No. 3304)*
No. 2 " " " " Martha "	*(No. 2 Dawes' Roll No. 3305)*

Chickasaw Enrollment Cards 1898-1914
Chickasaw by Blood   Volume III

No. 3 "   "   "   " Hardie Coleman Whithorne   *(No. 3 Dawes' Roll No. 4489)*
No. 3 Proof of Birth received and filed Sept. 26, 1902
No. 4 Enrolled Mar. 22/99   *(No. 4 Dawes' Roll No. 155)*
No. 5 Enrolled Aug. 21, 1900   *(No. 5 Dawes' Roll No. 3306)*
No. 5 <u>Died</u> April 19, 1901; Proof of Death filed Nov. 6th 1902; Additional proof of Death filed Nov. 21, 1901.
No. 6 Born May 26th 1902; Enrolled July 16th 1902.   *No. 6 Dawes' Roll No. 3307)*

P.O. Tishomingo, I.T.   Oct. 11/98.

RESIDENCE: Panola COUNTY					CARD NO.			
POST OFFICE: Colbert, Ind. Ter.					FIELD NO.			
NAME	RELATION-SHIP TO PERSON FIRST NAMED	AGE	SEX	BLOOD	TRIBAL ENROLLMENT			
					YEAR	COUNTY	PAGE	
1 Murray, Hinton	NAMED	25	M	3/8	1897	Panola	5	
2 " Mattie	Wife	19	F	1/8	1897	Tishomingo	35	
3 " ~~Lovard~~	~~Son~~	~~4mo~~	M	1/4				
4 " Lee Edward	"	2mo	"	1/4				

TRIBAL ENROLLMENT OF PARENTS						
NAME OF FATHER	YEAR	COUNTY	NAME OF MOTHER	YEAR	COUNTY	
1 Henry F. Murray I.W.	1897	Panola	Margaret Murray	Dead	Panola	
2 Ed Colling I.W.	1897	Tishomingo	Elsie Collins	"	Tishomingo	
3 ~~No. 1~~			~~No. 2~~			
4 No. 1			No. 2			

(NOTES)

No. 2 On Chickasaw Roll as Mattie Collins   *(No. 1 Dawes' Roll No. 3301)*
No. 3 Enrolled Oct. 16th 1900   *(No. 2 Dawes' Roll No. 3302)*
No. 3 Died May 26th 1902; Proof of Death filed Nov. 11, 1902   *(No. 3 Dawes' Roll No. 3303)*
No. 4 Born July 4th 1902; Enrolled Sept. 19, 1902.   *(No. 4 Dawes' Roll No. 4188)*
      Oct. 11/98.

RESIDENCE: Panola COUNTY					CARD NO.			
POST OFFICE: Colbert, Ind. Ter.					FIELD NO.			
NAME	RELATION-SHIP TO PERSON FIRST NAMED	AGE	SEX	BLOOD	TRIBAL ENROLLMENT			
					YEAR	COUNTY	PAGE	
1 Gooding, Charles Lemuel	NAMED	25	M	1/16	1897	Panola	2	
2 " Mouning **DEAD**	Mother	69	F	1/8	1897	"	2	
3 " Charles Holmes	Son	1mo	M	1/32				

TRIBAL ENROLLMENT OF PARENTS						
NAME OF FATHER	YEAR	COUNTY	NAME OF MOTHER	YEAR	COUNTY
1	C.E. Gooding	Dead	Non citizen	Mouning F. Gooding	1897	Panola
2	James Allen	"	" "	Elizabeth Allen	Dead	Chickasaw Roll
3	No. 1			Willie M. Gooding		Non Citizen

(NOTES)

No. 1 is the husband of Willie M. Gooding a non-citizen. Evidence of marriage filed April 4, 1901.
No. 1 On Chickasaw Roll as Lem Gooding   *(No. 1 Dawes' Roll No. 3299)*
No. 2 "   "   "   " Mrs. M.F. "   *(No. 3 Dawes' Roll No. 3300)*
No. 2 Died Feb. 14, 1899. Evidence of Death filed March 18th 1901
No. 3 Enrolled April 24th 1901.   Oct. 11/98.

RESIDENCE: Panola COUNTY   CARD No.
POST OFFICE: Colbert, Ind. Ter.   FIELD No.

NAME	RELATION-SHIP TO PERSON FIRST NAMED	AGE	SEX	BLOOD	TRIBAL ENROLLMENT		
					YEAR	COUNTY	PAGE
1	Murray, Meigs Colbert	NAMED	28	M	3/8	1897	Panola	5
2	" Maye	Wife	20	F	I.W.			
3	" Madge	Dau	3mo	"	3/16			
4	" Meigs Colbert, Jr.	Son	5mo	M	3/16			

TRIBAL ENROLLMENT OF PARENTS						
NAME OF FATHER	YEAR	COUNTY	NAME OF MOTHER	YEAR	COUNTY
1	Henry F. Murray	1897	Panola	Margaret Murray	Dead	Panola
2	Albert Parker		Non Citizen	Mary Parker	"	Non-citizen
3	No. 1			No. 2		
4	No. 1			No. 2		

(NOTES)

No. 1 On Chickasaw Roll as Meiges Murray   *(No. 1 Dawes' Roll No. 3296)*
No. 2 Admitted by United States Court, Settlement *(remainder illegible)*
(Notation illegible)   *(No. 3 Dawes' Roll No. 3297)*
No. 3 Enrolled Mar. 6/99.   *(No. 4 Dawes' Roll No. 3298)*
No. 4 Enrolled November 26th 1900
   Judgment of U.S. Ct. admitting No. 2 as a citizen by blood vacated and set aside by Decree of C.C.C.C. Dec. 17 '02
   No. 2 now in C.C.C.C. Case #1187
   No. 2 GRANTED Oct. 4, 1905.

                                                                           Oct. 11/98.

RESIDENCE: Choctaw Nation   COUNTY   CARD NO.

POST OFFICE: Boggy Depot, Ind. Ter.   FIELD NO.

	NAME	RELATIONSHIP TO PERSON FIRST NAMED	AGE	SEX	BLOOD	TRIBAL ENROLLMENT		
						YEAR	COUNTY	PAGE
1	Moore, Thomas Nowel		33	M	1/16	1897	Chick residing in Choctaw N. 3rd Dist.	74
2	" Samuel Riley	Son	8	"	1/32	1897	" " " "	74
3	" Lillie Armildia	Dau	5	F	1/32	1897	" " " "	74
4	" Cordelia	"	3	"	1/32	1897	" " " "	74
5	" Roxie Mildred	"	3mo	"	1/32			
6	" Nancy M.	"	3days	"	1/32			
7	" Louisa J.	Wife	32	F	I.W.			

TRIBAL ENROLLMENT OF PARENTS

	NAME OF FATHER	YEAR	COUNTY	NAME OF MOTHER	YEAR	COUNTY
1	Saml Blair	Dead	Chickasaw Roll	Jane Moore	Dead	Non-Citizen
2	No. 1			Louisa J. Moore		" "
3	No. 1			" " "		" "
4	No. 1			" " "		" "
5	No. 1			" " "		" "
6	No. 1			" " "		" "
7	Henry Livemore		non citizen	Cordelia Livemore	Dead	" "

(NOTES)

No. 1 On Chickasaw Roll as Thomas L. Moore   (No. 1 Dawes' Roll No. 3290)

No. 2 "   "   "   " Samuel   "   (No. 2 Dawes' Roll No. 3291)

No. 3 "   "   "   " Lillie   "   (No. 3 Dawes' Roll No. 3292)   (No. 4 Dawes' Roll No. 3293)

No. 5 Affidavit of attending physician to be supplied. Received Oct. 31/98,   (No. 5 Dawes' Roll No. 3294)

No. 6 Enrolled January 9th 1901   (No. 6 Dawes' Roll No. 3295)

No. 7 placed hereon under order of Commission to Five Civilized Tribes April 16, 1906, holding application was made for her enrollment within the time provide by Act of Congress of July 1, 1902 (32 Stat. 64)

Oct. 11/98.

RESIDENCE: Panola   COUNTY   CARD NO.

POST OFFICE: Silo, Ind. Ter.   FIELD NO.

	NAME	RELATIONSHIP TO PERSON FIRST NAMED	AGE	SEX	BLOOD	TRIBAL ENROLLMENT		
						YEAR	COUNTY	PAGE
1	Keirsey, William D.		29	M	I.W.	1897	Panola	76
2	" Mittie Josephine	Wife	27	F	1/8	1897	"	5
3	" James D.	Son	9	M	1/16	1897	"	5

4	" Clifford C.	"	7	"	1/16	1897	"	5
5	" Agnes Maude	Dau	5	F	1/16	1897	"	5
6	" William Conway	Son	4	M	1/16	1897	"	5
7	" Milton	"	11/2	"	1/16	1897	"	85
8	" Vivian	Dau	2mo	F	1/16			
9	" Benjamin C.	Son	2mo	M	1/16			

TRIBAL ENROLLMENT OF PARENTS

	NAME OF FATHER	YEAR	COUNTY	NAME OF MOTHER	YEAR	COUNTY
1	Jim Keirsey	Dead	Non Citizen	M.J. Keirsey		Non citizen
2	Dan Collins (I.W.)	1897	Panola	Sally Collins	1897	Panola
3	No. 1			No. 2		
4	No. 1			No. 2		
5	No. 1			No. 2		
6	No. 1			No. 2		
7	No. 1			No. 2		
8	No. 1			No. 2		
9	No. 1			No. 2		

(NOTES)

No. 1 On Chickasaw Roll as Will Kersey   *(No. 1 Dawes' Roll No. 154)*
No. 2 "   "   " " Mittie "   *(No. 2 Dawes' Roll No. 3283)*   *(No. 3 Dawes' Roll No. 3284)*
No. 4 "   "   " " Clifford "   *(No. 4 Dawes' Roll No. 3285)*
No. 5 "   "   " " Agnes M. "   *(No. 5 Dawes' Roll No. 3286)*
No. 6 "   "   " " William C. "   *(No. 6 Dawes' Roll No. 3287)*
No. 7 "   "   " " Melton   "; Proof of Birth received and filed Sept. 25, 1902 *(No. 7 Dawes' Roll No. 4187)*
No. 8 Enrolled Mar. 22/99.   *(No. 8 Dawes' Roll No. 3288)*
No. 9 Enrolled June 4th 1901.   *(No. 9 Dawes' Roll No. 3289)*
                                                                             Oct. 11/98.

RESIDENCE: Panola COUNTY						CARD NO.		
POST OFFICE: Colbert, Ind. Ter.						FIELD NO.		

	NAME	RELATIONSHIP TO PERSON FIRST NAMED	AGE	SEX	BLOOD	TRIBAL ENROLLMENT		
						YEAR	COUNTY	PAGE
1	Murray, Robert Lovard	NAMED	41	M	3/8	1897	Panola	5
2	" Louie	Wife	28	F	1/8	1897	"	5
3	" Mildred P.	Dau	6	"	1/4	1897	"	5
4	" Robert L. Jr.	Son	4	M	1/4	1897	"	5
5	" Lucile	Dau	2	F	1/4	1897	"	5
6	" Minnie Agnes	"	6mo	"	1/4			
7	" Cecil Collins	Son	3mo	M	1/4			

	TRIBAL ENROLLMENT OF PARENTS						
	NAME OF FATHER	YEAR	COUNTY	NAME OF MOTHER	YEAR	COUNTY
1	Henry F. Murray (I.W.)	1897	Panola	Margaret Murray	Dead	Panola
2	Dan Collins (I.W.)	1897	"	Sally Collins	1897	"
3	No. 1			No. 2		
4	No. 1			No. 2		
5	No. 1			No. 2		
6	No. 1			No. 2		
7	No. 1			No. 2		

(NOTES)

No. 1 On Chickasaw Roll as R.L. Murray   (No. 1 Dawes' Roll No. 3276)   (No. 2 Dawes' Roll No. 3277)
No. 3 "   "   "   " Mildred D. "   (No. 3 Dawes' Roll No. 3278)
No. 4 "   "   "   " Robert   "   Jr.   (No. 4 Dawes' Roll No. 3279)   (No. 5 Dawes' Roll No. 3280)
No. 6 Enrolled Feby 26th 1900   (No. 6 Dawes' Roll No. 3281)
No. 7 Born June 16, 1902; Enrolled Sept 18th 1902   (No. 7 Dawes' Roll No. 3282)

Oct. 11/98.

RESIDENCE: Panola COUNTY   CARD NO.
POST OFFICE: Colbert, Ind. Ter.   FIELD NO.

	NAME	RELATION-SHIP TO PERSON FIRST NAMED	AGE	SEX	BLOOD	TRIBAL ENROLLMENT		
						YEAR	COUNTY	PAGE
1	Murray, Henry F.		79	M	I.W.	1897	Panola	76

	TRIBAL ENROLLMENT OF PARENTS						
	NAME OF FATHER	YEAR	COUNTY	NAME OF MOTHER	YEAR	COUNTY
1	Robert Murray	Dead	Non-Citizen	Margaret Murray	Dead	Non-Citizen

(NOTES)

On Chickasaw Roll as H.F. Murray   (No. 1 Dawes' Roll No. 153)
No. 1 was formerly husband of Margaret H. James to whom he was married in 1854. She died in 1874.

Oct. 11/98.

RESIDENCE: Panola COUNTY   CARD NO.
POST OFFICE: Kemp, Ind. Ter.   FIELD NO.

	NAME	RELATION-SHIP TO PERSON FIRST NAMED	AGE	SEX	BLOOD	TRIBAL ENROLLMENT		
						YEAR	COUNTY	PAGE
1	Short, Serena J. **DEAD**	NAMED	52	F	Full	1897	Panola	3
2	" Thomas W.	Son	22	M	1/2	1897	"	3
3	Duncan, James	Ward	18	"	Full	1897	"	3
4	Short, Ethel	Gr.Dau	1mo	F	1/4			

	TRIBAL ENROLLMENT OF PARENTS					
NAME OF FATHER	YEAR	COUNTY	NAME OF MOTHER	YEAR	COUNTY
1 Joe Factor	Dead	Chickasaw Roll	Kin-he	Dead	Chickasaw Roll
2 Jesse Short	"	non-citizen	No. 1		
3 *(Name Illegible)*	"	Chickasaw Roll	Becky Duncan	Dead	Chickasaw Roll
4 No. 2			Cleo Short		non citizen

(NOTES)

No. 1 Died Feb. 3rd 1902; Proof of Death fied June 4, 1902
No. 1 On Chickasaw Roll as S.J. Short
No. 2 "   "   "   " Tom W. "   *(No. 2 Dawes' Roll No. 3273)*
No. 3 "   "   "   " Jimmie Duncan   *(No. 3 Dawes' Roll No. 3274)*
No. 4 Enrolled Nov. 22nd 1900   *(No. 4 Dawes' Roll No. 3275)*

Oct. 11/98.

RESIDENCE: Panola   COUNTY   CARD NO.
POST OFFICE: Kemp, Ind. Ter.   FIELD NO.

NAME	RELATION-SHIP TO PERSON FIRST NAMED	AGE	SEX	BLOOD	TRIBAL ENROLLMENT		
					YEAR	COUNTY	PAGE
1 Reynolds, Sarah Ann	NAMED	60	F	Full	1897	Panola	4

	TRIBAL ENROLLMENT OF PARENTS					
NAME OF FATHER	YEAR	COUNTY	NAME OF MOTHER	YEAR	COUNTY
1 Isohopy	Dead	Chickasaw Roll	Jennie	Dead	Chickasaw Roll

(NOTES)

On Chickasaw Roll as Sarahan Reynolds   *(No. 1 Dawes' Roll No. 3272)*

Oct. 11/98.

RESIDENCE: Panola   COUNTY   CARD NO.
POST OFFICE: Kemp, Ind. Ter.   FIELD NO.

NAME	RELATION-SHIP TO PERSON FIRST NAMED	AGE	SEX	BLOOD	TRIBAL ENROLLMENT		
					YEAR	COUNTY	PAGE
1 Kemp, Lina	NAMED	60	F	Full	1897	Panola	4

NAME OF FATHER	YEAR	COUNTY	NAME OF MOTHER	YEAR	COUNTY
1 Isohopy	Dead	Chickasaw Roll	Jennie	Dead	Chickasaw Roll

(NOTES)

(Notation illegible)   *(No. 1 Dawes' Roll No. 3271)*

Oct. 11/98.

Chickasaw Enrollment Cards 1898-1914
Chickasaw by Blood   Volume III

RESIDENCE: Tishomingo   COUNTY   CARD NO.

POST OFFICE: Emet, Ind. Ter.   FIELD NO.

	NAME		RELATION-SHIP TO PERSON FIRST NAMED	AGE	SEX	BLOOD	TRIBAL ENROLLMENT		
							YEAR	COUNTY	PAGE
1	McKinney, Laura	**DEAD**	NAMED	22	F	3/8	1897	Tishomingo	33
2	"	Lauretta	Dau	2	"	3/16	1897	"	38
3	"	Laurina	"	6mo	"	3/16			
4	"	Ben F.	Husband	31	M	I.W.	1897	Pickens	79
5	"	Clara Louisa	Void	S.Dau	11	F	1/4		
6	"	Ben A.	Void	S.Son	9	M	1/4		
7	"	Mattie	Void	S.Dau	7	F	1/4		

TRIBAL ENROLLMENT OF PARENTS

	NAME OF FATHER	YEAR	COUNTY	NAME OF MOTHER	YEAR	COUNTY
1	Taylor Potts	1897	Panola	Emily Potts	Dead	Panola
2	Ben F. McKinney (I.W.)		Choctaw residing in Chickasaw Dist.	No. I		
3	" " "		" "	No. I		
4	Alex McKinney	Dead	Non-citz	Maggie McKinney	Dead	Chick Roll
5	No. 4			" "	"	" "
6	No. 4			" "	"	" "
7	No. 4			" "	"	" "

(NOTES)

No. I Wife of Ben F. McKinney, Choctaw Card No. 361; No. I Died March 6, 1901
    Evidence of Death filed March 26th 1901   *(No. 2 Dawes' Roll No. 3270)*

No. 4 On 1896 Choctaw Roll No. 14889 as B.J. McKinney Chick Dist.
No. 5 " 1896   "   "   " 9528 " Louisa   "   "   "
No. 6 " 1896   "   "   " 9529   "   "
No. 7 " 1896   "   "   " 9530   "   "
    Transferred to Chickasaw Roll by Dawes Commission

No. 3 Enrolled Nov. 4, 1899

No. 4 Denied by United States Court Central District, Ind. Ter. July 13, 1897. Court Case No. 67

Nos. 4, 5, 6 and 7 were first enrolled on Choctaw Card Oct. 11 98. Declared to be Chickasaw and placed upon this Card Dec. 17/99 by order of Commission.

Nos. 5, 6 and 7 transferred to Choctaw Card No. 5421 Oct. 17, 1902.

Oct. 11/98.

Chickasaw Enrollment Cards 1898-1914
Chickasaw by Blood   Volume III

RESIDENCE: Panola COUNTY   CARD NO.

POST OFFICE: Mead, Ind. Ter.   FIELD NO.

	NAME	RELATION-SHIP TO PERSON FIRST	AGE	SEX	BLOOD	TRIBAL ENROLLMENT		
						YEAR	COUNTY	PAGE
1	Venable, Dollie	NAMED	21	F	3/4	1897	Panola	1
2	" Beulah	Dau	3wks	"	3/8			
3	" Laura	"	"	"	3/8			
4	" Robert L	husband	32	M	I.W.			

TRIBAL ENROLLMENT OF PARENTS

	NAME OF FATHER	YEAR	COUNTY	NAME OF MOTHER	YEAR	COUNTY
1	Johnson Calhoune	Dead	Chickasaw Roll	Emily Calhoune	Dead	Panola
2	R.L. Venable		white man	No. 1		
3	" " "		" "	No. 1		
4	Thomas Venable		Non Citizen	Rasanna[sic] Venable	Dead	Non Citizen

(NOTES)

On Chickasaw Roll as Dollie Franklin
Wife of R.L. Venable on Chickasaw Card D. #149
No. 3 Enrolled December 14, 1900
No. 4 transferred from Chickasaw Card #D.149. See decision of May, 190?   *(No. 4 Dawes' Roll No. 196)*

Oct. 11/98.

RESIDENCE: Tishomingo COUNTY   CARD NO.

POST OFFICE: Ravia, Ind. Ter.   FIELD NO.

	NAME	RELATION-SHIP TO PERSON FIRST	AGE	SEX	BLOOD	TRIBAL ENROLLMENT		
						YEAR	COUNTY	PAGE
1	Ravia, Joseph	NAMED	52	M	I.W.	1897	Tishomingo	89
2	" Mollie	Wife	49	F	1/8	1897	"	32

TRIBAL ENROLLMENT OF PARENTS

	NAME OF FATHER	YEAR	COUNTY	NAME OF MOTHER	YEAR	COUNTY
1	James Ravia	Dead	Non-Citizen	Rebecca Ravia	Dead	Non-Citizen
2	Christopher Moore	"	" "	Catherine Moore	"	Chickasaw Roll

(NOTES)

No. 1 On Chickasaw Roll as Joe Ravia   *(No. 1 Dawes' Roll No. 548)*
Nos. 1 & 2 separated about July 1, 1901 and have since been divorced   *(No. 2 Dawes' Roll No. 3266)*
No. 1 married Lottie Green, a white woman Dec. 19 1901. See testimony of No. 1 taken Nov. 6, 1902
No. 1 on 1893 Pay Roll No. 1, Page 130 as J.K. Ravia

P.O. Purcell, I.T. 1/29 - 04   Oct. 11/98.

RESIDENCE: Choctaw Nation ~~COUNTY~~   CARD NO.

POST OFFICE: Coalgate, Ind. Ter.   FIELD NO.

	NAME	RELATION-SHIP TO PERSON FIRST NAMED	AGE	SEX	BLOOD	TRIBAL ENROLLMENT		
						YEAR	COUNTY	PAGE
1	Thompson, Cyrus R.	NAMED	29	M	1/4			
2	" Clemmie	Wife	27	F	I.W.			
3	" Valley	Dau	8	"	1/8			
4	" Preemon C.	Son	6	M	1/8			
5	" Cyrus Waverly	"	4	"	1/8			
6	" James H.	"	1 1/2	"	1/8			
7	" Joseph B.	"	8mo	"	1/8			
8	" Robert H.	"	3mo	"	1/8			

TRIBAL ENROLLMENT OF PARENTS

	NAME OF FATHER	YEAR	COUNTY	NAME OF MOTHER	YEAR	COUNTY
1	Robert Thompson		Gaines Co Choctaw Roll	Siney Thompson	1897	Chick residing in Choctaw N. 3rd Dist.
2	James Gammons	Dead	Non Citizen	Martha Gammons		Non Citizen
3	No. 1			No. 2		
4	No. 1			No. 2		
5	No. 1			No. 2		
6	No. 1			No. 2		
7	No. 1			No. 2		
8	No. 1			No. 2		

(NOTES)

Nos. 1, 3, 4 & 5 on Choctaw Census Record No. 2, Page 450, transferred to Chickasaw Roll by Dawes Com

No. 2   "   "   Intermarried Roll   " 107   "   "   "   " "   "

Marriage Certificate on file in office of Dawes Com. Muskogee, Ind. Ter.

No. 2,3,4 & 5 Admitted by Dawes Com, Choctaw Card No. 75 and No appeal taken

No. 1 On Choctaw Roll as Cyrus W. Thompson

No. 5 "   "   "   " Cyrua W.   " ; Admitted by Dawes Com as Waverly

No. 6 Affidavit of attending physician to be supplied. Received Oct. 21, 1898

All except No. 6 on Choctaw Roll 1896. See list of names and numbers hereto attached.

No. 7 Enrolled Aug. 10/99

No. 8 Enrolled May 21, 1901

Oct. 11/98.

CANCELLED Stamped across card

Chickasaw Enrollment Cards 1898-1914
Chickasaw by Blood   Volume III

RESIDENCE: Panola COUNTY   CARD NO.

POST OFFICE: Colbert, Ind. Ter.   FIELD NO.

	NAME	RELATION-SHIP TO PERSON FIRST NAMED	AGE	SEX	BLOOD	TRIBAL ENROLLMENT		
						YEAR	COUNTY	PAGE
1	Webb, John M.	NAMED	48	M	I.W.	1897	Panola	76
2	" Isabella Abigale	Wife	38	F	1/2	1897	"	4
3	" Joel F.	Son	20	M	1/4	1897	"	4
4	" George W.	"	18	"	1/4	1897	"	4
5	" William H.	"	15	"	1/4	1897	"	4
6	" John M, Jr.	"	13	"	1/4	1897	"	4

TRIBAL ENROLLMENT OF PARENTS

	NAME OF FATHER	YEAR	COUNTY	NAME OF MOTHER	YEAR	COUNTY
1	Frank Webb	Dead	non citizen	Mary Ann Webb		non citizen
2	Joel Kemp	"	Tishomingo	Maria Kemp	Dead	Panola
3	No. 1			No. 2		
4	No. 1			No. 2		
5	No. 1			No. 2		
6	No. 1			No. 2		

(NOTES)

No. 1 On Chickasaw Roll as John Webb   *(No. 1 Dawes' Roll No. 152)*
No. 2 "   "   " " Abigale "
No. 3 "   "   " " Joe   "
No. 4 "   "   " " George "
No. 5 "   "   " " William "
No. 6 "   "   " " John   " Jr.

                                                                     Oct. 11/98.

RESIDENCE: Pickens COUNTY   CARD NO.

POST OFFICE: Lebanon, Ind. Ter. (Orphan Home)   FIELD NO.

	NAME	RELATION-SHIP TO PERSON FIRST NAMED	AGE	SEX	BLOOD	TRIBAL ENROLLMENT		
						YEAR	COUNTY	PAGE
1	Moore, Thomas W.	NAMED	18	M	1/8	1897	Pickens	18
2	" Monroe	Bro	13	"	1/8	1897	"	18

TRIBAL ENROLLMENT OF PARENTS

	NAME OF FATHER	YEAR	COUNTY	NAME OF MOTHER	YEAR	COUNTY
1	Wilson Moore	Dead	Chickasaw Roll	Sally Moore	Dead	Non citizen
2	" "	"	" "	" "	"	" "

Chickasaw Enrollment Cards 1898-1914
Chickasaw by Blood   Volume III

(NOTES)

No. 1 On Chickasaw Roll as Thomas Moore
Marriage certificate between parents of No. 1 & 2 filed at Atoka, I.T. Dec.4,1900.

Oct. 11/98.

RESIDENCE: Choctaw Nation ~~COUNTY~~   CARD NO.

POST OFFICE: Caddo, Ind. Ter.   FIELD NO.

	NAME	RELATION-SHIP TO PERSON FIRST NAMED	AGE	SEX	BLOOD	TRIBAL ENROLLMENT		
						YEAR	COUNTY	PAGE
1	Goforth, Sarah	NAMED	8	F	3/4	1897	Pontotoc	51
2	" Fred W.	Bro	6	M	3/4	1897	"	51
3	" Nora	Sister	4	F	3/4	1897	"	51

TRIBAL ENROLLMENT OF PARENTS

	NAME OF FATHER	YEAR	COUNTY	NAME OF MOTHER	YEAR	COUNTY
1	Wm H. Goforth		Blue County Choctaw Roll	Emma Goforth	Dead	Chick residing in Choctaw N. 3rd Dist.
2	" " "		" "	" "	"	" " " " "
3	" " "		" "	" "	"	" " " " "

(NOTES)

William H. Goforth, father of Nos. 1, 2, and 3 appears on Choctaw Card #366.

Oct. 11/98.

RESIDENCE: Panola COUNTY   CARD NO.

POST OFFICE: Mead, Ind. Ter.   FIELD NO.

	NAME	RELATION-SHIP TO PERSON FIRST NAMED	AGE	SEX	BLOOD	TRIBAL ENROLLMENT		
						YEAR	COUNTY	PAGE
1	Statons, Marina B.	NAMED	19	F	Full	1897	Panola	5
2	" Lillian Alma	Dau	14mo	"	1/2			
3	" Arthur Edward	Son	2wks	M	1/2			

TRIBAL ENROLLMENT OF PARENTS

	NAME OF FATHER	YEAR	COUNTY	NAME OF MOTHER	YEAR	COUNTY
1	Elijah Brown	Dead	Tishomingo	Amanda Kemp	Dead	Panola
2	H.A. Statons		non citizen	No. 1		
3	" " "		" "	No. 1		

(NOTES)

No. 1 On Chickasaw Roll as Merena P. Statons.
No. 3 Enrolled Aug. 20, 1901

Oct. 10/98.

Chickasaw Enrollment Cards 1898-1914
Chickasaw by Blood   Volume III

RESIDENCE: Panola   COUNTY   CARD NO.
POST OFFICE: Mead, Ind. Ter.   FIELD NO.

NAME	RELATION-SHIP TO PERSON FIRST NAMED	AGE	SEX	BLOOD	TRIBAL ENROLLMENT		
					YEAR	COUNTY	PAGE
1 Franklin, Martha A.	NAMED	62	F	1/8	1897	Panola	I
2 Ship, Susan	Ward	12	"	1/4	1897	"	I
3 " Mary	"	10	"	1/4	1897	"	I

TRIBAL ENROLLMENT OF PARENTS

	NAME OF FATHER	YEAR	COUNTY	NAME OF MOTHER	YEAR	COUNTY
1	Mirands Reynolds	Dead	Non Citizen	Pamelia Reynolds	Dead	Chickasaw Roll
2	John Ship	"	" "	Kittie Ship	"	Panola
3	" "	"	" "	" "	"	"

(NOTES)

No. 1 On Chickasaw Roll as M.A. Franklin

No. 2 P.O. Kemp, I.T. 7/27-04   Oct. 10/98.

RESIDENCE: Panola   COUNTY   CARD NO.
POST OFFICE: Colbert, Ind. Ter.   FIELD NO.

NAME	RELATION-SHIP TO PERSON FIRST NAMED	AGE	SEX	BLOOD	TRIBAL ENROLLMENT		
					YEAR	COUNTY	PAGE
1 Love, Henry	NAMED	56	M	1/4	1897	Panola	2
2 " Arthur	Son	11	"	1/8	1893	"	PR #2 P 7
3 Guess, Gabe	Step Dau	6	F	5/16			
4 Love, Benjamin	Son	10mo	M	1/8			
5 " Joseph Henry	"	1mo	"	1/8			
6 " Mary Aline	Dau	1mo	F	1/8			

TRIBAL ENROLLMENT OF PARENTS

	NAME OF FATHER	YEAR	COUNTY	NAME OF MOTHER	YEAR	COUNTY
1	Isaac Love	Dead	Chickasaw Roll	Eliza Love	Dead	Chickasaw Roll
2	No. 1			Jennie Love	"	Non-citizen
3	Jeff Guess	Dead	Panola	Ellen Love		" "
4	No. 1			" "		" "
5	No. 1			Marth[sic] Ellen Love		" "
6	No. 1			" " "		" "

Chickasaw Enrollment Cards 1898-1914
Chickasaw by Blood   Volume III

(NOTES)

No. 1 Died Nov. 22, 1901. Proof of Death filed Nov. 6, 1902.

Nos. 2 & 3 Enrolled Oct. 13/98.

Nos. 2 & 3 On Red Book of Nov. 5, 1896, Exhibit "A" Page 2

No. 3 Died Oct. 9th 1901. Proof of Death filed Nov. 6, 1902

No. 4 Enrolled Oct. 14/98.

No. 5 Enrolled May 24/99

No. 6 Enrolled November 28th 1900

(No. 2 Dawes' Roll No. 4186)

Oct. 10/98.

RESIDENCE: Panola COUNTY   CARD NO.

POST OFFICE: Silo, Ind. Ter.   FIELD NO.

	NAME	RELATION-SHIP TO PERSON FIRST NAMED	AGE	SEX	BLOOD	TRIBAL ENROLLMENT		
						YEAR	COUNTY	PAGE
1	Colbert, Sim	NAMED	45	M	Full	1897	Panola	5
2	" Kate	Wife	25	F	I.W.	1897	"	76
3	" Lizzie	Dau	17	"	Full	1897	"	5
4	" Jim	Son	11	M	"	1897	"	5
5	" Ben	"	10	"	"	1897	"	5
6	" Aden	"	2	"	1/2	1897	"	5
7	" Allie Lee	Dau	1	F	1/2			

TRIBAL ENROLLMENT OF PARENTS

	NAME OF FATHER	YEAR	COUNTY	NAME OF MOTHER	YEAR	COUNTY
1	Sham-mey	Dead	Chickasaw Roll	Ti-en-sie	Dead	Chickasaw Roll
2	A.W. Moore		Non-Citizen	E. Moore	"	Non-Citizen
3	No. 1			Rhody Colbert	"	Panola
4	No. 1			" "	"	"
5	No. 1			" "	"	"
6	No. 1			No. 2		
7	No. 1			No. 2		

(NOTES)

No. 1 is now husband of Lydia Wolf on Chickasaw Card #665, Oct. 3, 1901

No. 2 On Chickasaw Roll as Katie Colbert

No. 2 is Dead. Proof of Death requested Oct. 3, 1901. Received and filed Nov. 6th 1902

No. 3 is now wife of Sam Shirley a non-Citizen Aug 14/99

No. 6 On Chickasaw Roll as Edon.

Aug. 14/99 = No. 3 has been placed on card No. 1486 with her two children.

   She is now wife of Sam Shirley, a non-citizen

Oct. 10/98.

174

Chickasaw Enrollment Cards 1898-1914
Chickasaw by Blood   Volume III

RESIDENCE: Choctaw Nation ~~COUNTY~~   CARD No.

POST OFFICE: Ward, Ind. Ter.   FIELD No.

	NAME	RELATIONSHIP TO PERSON FIRST NAMED	AGE	SEX	BLOOD	TRIBAL ENROLLMENT		
						YEAR	COUNTY	PAGE
1	Burgevin, Josephine	NAMED	22	F	1/4			
2	" Basil Duke	Son	7mo	M	1/8			
3	" Agnes Elberta	Dau	2mo	F	1/8			
4	" Herbert Spencer	Son	1mo	M	1/8			

TRIBAL ENROLLMENT OF PARENTS

	NAME OF FATHER	YEAR	COUNTY	NAME OF MOTHER	YEAR	COUNTY
1	William Goforth	Dead	Non-Citizen	Jensie Goforth	Dead	Chickasaw Roll
2	Francis E. Burgevin		" "	No. 1		
3	" " "		" "	No. 1		
4	" " "		" "	No. 1		

(NOTES)
On Choctaw Census Record No. 2 Page 197. Transferred to Chickasaw Roll by Dawes Com.
On Choctaw Roll as Josephine Goforth
On Choctaw Roll, 1896, Sans Bois County, No. 4649 as Josephine Goforth
No. 2 Enrolled 6/16/99
No. 3 Enrolled May 24th 1900
No. 4 Enrolled Aug. 13th 1901

P.O. Spiro, I.T.   Oct. 10/98.

CANCELLED Stamped across card

RESIDENCE: Pickens   COUNTY   CARD No.

POST OFFICE: Lynn, Ind. Ter.   FIELD No.

	NAME	RELATIONSHIP TO PERSON FIRST NAMED	AGE	SEX	BLOOD	TRIBAL ENROLLMENT		
						YEAR	COUNTY	PAGE
1	McLaughlin, John Duke	NAMED	40	M	1/2	1897	Pickens	26
2	" Alice Dulcina	Wife	36	F	I.W.	1897	"	78
3	" Amanda Louisa	Dau	11	"	1/4	1897	"	26
4	" John Bunyan	Son	9	M	1/4	1897	"	26
5	" Benjamin	"	8	"	1/4	1897	"	26
6	" Tunkie	Dau	6	F	1/4	1897	"	26
7	" Cravens	Son	4	M	1/4	1897	"	26
8	" Duke	"	2	"	1/4	1897	"	26
9	" Easter	~~"~~	~~1mo~~	~~"~~	~~1/4~~	DIED PRIOR TO SEPTEMBER 25 1902		

TRIBAL ENROLLMENT OF PARENTS							
NAME OF FATHER	YEAR	COUNTY	NAME OF MOTHER	YEAR	COUNTY
1	Ben McLaughlin	Dead	Chickasaw Roll	Amanda McLaughlin	Dead	Chickasaw Roll
2	W.A.J. Finch	"	Non-citizen	Louisa Finch	"	Non-citizen
3	No. I			No. 2		
4	No. I			No. 2		
5	No. I			No. 2		
6	No. I			No. 2		
7	No. I			No. 2		
8	No. I			No. 2		
9	No. I			No. 2		

(NOTES)

No. 9 Died May 15, 1902
No. I On Chickasaw Roll as J.O. McLaughlin
No. 2 "   "   "   " A.B.   "   also called Dollie
No. 3 "   "   "   " Maudie L.   "
No. 4 "   "   "   " Bun   "
No. 5 "   "   "   " Ben   "
No. 7 "   "   "   " Craven   "
No. 8 Proof of Birth received & filed Nov. 10, 1902   *(No. 8 Dawes' Roll No. 4185)*
No. 9 nrolled May 25th 1900.
No. 2 Died Feb. 21st 1901; Proof of Death filed Nov. 10th 1902.   Oct. 10/98.

RESIDENCE: Choctaw Nation 3rd Dist.	COUNTY		CARD NO.
POST OFFICE: Durant, Ind. Ter.			FIELD NO.

NAME	RELATION-SHIP TO PERSON	AGE	SEX	BLOOD	TRIBAL ENROLLMENT		
					YEAR	COUNTY	PAGE
1	Thompson, Minnie	FIRST NAMED	23	F	1/2	1897	Chick residing in Choctaw N. 3rd Dist.	75
2	" ~~Leo Edward~~	~~Son~~	~~2~~	~~M~~	~~1/4~~			
3	" Rubie	Dau	6wks	F	1/4			

TRIBAL ENROLLMENT OF PARENTS							
NAME OF FATHER	YEAR	COUNTY	NAME OF MOTHER	YEAR	COUNTY
1	Charley Kingsberry		Non-Citizen	Minniw Graham	1897	Panola
2	~~Greenwood Thompson~~		~~Blue County Choctaw Roll~~	~~No. I~~		
3	" "		" "	No. I		

(NOTES)

No. I is wife of Green Thompson Choctaw Card #3439
No. 2 On Choctaw Census Record No. 2 Page 449 as Leo Ed. Thompson,

Chickasaw Enrollment Cards 1898-1914
Chickasaw by Blood   Volume III

transferred to Chickasaw Roll by Dawes Com
No. 2 On Choctaw Roll, 1896, Blue County, No. 12140 as Lee Ed. Thompson
No. 3 Enrolled Feb. 12th 1901.
(Notation illegible)

Oct. 10/98.

RESIDENCE: Panola   COUNTY   CARD NO.
POST OFFICE: Yarnaby, Ind. Ter.   FIELD NO.

| | NAME | RELATION-SHIP TO PERSON FIRST NAMED | AGE | SEX | BLOOD | TRIBAL ENROLLMENT | | |
						YEAR	COUNTY	PAGE
1	Barker, Thomas S.	NAMED	57	M	I.W.	1897	Panola	83
2	Halsell, Susan	Dau	18	F	1/4	1897	"	3
3	Barker, Eula	"	16	"	1/4	1897	"	3
4	" Minnie	"	14	"	1/4	1897	"	3
5	" Thomas M	Son	10	M	1/4	1897	"	3
6	Halsell, Annie Laurie	Gr.Dau	6wk	F	1/8			
7	" Samuel D.	Husband of No. 2	30	M	I.W.			

TRIBAL ENROLLMENT OF PARENTS

	NAME OF FATHER	YEAR	COUNTY	NAME OF MOTHER	YEAR	COUNTY
1	John Barker	Dead	Non-Citizen	Susan Barker	Dead	Non-Citizen
2	No. 1			Catherine Barker	"	Panola
3	No. 1			" "	"	"
4	No. 1			" "	"	"
5	No. 1			" "	"	"
6	Saml. D. Halsell		Non-Citizen	No. 2		
7	R.R. Halsell		" "	Nora A. Halsell	Dead	Non-Citz.

(NOTES)

No. 5 On Chickasaw Roll as Tom Barker, Jr.   *(No. 1 Dawes' Roll No. 290)*
   Surname on Chickasaw Roll Braker   *(No. 2 Dawes' Roll No. 1792)*
No. 2 is now the wife of Samuel D. Halsell on Chickasaw Card #D.289.   *(No. 3 Dawes' Roll No. 1793)*
No. 6 Enrolled Oct. 16th 1900   *(No. 4 Dawes' Roll No. 1794)*
   All admitted by Dawes Commission in 1896 on Chickasaw Card No. 269   *(No. 5 Dawes' Roll No. 4795)*
No. 7 transferred from Chickasaw Card #D.289.   *(No. 6 Dawes' Roll No. 4796)*
   See decision of August 21, 1904. Sept. 15, 1904.
Nos. *(illegible)* 6 incl See decision of March 9 '04.   *(No. 7 Dawes' Roll No. 173)*

P.O. Yuba, I.T. 11/17/02.   Oct. 10/98.

177

Chickasaw Enrollment Cards 1898-1914
Chickasaw by Blood   Volume III

RESIDENCE: Panola COUNTY   CARD NO.

POST OFFICE: Robbersroost, Ind. Ter.   FIELD NO.

	NAME	RELATION-SHIP TO PERSON FIRST NAMED	AGE	SEX	BLOOD	TRIBAL ENROLLMENT		
						YEAR	COUNTY	PAGE
1	Keffer, Nick	NAMED	72	M	I.W.	1897	Panola	76
2	" Alvira	Wife	48	F	Full	1897	"	6
3	Godfrey, Annie	Dau	15	F	1/2	1897	"	6
4	Keffer, Willie	Son	10	M	1/2	1897	"	6
5	Godfrey, Wilber Elmer	Gr.Son	8mo	"	1/4			

TRIBAL ENROLLMENT OF PARENTS

	NAME OF FATHER	YEAR	COUNTY	NAME OF MOTHER	YEAR	COUNTY
1	John H. Keffer	Dead	Non-Citiwn	Mattie Keffer	Dead	Non Citizen
2	Marshal		Chickasaw Roll	Shim-a-yo-ka	"	Chickasaw Roll
3	No. 1			No. 2		
4	No. 1			No. 2		
5	Ed. Godfrey		non-citizen	No. 3		

(NOTES)

No. 1 See decision of June 13 '04.   *(No. 1 Dawes' Roll No. 400)*

No. 1 On Chickasaw Roll as Nick Keiffer

   Married in 1862. Copy of record to be supplied. Received Oct. 10/98

No. 3 is now the wife of Ed. Godfrey, a non-citizen, Oct. 16th 1901

No. 3 " " " " " " " on Chickasaw Card #D350. Oct. 24th 1901

No. 5 Born Feb. 22nd 1901; and enrolled Oct. 16th 1901   Oct. 10/98.

RESIDENCE: Panola COUNTY   CARD NO.

POST OFFICE: Robbersroost, Ind. Ter.   FIELD NO.

	NAME		RELATION-SHIP TO PERSON FIRST NAMED	AGE	SEX	BLOOD	TRIBAL ENROLLMENT		
							YEAR	COUNTY	PAGE
1	Miller, Joe Daniel	DIED	NAMED	6wks	M	1/4			

TRIBAL ENROLLMENT OF PARENTS

	NAME OF FATHER	YEAR	COUNTY	NAME OF MOTHER	YEAR	COUNTY
1	W.C. Miller		non-citizen	Ida Miller	Dead	Panola

(NOTES)

William C. Miller father of No 1 on Chickasaw R462

Mother of No. 1 on 1896 Chick Census Roll, Page 4 as Ida McCoy

                                                         Oct. 10/98.

RESIDENCE: Panola COUNTY					CARD NO.			
POST OFFICE: Mead, Ind. Ter.					FIELD NO.			

	NAME	RELATION-SHIP TO PERSON FIRST NAMED	AGE	SEX	BLOOD	TRIBAL ENROLLMENT		
						YEAR	COUNTY	PAGE
1	Krouse, Christian	NAMED	53	M	I.W.	1897	Panola	76
2	Krouse, Frances	Wife	44	F	Full	1897	"	5
3	" Lewis	Son	20	M	1/2	1897	"	5
4	" Johnson	"	18	M	1/2	1897	"	5
5	" Lucy	Dau	16	F	1/2	1897	"	5
6	" Martin	Son	12	M	1/2	1897	"	5
7	" Lena M	Dau	8	F	1/2	1897	"	5
8	" Margaret	"	5	"	1/2	1897	"	5
9	" Rosa	"	2	"	1/2	1897	"	5

TRIBAL ENROLLMENT OF PARENTS

	NAME OF FATHER	YEAR	COUNTY	NAME OF MOTHER	YEAR	COUNTY
1	Christian Krouse	Dead	Non-Citizen	Margaret Krouse	Dead	Non-Citizen
2	Lewis Newberry	"	Panola	Lucy Newberry	1897	Panola
3	No. 1			No. 2		
4	No. 1			No. 2		
5	No. 1			No. 2		
6	No. 1			No. 2		
7	No. 1			No. 2		
8	No. 1			No. 2		
9	No. 1			No. 2		

(NOTES)

No. 2 On Chickasaw Roll as Francis Krouse   (No. I Dawes' Roll No. 337)

No. 3 "   "   " " Louis   "

No. 5 is now the wife of J.E. Rowler, non-citizen. Evidence of marriage filed Nov. 7th 1902

See certificate of William Kaney relative to marriage between Nos. 1 & 2 filed March 31, 1902.

Oct. 10/98.

RESIDENCE: Panola COUNTY					CARD NO.			
POST OFFICE: Mead, Ind. Ter.					FIELD NO.			

	NAME	RELATION-SHIP TO PERSON FIRST NAMED	AGE	SEX	BLOOD	TRIBAL ENROLLMENT		
						YEAR	COUNTY	PAGE
1	Newberry, Lucy	NAMED	65	F	Full	1897	Panola	5

TRIBAL ENROLLMENT OF PARENTS

NAME OF FATHER	YEAR	COUNTY	NAME OF MOTHER	YEAR	COUNTY
1 Hawkins	Dead	Chickasaw Roll	Sha-thlock-ker	Dead	Chickasaw Roll

(NOTES)

Oct. 10/98.

RESIDENCE: Choctaw Nation 3rd Dist.   ~~COUNTY~~   **CARD NO.**

POST OFFICE: Tuskahoma, Ind. Ter.   **FIELD NO.**

NAME	RELATION-SHIP TO PERSON FIRST NAMED	AGE	SEX	BLOOD	TRIBAL ENROLLMENT		
					YEAR	COUNTY	PAGE
1 Anderson, Zodick		20	M	1/2			

TRIBAL ENROLLMENT OF PARENTS

NAME OF FATHER	YEAR	COUNTY	NAME OF MOTHER	YEAR	COUNTY
1 Solomon Anderson	Dead	Chickasaw Roll	Lucy Anderson	Dead	Chickasaw Roll

(NOTES)

On Choctaw Census Record No. 2, Page 22 as Verdick Anderson; Transferred to Chickasaw Roll by Dawes Com.
On Choctaw Roll, 1896, Jacks Fork County, No. 532 as Verdick Anderson.

Oct. 10/98.

CANCELLED Stamped across card

RESIDENCE: Choctaw Nation 3rd Dist.   **COUNTY**   **CARD NO.**

POST OFFICE: Hartshorn, I.T.   **FIELD NO.**

NAME		RELATION-SHIP TO PERSON FIRST NAMED	AGE	SEX	BLOOD	TRIBAL ENROLLMENT		
						YEAR	COUNTY	PAGE
1 Thompson, Siney		NAMED	51	F	1/2	1897	Chick residing in Choctaw N. 3rd Dist.	73
2 " ~~William C.~~	Void	~~Son~~	~~23~~	~~M~~	~~1/4~~			
3 " ~~Ella~~	Void	~~Dau~~	~~19~~	F	~~1/4~~			
4 " ~~Lewis~~	Void	~~Son~~	~~16~~	M	~~1/4~~			
5 " ~~Burney~~	Void	~~"~~	~~14~~	~~"~~	~~1/4~~			

TRIBAL ENROLLMENT OF PARENTS

NAME OF FATHER	YEAR	COUNTY	NAME OF MOTHER	YEAR	COUNTY
1 Silas Ward		Non-Citizen	Mary Pickens Ward	Dead	Chickasaw Roll
2 ~~Robert Thompson~~		~~Kiamitia County Choctaw Roll~~	~~No. 1~~		
3 " "		" "	~~No. 1~~		
4 " "		" "	~~No. 1~~		
5 " "		" "	~~No. 1~~		

Chickasaw Enrollment Cards 1898-1914
Chickasaw by Blood   Volume III

(NOTES)

All except No. 1 on Choctaw Census Record No. 2, Kiamitia County, Page 448;
transferred to Chickasaw Roll by Dawes Com.

No. 2 On Choctaw Roll, 1896, Kiamitia County, No. 12361

No. 3 "   "   " 1896   "   "   " 12362

No. 4 "   "   " 1896   "   "   " 12363

No. 5 "   "   " 1896   "   "   " 12364 as Burnie Thompson

Nos. 2,3,4 & 5 transferred to Choctaw Card #541 *(remainder illegible)*

P.O. Dowell, I.T.   Oct. 10/98.

	NAME	RELATION-SHIP TO PERSON FIRST NAMED	AGE	SEX	BLOOD	TRIBAL ENROLLMENT		
						YEAR	COUNTY	PAGE
1	Anderson, Nicholas	NAMED	30	M	1/2			
2	" Louisa	niece	16	F	3/4			

RESIDENCE: Choctaw Nation 3rd Dist.   ~~COUNTY~~   CARD NO.
POST OFFICE: Antlers, Ind. Ter.   FIELD NO.

TRIBAL ENROLLMENT OF PARENTS

	NAME OF FATHER	YEAR	COUNTY	NAME OF MOTHER	YEAR	COUNTY
1	Allington Anderson	Dead	Choctaw Roll	Louisa Impson	1897	Chick residing in Choctaw N. 3rd Dist.
2	Gooden "	"	Chick residing in Choctaw N. 3rd Dist.	Nancy Anderson	Dead	" " " "

(NOTES)

No. 1 Husband of Amanda Anderson, Choctaw Roll Card No. 357

No. 1 On Choctaw Census Record No. 2 Page 19;   Transferred to Chickasaw Roll by Dawes Com

No. 2 "   "   "   "   "   " 268 as Louisa Impson "   "   "   "   "

No. 1 On Choctaw Roll, 1896, Jacks Fork County, No. 463 as Nicholas E. Anderson

No. 2 "   "   " 1896   "   "   " 6342 " Louisa Impson

Oct. 10/98.

CANCELLED Stamped across card

RESIDENCE: Choctaw Nation 3rd Dist.   ~~COUNTY~~   CARD NO.
POST OFFICE: Tuskahoma, Ind. Ter.   FIELD NO.

	NAME	RELATION-SHIP TO PERSON FIRST NAMED	AGE	SEX	BLOOD	TRIBAL ENROLLMENT		
						YEAR	COUNTY	PAGE
1	Impson, Louisa	NAMED	58	F	Full			
2	Anderson, Tandy	Son	23	M	1/2			
3	Impson, Ida	Dau	17	F	Full			

4	Anderson, Clarence J.		Gr.Son	2mo	M	1/2				

TRIBAL ENROLLMENT OF PARENTS

	NAME OF FATHER	YEAR	COUNTY	NAME OF MOTHER	YEAR	COUNTY
1	Hotubby Moore	Dead	Chickasaw Roll	Hettie Anderson	Dead	Chickasaw Roll
2	Allington Anderson		Choctaw Roll	No. 1		
3	Sydney Burris	1897	Chick residing in Choctaw N. 3rd Dist	No. 1		
4	Jackman Anderson	1896	Choctaw Roll	No. 3		

(NOTES)

All transferred to Chickasaw Roll by Dawes Com

Nos. 1 & 3 On Choctaw Census Record No. 2 Page 268

No. 2   "   "   "   "   " 2   " 19

No. 2 is now the Husband of Lyles Hotubbee on Choctaw Card #1993 Sept. 15, 1902

No. 3 is now the wife of Jackman Anderson on Choctaw Card #1883. Evidence of marriage requested
     May 13th 1902, Received & filed June 9th 1902.

No. 4 Born March 8th 1902; Enrolled May 13, 1902.

No. 1 On Choctaw Roll, 1896, Jacks Fork County, No. 6340

No. 2 "   "   " 1896 "   "   "   " 461

No. 3 "   "   " 1896 "   "   "   " 6341

Oct. 10/98.

CANCELLED Stamped across card

RESIDENCE: Choctaw Nation 3rd Dist.   COUNTY   CARD NO.

POST OFFICE: Tuskahoma, Ind. Ter.   FIELD NO.

	NAME	RELATION-SHIP TO PERSON FIRST NAMED	AGE	SEX	BLOOD	TRIBAL ENROLLMENT		
						YEAR	COUNTY	PAGE
1	Anderson, Elsey		60	F	Full	1893	Choc. Dist.	#2 Maytubby
2	" ~~Norton~~	~~Son~~	~~25~~	~~M~~	~~1/2~~			
3	" ~~Missie~~	~~Dau~~	~~17~~	~~F~~	~~1/2~~			

	NAME OF FATHER	YEAR	COUNTY	NAME OF MOTHER	YEAR	COUNTY
1	Ay-ko-ches	Dead	Chickasaw Roll	(Name Illegible)	Dead	Chickasaw Roll
2	~~Bartlett Anderson~~	"	~~Choctaw Roll~~	~~No. 1~~		
3	" "	"	" "	~~No. 1~~		

(NOTES)

No. 1 On Maytubby Pay Roll No. 2

Nos. 2 & 3 On Choctaw Census Record No. 2, Jacks Fork County, Page 20. Transferred to Chickasaw Roll by
     Dawes Com.

No. 2 On Choctaw Roll as M.J. Anderson

No. 2 is the Husband of Mary Anderson on Choctaw Card #1972

No. 2 On Choctaw Roll 1896, Jacks Fork County, No. 498, as M.J. Anderson

No. 3 "   "   "   1896, "   "   "   " 496
Nos. 2 & 3 transferred to Choctaw Card No. *(remainder illegible)*

Oct. 10/98.

RESIDENCE: Tishomingo COUNTY					CARD No.			
POST OFFICE: Tishomingo. Ind. Ter.					FIELD No.			
NAME	RELATION-SHIP TO PERSON FIRST NAMED	AGE	SEX	BLOOD	TRIBAL ENROLLMENT			
					YEAR	COUNTY	PAGE	
1 Robinson, Eliza	NAMED	55	F	Full	1897	Tishomingo	33	

	TRIBAL ENROLLMENT OF PARENTS						
NAME OF FATHER	YEAR	COUNTY	NAME OF MOTHER	YEAR	COUNTY		
1 Marshal	Dead	Chickasaw Roll	Chini-e-o-ka	Dead	Chickasaw Roll		

(NOTES)

Oct. 10/98.

RESIDENCE: Panola COUNTY					CARD No.			
POST OFFICE: Emmet, Ind. Ter.					FIELD No.			
NAME	RELATION-SHIP TO PERSON FIRST NAMED	AGE	SEX	BLOOD	TRIBAL ENROLLMENT			
					YEAR	COUNTY	PAGE	
1 Brown, Edmonson	NAMED	28	M	Full	1897	Panola	4	
2 " Malinda	Wife	30	F	"	1897	"	4	
3 " Julia	Dau	12	"	"	1897	"	4	
4 " Lulu	"	6	"	"	1897	"	4	
5 " Nannie	"	2	"	"				
6 " Bettie	"	1mo	"	"				

	TRIBAL ENROLLMENT OF PARENTS						
NAME OF FATHER	YEAR	COUNTY	NAME OF MOTHER	YEAR	COUNTY		
1 Ebil Brown	Dead	Chickasaw Roll	Jincy Brown	Dead	Chickasaw Roll		
2 Sampson Carney	"	" "	S//phey Carney	"	" "		
3 No. 1			No. 2				
4 No. 1			No. 2				
5 No. 1			No. 2				
6 No. 1			No. 2				

(NOTES)

No. 3 also on Chickasaw Roll Page 92 as Julia Conaway
No. 4 On Chickasaw Roll as Lulua Brown
No. 6 Enrolled November 16, 1900

Oct. 10/98.

Chickasaw Enrollment Cards 1898-1914
Chickasaw by Blood   Volume III

RESIDENCE: Panola   COUNTY   CARD NO.

POST OFFICE: Silo, Ind. Ter.   FIELD NO.

NAME	RELATION-SHIP TO PERSON FIRST NAMED	AGE	SEX	BLOOD	TRIBAL ENROLLMENT		
					YEAR	COUNTY	PAGE
1 Phelps, Emma	NAMED	21	F	1/2	1897	Panola	6
2 " Willie	Son	14mo	M	1/4	1897	"	25
3 " Bessoe	Dau	2mo	F	1/4			

TRIBAL ENROLLMENT OF PARENTS

NAME OF FATHER	YEAR	COUNTY	NAME OF MOTHER	YEAR	COUNTY
1 Nick Keffer		Non-citizen	Elvira Keffer	1897	Panola
2 Andrew Phelps		" "	No. 1		
3 " "		" "	No. 1		

(NOTES)

No. 1 On Chickasaw Roll as Emly Keffer

No. 2 Proof of Death received and filed Dec. 4, 1902   (No. 2 Dawes' Roll No. 4184)

No. 3 Enrolled Sept. 24, 1902

P.O. Address is now Robbers Roost I.T.

P.O. Antlers I.T. 12/4/02.   Oct. 10/98.

RESIDENCE: Panola   COUNTY   CARD NO.

POST OFFICE: Mead, Ind. Ter.   FIELD NO.

NAME	RELATION-SHIP TO PERSON FIRST NAMED	AGE	SEX	BLOOD	TRIBAL ENROLLMENT		
					YEAR	COUNTY	PAGE
1 Underwood, Edgar	NAMED	5	M	1/2	1897	Panola	1
2 " Allen	Bro	3	"	1/2	1897	"	1
3 " Lewis	"	6mo	"	1/2			

TRIBAL ENROLLMENT OF PARENTS

NAME OF FATHER	YEAR	COUNTY	NAME OF MOTHER	YEAR	COUNTY
1 Joe Underwood	1897	Tishomingo	Fannie Underwood		Non-citizen
2 " "	"	"	" "		" "
3 " "	"	"	" "		" "

(NOTES)

No. 1 On Chickasaw Roll as Ed. Underwood

Joe Underwood, father of No. 1, 2, & 3 on Chickasaw Card #864.

Oct. 10/98.

RESIDENCE: Choctaw Nation ~~COUNTY~~   CARD NO.

POST OFFICE: Kiowa, Ind. Ter.   FIELD NO.

	NAME	RELATION-SHIP TO PERSON FIRST NAMED	AGE	SEX	BLOOD	TRIBAL ENROLLMENT		
						YEAR	COUNTY	PAGE
1	Duncan, Lewis	FIRST NAMED	37	M	3/4	1897	Chick residing in Choctaw N. 1st Dist.	71
2	" Martha E.	Wife	30	F	I.W.			

TRIBAL ENROLLMENT OF PARENTS

	NAME OF FATHER	YEAR	COUNTY	NAME OF MOTHER	YEAR	COUNTY
1	Howard Duncan	Dead	Panola	Villy Duncan	Dead	Chickasaw Roll
2	Hardy Van Camp		Non-Citizen	Sallie Van Camp		Non-citizen

(NOTES)

No. 2 See Decision of June 13 '04.   *(No. 2 Dawes' Roll No. 398)*

    Marriage license & certificate under U.S. Law filed 7/31/1900

No. 2 Enrolled July 31st 1900

    Certified copy of Divorce proceedings between No. 1 and Esther Ann Duncan filed Feb. 16, 1903

P.O. Coalgate, I.T. 9/17/02   Oct. 10/98.

RESIDENCE: Panola COUNTY   CARD NO.

POST OFFICE: Mead, Ind. Ter.   FIELD NO.

	NAME	RELATION-SHIP TO PERSON FIRST	AGE	SEX	BLOOD	TRIBAL ENROLLMENT		
						YEAR	COUNTY	PAGE
1	Calhoune, Emily	NAMED	5	F	1/2	1897	Panola	9
2	Lamar, Hattie	Mother	26	F	I.W.			

TRIBAL ENROLLMENT OF PARENTS

	NAME OF FATHER	YEAR	COUNTY	NAME OF MOTHER	YEAR	COUNTY
1	Sam Calhoune	Dead	Panola	Hattie Lamar		non-citizen
2	Moses Meeks		non citizen	Martha Meeks		non citizen

(NOTES)

On Chickasaw Roll as Emerly Calhoune

No. 2 placed on this card September 28th 1905, in accordance with order of the Commissioner to the Five Civilized Tribes of that date holding application was madewithin time prescribed by Act of Congress approved July 1, 1902

Oct. 10/98.

Chickasaw Enrollment Cards 1898-1914
Chickasaw by Blood   Volume III

RESIDENCE: Panola   COUNTY   CARD NO.

POST OFFICE: Mead, Ind. Ter.   FIELD NO.

	NAME	RELATION-SHIP TO PERSON FIRST	AGE	SEX	BLOOD	TRIBAL ENROLLMENT		
						YEAR	COUNTY	PAGE
1	Meeks, Betsey	NAMED	40	F	3/4	1897	Panola	2
2	" Reubin	Son	7	M	3/8	1897	"	2
3	" Cruce	"	14mo	"	3/8			
4	" Dosia	St.Dau	9	F	3/8	1897	Panola	2
5	Alberson, Jim	St.Son	18	M	Full	1897	"	1

TRIBAL ENROLLMENT OF PARENTS

	NAME OF FATHER	YEAR	COUNTY	NAME OF MOTHER	YEAR	COUNTY
1	Isaac Jefferson	Dead	Chickasaw Roll	Julia Kemp	1897	Panola
2	Henry Meeks		White man	No. 1		
3	" "		" "	No. 1		
4	" "		" "	Amanda Kemp Meeks	Dead	Panola
5	Wilburn Alberson	Dead	Panola	Jennie James	"	"

(NOTES)

Henry Meeks, husband of No. 1 on Chickasaw D.148

No. 3 Died Feb. 22 1898. Proof filed Oct. 25th 1902

Oct. 10/98.

RESIDENCE: Panola   COUNTY   CARD NO.

POST OFFICE: Silo, Ind. Ter.   FIELD NO.

	NAME	RELATION-SHIP TO PERSON FIRST	AGE	SEX	BLOOD	TRIBAL ENROLLMENT		
						YEAR	COUNTY	PAGE
1	Kemp, Julia	NAMED	60	F	1/2	1897	Panola	2
2	Miller, Julia	G.Dau	18	"	3/4	1897	"	2
3	Alberson, Isaac	G.Son	13	M	3/4	1897	"	2
4	Miller, Robert Johnston	Son of No. 2	1mo	"	3/8			

TRIBAL ENROLLMENT OF PARENTS

	NAME OF FATHER	YEAR	COUNTY	NAME OF MOTHER	YEAR	COUNTY
1	Jim Merritt	Dead	Non-Citizen	Em-mo-holl-le	Dead	Chickasaw Roll
2	Walter Porter	"	Tishomingo	Betsey Meeks	1897	Panola
3	Wilburn Alberson	"	Panola	" "	"	"
4	Tom A. Miller		Non-Citizem	No. 2		

(NOTES)

No. 1 Wife of Robinson Kemp, Choctaw Roll Card No. 354

No. 2 now the wife of T.A. Miller, Evidence of marriage filed June 25th 1902
No. 4 Born May 25th 1902. Enrolled June 20th 1902

Oct. 10th 1898.

	NAME	RELATIONSHIP TO PERSON FIRST NAMED	AGE	SEX	BLOOD	TRIBAL ENROLLMENT		
						YEAR	COUNTY	PAGE
1	Turnbull, George W.	NAMED	37	M	1/2			
2	" Jessie James	Son	4mo	"	1/4			

RESIDENCE: Choctaw Nation ~~COUNTY~~   CARD NO.
POST OFFICE: Caddo   FIELD NO.

TRIBAL ENROLLMENT OF PARENTS

	NAME OF FATHER	YEAR	COUNTY	NAME OF MOTHER	YEAR	COUNTY
1	Leroy Turnbull	Dead	Choctaw Roll	Mary J. Turnbull	1897	Tishomingo
2	No. 1			Ettie Turnbull		non citizen

(NOTES)
On Choctaw Census Record No. 2 Page 449; transferred to Chickasaw Roll by Dawes Com.
Father of Emma Turnbull, Choctaw Roll card 353
On Choctaw Roll 1896 No. 12418, Blue County
No. 1 is the husband of Ettie Turnbull, a non-citizen. Evidence of marriage filed March 25th 1901
No. 2 Enrolled March 25th 1902.

Oct. 10/98.

CANCELLED Stamped across card

	NAME	RELATIONSHIP TO PERSON FIRST NAMED	AGE	SEX	BLOOD	TRIBAL ENROLLMENT		
						YEAR	COUNTY	PAGE
1	Brown, Willis	NAMED	47	M	Full	1897	Panola	3
2	Maxwil, Tommie	Nephew	11	"	"	1897	"	4

RESIDENCE: Panola COUNTY   CARD NO.
POST OFFICE: Yarnaby, Ind. Ter.   FIELD NO.

TRIBAL ENROLLMENT OF PARENTS

	NAME OF FATHER	YEAR	COUNTY	NAME OF MOTHER	YEAR	COUNTY
1	Ya-ka-pe-cha	Dead	Chickasaw Roll	Ste-ke-ye	Dead	Chickasaw Roll
2	Maxwil	"	Panola	Siney Maxwil	"	Panola

(NOTES)
P.O. Kemp, I.T.

Oct. 10/98.

Chickasaw Enrollment Cards 1898-1914
Chickasaw by Blood   Volume III

RESIDENCE: Panola   COUNTY   CARD NO.

POST OFFICE: Yarnaby, Ind. Ter.   FIELD NO.

NAME	RELATION-SHIP TO PERSON FIRST NAMED	AGE	SEX	BLOOD	TRIBAL ENROLLMENT		
					YEAR	COUNTY	PAGE
1 Brown, Gipson	NAMED	25	M	Full	1897	Panola	1
2 " Lolah Rachel	Dau	7mo	F	1/2			
3 " Nealie	"	17mo	"	1/2			
4 " Gipson Albert	Son	6mo	M	1/2			

TRIBAL ENROLLMENT OF PARENTS

	NAME OF FATHER	YEAR	COUNTY	NAME OF MOTHER	YEAR	COUNTY
1	Willis Brown	1897	Panola	Harriet Brown	Dead	Panola
2	No. 1			Ada Brown		Non citizen
3	No. 1			" "		" "
4	No. 1			" "		" "

(NOTES)

No. 3 Enrolled June 24, 1900.

No. 4 Born April 6th 1902. Enrolled Oct. 24, 1902.   *(No. 4 Dawes' Roll No. 4183)*

Oct. 10/98.

RESIDENCE: Panola   COUNTY   CARD NO.

POST OFFICE: Colbert, Ind. Ter.   FIELD NO.

NAME	RELATION-SHIP TO PERSON FIRST NAMED	AGE	SEX	BLOOD	TRIBAL ENROLLMENT		
					YEAR	COUNTY	PAGE
1 Kemp, Willington Martin	NAMED	38	M	3/4	1897	Panola	3
2 " Susan A.	Wife	28	F	I.W.	1897	"	76
3 " Levi Pitman	Son	2	M	3/8	1897	"	3
4 " Lela	Dau	1	F	3/8	~~1897~~	"	~~85~~
5 " Ethel	"	2wks	"	3/8			
6 " Elzira	Mother	56	"	Full	1897	Panola	3
7 " Will	Son	3wks	M	3/8			
8 " Eva	Dau	3wks	F	3/8			

TRIBAL ENROLLMENT OF PARENTS

	NAME OF FATHER	YEAR	COUNTY	NAME OF MOTHER	YEAR	COUNTY
1	Levi Kemp	Dead	Choctaw Roll	Elzira Kemp	1897	Panola
2	C.C. Jackson		Non Citizen	Julia A. Jackson		Non Citizen
3	No. 1			No. 2		
4	No. 1			No. 2		
5	No. 1			No. 2		

Chickasaw Enrollment Cards 1898-1914
Chickasaw by Blood   Volume III

6	Robert Colbert	Dead	Chickasaw Roll	Elsey Colbert		Dead	Chickasaw Roll
7	No. 1			No. 2			
8	No. 1			No. 2			

(NOTES)

No. 1 On Chickasaw Roll as W.M. Kemp
No. 2 "   "   "   " S.J.   "   *(No. 2 Dawes' Roll No. 151)*
No. 3 "   "   "   " Levi P. "
No. 4 Proof of Birth received and file Sept 30ᵗʰ 1902   *(No. 4 Dawes' Roll No. 4181)*
No. 5 Died Nov. 13ᵗʰ 1900. Proof of Death filed Aug. 15ᵗʰ 1902
No. 7 Enrolled Jan. 2ⁿᵈ 1901; Died July 4ᵗʰ 1901. Proof of Death filed Aug. 15ᵗʰ 1902
Born Sept. 8ᵗʰ 1902; Enrolled Sept. 30ᵗʰ 1902   *(No. 8 Dawes' Roll No. 4182)*

P.O. Paucaunda, I.T.   Oct. 10/98.

RESIDENCE: Choctaw Nation   COUNTY   CARD NO.
POST OFFICE: Sterrett, Ind. Ter.   FIELD NO.

NAME	RELATION-SHIP TO PERSON FIRST NAMED	AGE	SEX	BLOOD	TRIBAL ENROLLMENT		
					YEAR	COUNTY	PAGE
1 Parker, Wesley		20	M	1/2	1897	Chick residing in Choctaw N. 3ʳᵈ Dist.	74

TRIBAL ENROLLMENT OF PARENTS

	NAME OF FATHER	YEAR	COUNTY	NAME OF MOTHER	YEAR	COUNTY
1	Edward Parker	Dead	Pickens	Susan Parker	Dead	Pickens

(NOTES)
                                                            Oct. 10/98.

RESIDENCE: Choctaw Nation   COUNTY   CARD NO.
POST OFFICE: Caddo, Ind. Ter.   FIELD NO.

NAME	RELATION-SHIP TO PERSON FIRST NAMED	AGE	SEX	BLOOD	TRIBAL ENROLLMENT		
					YEAR	COUNTY	PAGE
1 Goforth, Solomon		63	M	1/2	1897	Chick residing in Choctaw N. 2ⁿᵈ Dist.	74

TRIBAL ENROLLMENT OF PARENTS

	NAME OF FATHER	YEAR	COUNTY	NAME OF MOTHER	YEAR	COUNTY
1	*(Name Illegible)*	Dead	Non citizen	Ma?ate	Dead	Chick residing in Choctaw N. 3ʳᵈ Dist.

(NOTES)
No. 1 On Chickasaw Roll as Soloman Goforth
No. 1 is the Husband of Mary A. Goforth, Choctaw Card #D.722.   Oct. 10/98.

189

RESIDENCE:	Panola	COUNTY					CARD NO.			
POST OFFICE:	Mead, Ind. Ter.						FIELD NO.			

	NAME	RELATION-SHIP TO PERSON FIRST NAMED	AGE	SEX	BLOOD	TRIBAL ENROLLMENT			
						YEAR	COUNTY		PAGE
1	Kemp, Levi	NAMED	40	M	Full	1897	Panola		1
2	" Lulu	Dau	15	F	1/2	1897	"		1
3	" Mary	Wife	36	F	I.W.				

	NAME OF FATHER	YEAR	COUNTY	NAME OF MOTHER	YEAR	COUNTY
1	Reuben Kemp	Dead	Chickasaw Roll	Katesy Kemp	Dead	Chickasaw Roll
2	No. 1			Mary Kemp		white woman
3	(Illegible) Bohannan	Dead	non citiz.	Peggy Bohannon	dead	non citz

(NOTES)

Mary Kemp wife of No. 1 on Chickasaw Card D.147
No. 3 transferred from Chickasaw Card #D.147 March 29, 1903.   *(No. 3 Dawes' Roll No. 51)*
See decision of March 13, 1903.

Oct. 10/98.

RESIDENCE:	Panola	COUNTY					CARD NO.			
POST OFFICE:	Robbinroost, Ind. Ter.						FIELD NO.			

	NAME	RELATION-SHIP TO PERSON FIRST NAMED	AGE	SEX	BLOOD	TRIBAL ENROLLMENT			
						YEAR	COUNTY		PAGE
1	Seely, George	NAMED	30	M	Full	1897	Panola		2

TRIBAL ENROLLMENT OF PARENTS						
	NAME OF FATHER	YEAR	COUNTY	NAME OF MOTHER	YEAR	COUNTY
1	Simon Seely	Dead	Panola	Bicey Seely	Dead	Tishomingo

(NOTES)

On Chickasaw Roll as George Sealy
No. 1 and her husband Frazier McLish are separated. See testimony of No. 1 of May 20, 1903.

Oct. 10/98.

RESIDENCE:	Panola	COUNTY					CARD NO.			
POST OFFICE:	Emmet, Ind. Ter.						FIELD NO.			

	NAME	RELATION-SHIP TO PERSON FIRST NAMED	AGE	SEX	BLOOD	TRIBAL ENROLLMENT			
						YEAR	COUNTY		PAGE
1	Peter, Harvey	NAMED	26	M	Full	1897	Panola		56
2	" Jane	Wife	21	F	"	1897	Panola		6
3	" Simon	Son	3mo	M	"				

4	" Rosa Anna		Dau	2mo	F	"				

TRIBAL ENROLLMENT OF PARENTS

	NAME OF FATHER	YEAR	COUNTY	NAME OF MOTHER	YEAR	COUNTY
1	William Peter	Dead	Panola	Shem-be-by	Dead	Panola
2	Joel Conway	1897	"	Nancy Conway	1897	"
3	No. 1			No. 2		
4	No. 1			No. 2		

(NOTES)

No. 1 On Chickasaw Roll as Harvy Peter
No. 2 "   "   "   " Jane Conway
No. 3 Enrolled Oct. 4/99
No. 4 Born May 9th 1902. Enrolled June 30th 1902

Oct. 10/98.

RESIDENCE: Panola COUNTY		CARD NO.	
POST OFFICE: Yarnaby, Ind. Ter.		FIELD NO.	

	NAME	RELATION-SHIP TO PERSON FIRST NAMED	AGE	SEX	BLOOD	TRIBAL ENROLLMENT		
						YEAR	COUNTY	PAGE
1	Perry, Henry Kilpatrick	NAMED	13	M	3/8	1897	Panola	3
2	" Lucian Rains	Bro	8	"	3/8	1897	"	3
3	" Mattie Louise	Sis	5	F	3/8	1897	"	3
4	" Eli Leon	Bro	3	M	3/8	1897	"	3

TRIBAL ENROLLMENT OF PARENTS

	NAME OF FATHER	YEAR	COUNTY	NAME OF MOTHER	YEAR	COUNTY
1	Eli Perry		Choctaw residing in Chickasaw Dist.	Minnie E. Perry	Dead	Panola
2	" "		" "	" " "	"	"
3	" "		" "	" " "	"	"
4	" "		" "	" " "	"	"

(NOTES)

Father Eli Perry on Choctaw Roll Card No. 352
No. 1 On Chickasaw Roll as Henry K. Perry
No. 2 "   "   "   " Lucian   "
No. 3 "   "   "   " Mattie L.   "
No. 4 "   "   "   " Eli L.   "
No. 3 Died April 9, 1899. Proof of Death filed Sept 12th 1902
No. 4 Died April 10, 1899. Proof of Death filed Sept. 12th 1902

Oct. 10/98

Chickasaw Enrollment Cards 1898-1914
Chickasaw by Blood   Volume III

RESIDENCE: Panola COUNTY   CARD NO.
POST OFFICE: Emmett, Ind. Ter.   FIELD NO.

NAME	RELATION-SHIP TO PERSON FIRST NAMED	AGE	SEX	BLOOD	TRIBAL ENROLLMENT		
					YEAR	COUNTY	PAGE
1 ~~Reel, Mitchel~~	NAMED	40	M	~~Full~~	~~1897~~	~~Panola~~	~~6~~

TRIBAL ENROLLMENT OF PARENTS

NAME OF FATHER	YEAR	COUNTY	NAME OF MOTHER	YEAR	COUNTY
1 ~~Christopher Reel~~	~~Dead~~	~~Chickasaw Roll~~	~~Silbey Reel~~	~~Dead~~	~~Chickasaw Roll~~

(NOTES)

No. 1 died in December, 1899; Enrollment cancelled by Department Dec. 28, 1904

Oct. 10/98

RESIDENCE: Pontotoc COUNTY   CARD NO.
POST OFFICE: Emmet Ind. Ter.   FIELD NO.

	NAME	RELATION-SHIP TO PERSON FIRST NAMED	AGE	SEX	BLOOD	TRIBAL ENROLLMENT		
						YEAR	COUNTY	PAGE
1	Carney, Cicen	NAMED	36	F	Full	1897	Pontotoc	58
2	Brown, Sibby	Dau	11	"	"	1897	"	58
3	John, Sanders	Son	5	M	"	1897	"	58
4	" Grover	"	14mo	"	"			

TRIBAL ENROLLMENT OF PARENTS

	NAME OF FATHER	YEAR	COUNTY	NAME OF MOTHER	YEAR	COUNTY
1	Sampson Carney	Dead	Chickasaw Roll	Sylvie Carney	Dead	Chickasaw Roll
2	Edmon Brown	"	Pontotoc	No. 1		
3	Stephen John	1897	"	No. 1		
4	" "	"	"	No. 1		

(NOTES)

No. 1 also on Page 53, Pontotoc Co as Cicin Brown
No. 4 Born Sept. 14th 1901; Enrolled Nov. 8, 1902.

(No. 4 Dawes' Roll No. 4180)
Oct. 10/98.

RESIDENCE: Tishomingo COUNTY   CARD NO.
POST OFFICE: Davis, Ind. Ter.   FIELD NO.

	NAME	RELATION-SHIP TO PERSON FIRST NAMED	AGE	SEX	BLOOD	TRIBAL ENROLLMENT		
						YEAR	COUNTY	PAGE
1	Alexander, James	NAMED	24	M	Full	1897	Tishomingo	30
2	" Mollie	Wife	27	F	I.W.			

3	"	Flossie		Dau	3days	F	1/2			

TRIBAL ENROLLMENT OF PARENTS

	NAME OF FATHER	YEAR	COUNTY	NAME OF MOTHER	YEAR	COUNTY
1	Chili Alexander	1897	Tishomingo	Caroline Alexander	Dead	Tishomingo
2	Jim Thompson		Non-Citizen	Sarah Thompson		Non-Citizen
3	No. 1			Mollie Alexander		White woman

(NOTES)

On Chickasaw Roll as Jim Alexander
Evidence of marriage of parents of No. 2 attached to card of Mollie Alexander No. D.146
No. 3 Enrolled Nov. 25/98.
No. 1 is in Ft. Leavenworth Penitentiary
Sentencing is June 13, 1903.
No. 2 transferred from Chickasaw Card #D.146   *(No. 2 Dawes' Roll No. 195)*
    See decision of May 1, 1902

Oct. 10/98.

RESIDENCE:	Panola	COUNTY			CARD NO.			
POST OFFICE:	Emmet, Ind. Ter.				FIELD NO.			

	NAME	RELATIONSHIP TO PERSON FIRST NAMED	AGE	SEX	BLOOD	TRIBAL ENROLLMENT		
						YEAR	COUNTY	PAGE
1	Shico, Frank	NAMED	29	M	Full	1897	Panola	6
2	" Louisa	Wife	24	F	"	1897	"	6
3	" Mamie	Dau	2	"	"			
4	" ~~Able~~	~~Son~~	~~4mo~~	~~M~~	~~"~~	DIED PRIOR TO SEPTEMBER 25 1902		
5	" Douglas	"	17da	"	"			

TRIBAL ENROLLMENT OF PARENTS

	NAME OF FATHER	YEAR	COUNTY	NAME OF MOTHER	YEAR	COUNTY
1	Eastman Shico	Dead	Panola	Rhody Shico	Dead	Panola
2	Aaron Apala	1897	Chick residing in Choctaw N. 1st Dist.	Biley Mosley	1897	"
3	No. 1			No. 2		
4	~~No. 1~~			~~No. 2~~		
5	No. 1			No. 2		

(NOTES)

No. 4 Enrolled May 24th 1900
No. 4 Died June 8th 1901; Proof of Death filed Nov. 6, 1902
No. 5 Born June 2nd 1902; Enrolled June 19th 1902

Oct. 10/98.

Chickasaw Enrollment Cards 1898-1914
Chickasaw by Blood   Volume III

RESIDENCE: Choctaw Nation   ~~COUNTY~~   CARD NO.

POST OFFICE: Stringtown, Ind. Ter.   FIELD NO.

NAME	RELATION-SHIP TO PERSON FIRST NAMED	AGE	SEX	BLOOD	TRIBAL ENROLLMENT		
					YEAR	COUNTY	PAGE
1 Noah, Annie	NAMED	27	F	Full			
2 " Rindie	Dau	10	"	1/2			
3 " Robert	Son	5	M	1/2			
4 " Reuben	"	3	"	1/2			

TRIBAL ENROLLMENT OF PARENTS

NAME OF FATHER	YEAR	COUNTY	NAME OF MOTHER	YEAR	COUNTY
1 Huscha	Dead	Chickasaw Roll	Te-ho-ya	Dead	Chickasaw Roll
2 David Noah		Jacks Fork Co. Choctaw Roll	No. 1		
3 " "		" "	No. 1		
4 " "		" "	No. 1		

(NOTES)

All on Choctaw Census Record No. 2. Page 384; Transferred to Chickasaw Roll by Dawes Com
No. 1 On Choctaw Roll 1896 Jacks Fork Co, No. 9860
No. 2 "   "   " 1896 "   " "   " 9863 as Ranty Noah
No. 3 "   "   " 1896 "   " "   " 9864
No. 4 "   "   " 1896 "   " "   " 9865

Oct. 10/98

CANCELLED Stamped across card

RESIDENCE: Choctaw Nation   ~~COUNTY~~   CARD NO.

POST OFFICE: Stringtown, Ind. Ter.   FIELD NO.

NAME	RELATION-SHIP TO PERSON FIRST NAMED	AGE	SEX	BLOOD	TRIBAL ENROLLMENT		
					YEAR	COUNTY	PAGE
1 Noletubby, John Anderson	NAMED	44	M	3/4	1897	Chick residing in Choctaw N 3rd Dist.	73
2 " Laud	Wife	26	F	I.W.	1897	" " " "	82
3 " Jessie	Dau	4 1/2	"	3/8	1897	" " " "	73
4 " Jackson	Son	3	M	3/8	1897	" " " "	73
5 " Tandy	"	2wks	"	3/8			

TRIBAL ENROLLMENT OF PARENTS

NAME OF FATHER	YEAR	COUNTY	NAME OF MOTHER	YEAR	COUNTY
1 Kissen Noletubby	Dead	Choctaw Roll	Lottie Noletubby	Dead	Chickasaw Roll
2 J.W. Mackey	"	non citizen	Mrs. J.W. Mackey	"	non citizen
3 No. 1			No. 2		

194

4	No. 1			No. 2		
5	No. 1			No. 2		

(NOTES)

No. 2 See Decision of June 13 '04   *(No. 2 Dawes' Roll No. 398)*

No. 1 On Chickasaw Roll as J.A. Noletubby

No. 2 "   "   " " "Nolatubby"

    Marriage certificate to be recorded and *(illegible)* Received Oct. 10/98.

    Tandy, Son of Nos. 1 & 2, born Dec. 4th/99 on Card D.303

No. 5 Born December 4th 1899. Transferred to this Card Feb. 1st 1902.

Oct. 10/98.

RESIDENCE: Choctaw Nation ~~COUNTY~~   **CARD NO.**

POST OFFICE: Hartshorne, Ind. Ter.   **FIELD NO.**

NAME	RELATION-SHIP TO PERSON FIRST NAMED	AGE	SEX	BLOOD	TRIBAL ENROLLMENT		
					YEAR	COUNTY	PAGE
4 ~~Thompson, Willis~~		50	M	~~Full~~	~~1897~~	~~Chick residing in Choctaw N. 1st Dist.~~	~~71~~

TRIBAL ENROLLMENT OF PARENTS

NAME OF FATHER	YEAR	COUNTY	NAME OF MOTHER	YEAR	COUNTY
4 ~~Poche~~	~~Dead~~	~~Chickasaw Roll~~	~~A-li-key~~	~~Dead~~	~~Chickasaw Roll~~

(NOTES)

On Chickasaw Roll as Willie Thompson

Also known as Willie Pochie

No. 1 died in Nov. 1899. Evidence of death filed Jn. 29, 1905.   Oct. 10/98.

CANCELLED Stamped across card

RESIDENCE: Panola   **COUNTY**   **CARD NO.**

POST OFFICE: Emmet, Ind. Ter.   **FIELD NO.**

NAME	RELATION-SHIP TO PERSON FIRST NAMED	AGE	SEX	BLOOD	TRIBAL ENROLLMENT		
					YEAR	COUNTY	PAGE
1 ~~Apala, Simon~~		~~20~~	M	~~Full~~	~~1897~~	~~Panola~~	~~34~~
2 " Leticia	Wife	17	F	"	1897	Tishomingo	34
3 " ~~Dora~~	~~Dau~~	~~5mo~~	"	"			
4 " Joseph	Son	5mo	M	"			

TRIBAL ENROLLMENT OF PARENTS

NAME OF FATHER	YEAR	COUNTY	NAME OF MOTHER	YEAR	COUNTY
1 ~~Jimpson Apala~~	~~Dead~~	~~Chick residing in Choctaw N. 1st Dist.~~	~~Nicey Apala~~	~~Dead~~	~~Panola~~
2 Leonder Colbert		Tishomingo	Delphie Colbert	1897	Tishomingo

3	~~No. 1~~			~~No. 2~~		
4	No. 1			No. 2		

(NOTES)

No. 1 <u>Died</u> April 3rd 1902; Proof of Death filed Nov. 7th 1902

No. 2 On Chickasaw Roll as Latty cei Colbert

No. 3 Enrolled Nov. 4/99

No. 3 <u>Died</u> Jan. 9th 1902; Proof of Death filed Nov. 7th 1902

No. 4 Enrolled June 27th 1901

Oct. 10/98.

RESIDENCE: Panola COUNTY					CARD NO.		
POST OFFICE: Emmett, Ind. Ter.					FIELD NO.		

	NAME	RELATION-SHIP TO PERSON FIRST NAMED	AGE	SEX	BLOOD	TRIBAL ENROLLMENT		
						YEAR	COUNTY	PAGE
1	Mosley, Biley	NAMED	50	F	Full	1897	Panola	6
2	Beavers, Harriet	Dau	14	"	"	1897	"	6
3	" Rachel	"	12	"	"	1897	"	6

TRIBAL ENROLLMENT OF PARENTS							
NAME OF FATHER	YEAR	COUNTY	NAME OF MOTHER	YEAR	COUNTY		
1	Jackson Conway	Dead	Chickasaw Roll	Sylphie Conway	Dead	Chickasaw Roll
2	Watkin Beaver	"	Panola	No. 1		
3	" "	"	"	No. 1		

(NOTES)

No. 1 On Chickasaw Roll as Billy Mosley

No. 2 "   "   "   " Marriet "

No. 3 "   "   "   " Rachal Beavers

Oct. 10/98.

RESIDENCE: Panola COUNTY					CARD NO.		
POST OFFICE: Mead, Ind. Ter.					FIELD NO.		

	NAME	RELATION-SHIP TO PERSON FIRST NAMED	AGE	SEX	BLOOD	TRIBAL ENROLLMENT		
						YEAR	COUNTY	PAGE
1	Newberry, Joe	NAMED	33	M	Full	1897	Panola	1
2	" Franklin	Son	8	"	1/2	1897	"	1
3	" Calvin	"	4	"	1/2	1897	"	1
4	" Burney	"	3mo	"	1/2			
5	" Mattie Avd.	Dau	2mo	F	1/2			
6	" Wilson	Son	1mo	M	1/2			

196

	TRIBAL ENROLLMENT OF PARENTS					
	NAME OF FATHER	YEAR	COUNTY	NAME OF MOTHER	YEAR	COUNTY
1	Louis newberry	Dead	Panola	Lucy Newberry	1897	Panola
2	No. 1			" "	"	"
3	No. 1			" "	"	"
4	No. 1			" "	"	"
5	No. 1			" "	"	"
6	No. 1			" "	"	"

(NOTES)

No. 5 Enrolled May 25, 1900
No. 6 Born Jany 4, 1902; Enrolled Jany. 22nd 1902

Oct. 10/98.

RESIDENCE: Panola COUNTY   CARD NO.

POST OFFICE: Colbert, Ind. Ter.   FIELD NO.

	NAME	RELATION-SHIP TO PERSON FIRST NAMED	AGE	SEX	BLOOD	TRIBAL ENROLLMENT		
						YEAR	COUNTY	PAGE
1	Newberry, Martin	NAMED	42	M	Full	1897	Panola	4
2	" Mattie	Wife	33	F	I.W.	1897	"	76

	TRIBAL ENROLLMENT OF PARENTS					
	NAME OF FATHER	YEAR	COUNTY	NAME OF MOTHER	YEAR	COUNTY
1	Louis Newberry	Dead	Panola	Lucy Newberry	1897	Panola
2	Jim Franklin		non citizen	Nannie Franklin	Dead	non citizen

(NOTES)

No. 2 See decision of June 16 '04   (No. 2 Dawes' Roll No. 897)
No. 2 On Chickasaw Roll as Mrs. Mattie Newberry
Certified copy of marriage license and certificate of Nos. 1 and 2 filed April 4, 1903.

Oct. 10/98.

RESIDENCE: Panola COUNTY   CARD NO.

POST OFFICE: Colbert, Ind. Ter.   FIELD NO.

	NAME	RELATION-SHIP TO PERSON FIRST NAMED	AGE	SEX	BLOOD	TRIBAL ENROLLMENT		
						YEAR	COUNTY	PAGE
1	Gooding, John Franklin	NAMED	39	M	1/16	1897	Panola	2
2	" Sarah W.	Wife	48	F	I.W.	1897	"	76

	TRIBAL ENROLLMENT OF PARENTS					
	NAME OF FATHER	YEAR	COUNTY	NAME OF MOTHER	YEAR	COUNTY
1	Charles Gooding	Dead	Non Citizen	M.T. Gooding	1897	Panola
2	Martin Steadman	"	" "	Barbara Steadman	Dead	Non-Citizen

(NOTES)

No. 1 On Chickasaw Roll as Frank Gooding
No. 2 "   "   "   " Mrs. S.W. "

(No. 2 Dawes' Roll No. 150)
Oct. 10/98.

RESIDENCE: Choctaw Nation   ~~COUNTY~~   **CARD NO.**
POST OFFICE: South Canadian, Ind. Ter.   **FIELD NO.**

	NAME	RELATION-SHIP TO PERSON FIRST NAMED	AGE	SEX	BLOOD	TRIBAL ENROLLMENT		
						YEAR	COUNTY	PAGE
1	Phillips, Joseph R.	FIRST NAMED	24	M	1/32	1897	Chick residing in Choctaw N. 1st Dist.	68
2	" Mary M	Wife	24	F	I.W.	1897	" " " "	84
3	" Harry H.	Son	2	M	1/64	1897	" " " "	68

TRIBAL ENROLLMENT OF PARENTS

	NAME OF FATHER	YEAR	COUNTY	NAME OF MOTHER	YEAR	COUNTY
1	J.J. Phillips (I.W.)	1897	Chick residing in Choctaw N. 1st Dist.	Mary Phillips	Dead	Chickasaw Roll
2	Wm Morgan		non citizen	Louisa Morgan		non citizen
3	No. 1			No. 2		

(NOTES)

No. 1 On Chickasaw Roll as J.R. Phillips
No. 2 Enrolled Oct. 13, 1898

(No. 2 Dawes' Roll No. 149)

P.O. Paola, I.T. 10/24/02
Womack, I.T. 7/8/00

Oct. 10/98.

RESIDENCE: Choctaw Nation   **COUNTY**   **CARD NO.**
POST OFFICE: Calvin, Ind. Ter.   **FIELD NO.**

	NAME	RELATION-SHIP TO PERSON FIRST NAMED	AGE	SEX	BLOOD	TRIBAL ENROLLMENT		
						YEAR	COUNTY	PAGE
1	Scales, George W.	FIRST NAMED	44	M	I.W.	1897	Chick residing in Choctaw N. 1st Dist.	82
2	" Mattie	Wife	40	F	1/16	1897	" " " "	67
3	" Claude	Son	14	M	1/32	1897	" " " "	67
4	" Mamie	Dau	12	F	1/32	1897	" " " "	67
5	" Winnie	"	9	"	1/32	1897	" " " "	67
6	" Grace	"	5		1/32	1897	" " " "	67

	TRIBAL ENROLLMENT OF PARENTS						
	NAME OF FATHER	YEAR	COUNTY	NAME OF MOTHER	YEAR	COUNTY	
1	Tobe Scales	Dead	Non Citizen	Amanda Scales		Non Citizen	
2	Reuben Bourland		" "	Eliza Bourland	Dead	Chickasaw Roll	
3	No. 1			No. 2			
4	No. 1			No. 2			
5	No. 1			No. 2			
6	No. 1			No. 2			

(NOTES)

(No. 1 Dawes' Roll No. 386)   Oct. 10/98.

RESIDENCE: Panola COUNTY					CARD NO.		
POST OFFICE: Emmet, Ind. Ter.					FIELD NO.		

NAME	RELATION-SHIP TO PERSON FIRST NAMED	AGE	SEX	BLOOD	TRIBAL ENROLLMENT		
					YEAR	COUNTY	PAGE
1 Apala, Nicholas	NAMED	23	M	Full	1897	Panola	4
2 " Martha	Dau	4	F	"	1897	"	4
3 " ~~Lena~~	"	~~2~~	"	"	~~1897~~	"	4
4 " Sophia	Sister	22	"	"	1897	"	4

	TRIBAL ENROLLMENT OF PARENTS						
	NAME OF FATHER	YEAR	COUNTY	NAME OF MOTHER	YEAR	COUNTY	
1	Jimpson Apala	Dead	Chickasaw Roll	Nicey Apala	Dead	Panola	
2	No. 1			Lottie Apala	"	"	
3	~~No. 1~~			" "	"	"	
4	Jimpson Apala	Dead	Chickasaw Roll	Nicey Apala	"	"	

(NOTES)

No. 1 is now the husband of Isabelle Greer on Choctaw Card #4169 Nov. 8th 1902

No. 3 On Chickasaw Roll as Francis Apala

No. 3 died in November 1900; Enrollment cancelled by Department Dec. 28, 1904

Oct. 10/98

RESIDENCE: Choctaw Nation ~~COUNTY~~					CARD NO.		
POST OFFICE: Stringtown, Ind. Ter.					FIELD NO.		

NAME	RELATION-SHIP TO PERSON FIRST NAMED	AGE	SEX	BLOOD	TRIBAL ENROLLMENT		
					YEAR	COUNTY	PAGE
1 Bond, Calvin	NAMED	21	M	1/2			

TRIBAL ENROLLMENT OF PARENTS

	NAME OF FATHER	YEAR	COUNTY	NAME OF MOTHER	YEAR	COUNTY
1	Jesse Bond		Jacks Fork County Choctw Roll	Mary Bond	1897	Chick residing in Choctaw N. 3rd Dist.

(NOTES)

On Choctaw Census Record No. 2 Page 76 as Campbell Bond; Transferred to Chickasaw Roll by Dawes Com

On Choctaw Roll, 1896 Jacks Fork County, No. 1881 as Campbell Bond

No. 1 is the husband of Sallie Bond on Choctaw Card #3993.

Oct. 10/98.

CANCELLED Stamped across card

RESIDENCE: Panola **COUNTY**   **CARD NO.**

POST OFFICE: Emet, Ind. Ter.   **FIELD NO.**

	NAME	RELATION-SHIP TO PERSON FIRST	AGE	SEX	BLOOD	TRIBAL ENROLLMENT		
						YEAR	COUNTY	PAGE
1	Conway, Joel	NAMED	45	M	Full	1897	Panola	6
2	" Nancy	Wife	40	F	"	1897	"	6
3	" Lizzie	Dau	15	"	"	1897	"	6
4	" Bessie	"	3	"	"	1897	"	6
5	" ~~William~~	~~Nephew~~	~~14~~	~~M~~	~~"~~	~~1893~~	~~"~~	~~2~~
6	~~Colbert, Joel~~	~~Gr. Son~~	~~2mo~~	~~"~~	~~1/2~~			
7	" Been	" "	7mo	"	1/2			

TRIBAL ENROLLMENT OF PARENTS

	NAME OF FATHER	YEAR	COUNTY	NAME OF MOTHER	YEAR	COUNTY
1	Jackson Conway	Dead	Chickasaw Roll	Tash-ke	Dead	Chickasaw Roll
2	Ah-ne-le-tubby	"	" "	(Name Illegible)	"	" "
3	No. 1			No. 2		
4	No. 1			No. 2		
5	~~Eastman Conway~~	~~Dead~~	~~Panola~~	~~Liney Conway~~	~~Dead~~	~~Pontotoc~~
6	~~Jeff Colbert~~			~~No. 3~~		
7	" "			No. 3		

(NOTES)

No. 3 is now the wife of Jeff Colbert on Chickasaw Card #735 certificate of marriage received & filed Nov. 1, 1902

No. 5 On Chickasaw Roll as W.M. Conway

No. 5 Also on 1896 Census Roll Page 92

No. 5 On 1893 Chickasaw Pay Roll No. 2 Page 15 as William Conaway

No. 5 <u>Died</u> Jan 1900; Proof of Death filed Nov. 7 1902

No. 6 Enrolled May 25, 1900

No. 6 <u>Died</u> Nov. 1901; Proof of Death filed Nov. 8th 1902

No. 7 Born March 23rd 1902; Enrolled Oct. 20th 1902.

Oct. 10/98.

Index

Index

Index

Index

Index

www.ingramcontent.com/pod-product-compliance
Lightning Source LLC
Chambersburg PA
CBHW030241030426
42336CB00009B/199